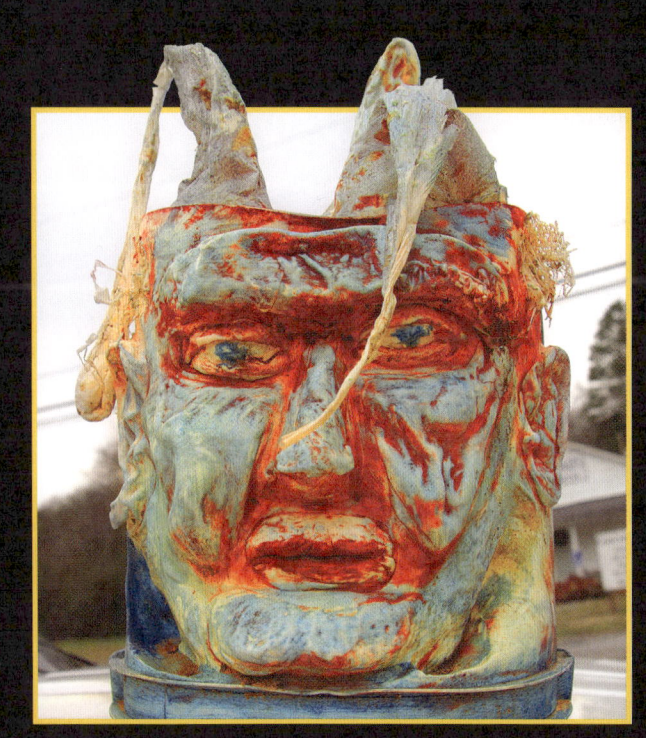

WEIRD TENNESSEE

Weird Tennessee

Your Travel Guide to Tennessee's Local Legends and Best Kept Secrets

By Roger Manley

Mark Sceurman and Mark Moran,
Executive Editors

STERLING

New York / London
www.sterlingpublishing.com

WEIRD TENNESSEE

STERLING and the distinctive Sterling logo are registered trademarks of Sterling Publishing Co., Inc.

Published by Sterling Publishing Co., Inc.
387 Park Avenue South, New York, NY 10016
© 2010 Mark Moran and Mark Sceurman
Distributed in Canada by Sterling Publishing
c/o Canadian Manda Group, 165 Dufferin Street
Toronto, Ontario, Canada M6K 3H6
Distributed in the United Kingdom by GMC Distribution Services,
Castle Place, 166 High Street, Lewes,
East Sussex, England BN7 1XU
Distributed in Australia by Capricorn Link
(Australia) Pty. Ltd. P. O. Box 704, Windsor, NSW 2756, Australia

10 9 8 7 6 5 4 3 2

Manufactured in China.
All rights reserved.

Photography and illustration credits are found on page 270 and constitute an extension of this copyright page.

Layout and production by bobsteimle.com

Sterling ISBN: 978-1-4027-5465-4

For information about custom editions, special sales, premium and corporate purchases, please contact Sterling Special Sales Department at 800-805-5489 or specialsales@sterlingpublishing.com.

DEDICATION

This book is dedicated to the memory of two patron saints—the late, great Grace Profitt of Bluff City, who must now be making barbecue for the Lord and all His Angels if they really do know what Righteous is, and for Jonathan Williams, undoubtedly there among them with the sauce running clear down to his elbows. He could always tell when a poem, a photo, or a fine plate of pork was truly worth paying attention to.

CONTENTS

Foreword: A Note from the Marks	6
Introduction	8
Local Legends	10
Ancient Mysteries	36
Fabled People and Places	60
Unexplained Phenomena	82
Bizarre Beasts	108
Local Heroes and Villains	126
Personalized Properties	150
Roadside Oddities	174
Roads Less Traveled	192
Tennessee Ghosts	212
Cemetery Safari	234
Abandoned Tennessee	252
Index	264
Acknowledgments	270
Picture Credits	271

Weird Tennessee is intended as entertainment to present a historical record of local legends, folklore, and sites throughout Tennessee. Many of these legends and stories cannot be independently confirmed or corroborated, and the authors and publisher make no representation as to their factual accuracy. The reader should be advised that many of the sites described in *Weird Tennessee* are located on private property and such sites should not be visited, or you may face prosecution for trespassing.

A Note from the Marks

Our weird journey began a long, long time ago in a far off land called New Jersey. Once a year or so we'd compile a homespun newsletter to hand out to our friends called *Weird NJ*. The pamphlet was a collection of odd news clippings, bizarre facts, little-known historical anecdotes, and anomalous encounters from our home state. The newsletter also focused on the kind of very localized legends that were often whispered around a particular town, but seldom heard outside the boundaries of the community where they first originated.

We had started the publication with the simple theory that every town in the state had at least one good tale to tell. *Weird NJ* soon become a full-fledged magazine and we made the decision to actually do all of our own investigating and see if we couldn't track down just where all of these seemingly unbelievable stories were coming from. Was there, we wondered, any factual basis for these fantastic local legends that people were telling us? Armed with not much more than a camera and notepad, we set off on a mystical journey of discovery. Much to our surprise and amazement, much of what we had initially presumed to be nothing more than urban legend actually turned out to be real, or at least contained a grain of truth that had originally sparked the lore.

After about a dozen years of documenting the bizarre we were asked to write a book about our adventures, and so *Weird NJ: Your Guide to New Jersey's Local Legends and Best Kept Secrets* was published in 2003. Soon people from all over the country began writing to us, telling us strange tales from their home states. As it turned out, what we had first perceived to be a very local-interest genre was actually just a small part of a much larger and more universal phenomenon. People from all over the United States had strange tales to tell, which they believed to be true, and they all wanted somebody to tell them to.

When our publisher asked us what we wanted to do next, for us the choice was simple: "We'd like to do a book called *Weird U.S.*, in which we could document the local legends and strangest stories from all over the entire country," we told them. So for the next twelve months we set out in search of weirdness wherever it might be found in these fifty states.

In 2004, after *Weird U.S.* was published, our publisher asked us once more where we wanted to go next. In the year that it had taken us to put together *Weird U.S.* we had come to the conclusion that this country had more great tales waiting to be told than could be contained in just one book. We had discovered—somewhat to our surprise—that every state we researched seemed to have more fascinating stories to offer than we actually had pages to accommodate. Everywhere we looked we found unwritten folklore, creepy cemeteries, cursed locations and outlandish roadside oddities. With this in mind we told our publisher that we wanted to document it *all*, and to do it in a series of books, each focusing on the peculiarities of a particular state.

When it came time to document the weirdness of Tennessee, the first and only author we considered asking to help us was our old friend and collaborator Roger Manley. Over the past few years Roger has become sort of our "go-to guy" south of the Mason-Dixon Line. He is the author of our books for this series on the states of North Carolina, South Carolina, and Louisiana. While working on those titles with Roger we were truly astonished by the almost incomprehensible volume of bizarre material he was able to dig up. Not only is he a dogged investigator of the weird, but he also possesses the photographic and storytelling expertise required to bring his unusual subjects to life in the pages of a book. He is a true kindred spirit with a wanderlust, who also happened to harbor a deep-rooted fascination for the weird. Having lived all over the South, Roger has spent most of his life collecting tales known only to the locals. He has a rare gift for being able to recognize a site or story for its strangeness and then to convey its inherent uniqueness to his readers.

So volunteer yourself to come with us now and let Roger take you on a tour of the Hog and Hominy State, with all of its haints, hillbillies, and history. It's an unusually interesting state of mind we like to call *Weird Tennessee*. —*Mark Moran and Mark Sceurman*

Introduction

Anyone who's ever been to a potluck supper knows that there's a certain art to cutting into pies, cakes, or casseroles so that you end up getting the perfect piece. You have to angle the knife a certain way so you get the smooth, tasty parts in the middle but also the icing, crust, or yummies around the edges, too. The ideal piece is one that gives you a cross-section of everything that particular dish has to offer.

In a way, Tennessee is like that perfect serving. It's a cross-section of everything our nation dishes up between the Great Smokies and the Mississippi. "You know," Tennesseeans told me, "we've got the eastern mountains, the highland hills, and the western flatlands. That's why we've got three stars on the state flag. So don't go thinking you've seen it all just because you've been to Graceland."

Others told me there were really more like six regions, including the Gulf Plain, Highland Rim, Central Basin, Cumberland Plateau, Great Valley, and the Unaka Mountains.

Then I began hearing how *those regions* were further divvied up, with the Gulf Plain really being the Mississippi Alluvial Plain, the Gulf Coastal Plain, the Western Valley of the Tennessee Valley . . . until I had to hold up my hands and surrender. There was no way I could randomly drive around and hope to spot the all the available weirdness with a mere "windshield survey." I would need to plan well.

"I'm looking for abandoned hospitals, blood springs, and cursed railroad crossings," I'd say to the staffs in sheriff's offices, town libraries, historical societies, and heritage museums. "Add to that the forest midgets, secret cults, snake-oil salesmen, upside-down trees, and werewolves . . ." They got the idea, and they sent me in the right directions so I could shake the bushes to see what would fall out.

An amazing amount did. Way more, in fact, than I could ever hope to cram between the two covers of this book. Let me assure you, Tennessee is one weird state.

"Anybody tell you about the Harpe brothers?" a historian asked. "Sewed rocks up in their victims to keep them from floating." Were they really America's first serial killers?

"Go to Calfkiller Bridge," said one young correspondent. "There's a ghost of an angry dead woman who hangs out there at midnight and attacks people. If you turn off your car it won't start again." I left the key in the ignition, just in case.

Convenience store clerks and town cops filled me in. "You been out to the Red Ash coal tower on Royal Blue Road?" a cashier in Caryville asked. "Some poor guy fell off it about fifty years ago and died, but they say his ghost is still out there, looking for something." A boy standing near racks of Little Debbies overheard us and chimed in. "My big brother was out there one night and saw a blue light on the way to Turleys, and it wasn't a police car, either." Not to be outdone, a man in a camouflaged hunter's cap in the back near the coolers full of RC colas chimed in. "Over on Bacchus Road in Claiborne County we got us green lights, orange lights, fire balls, and all kinds of other stuff floating around."

Not everything wound up in the book, of course. There just wasn't enough room. If there was more than one decapitated brakeman out looking for his head, I went with the one that sounded most interesting. And some things, while plenty weird, just didn't seem to fit the goals of the book. Lots of people, for example, mentioned the famous "Body Farm" (aka the Outdoor Research Facility of the Forensic Anthropology Center) near UT Medical Center in Knoxville, but most people (including me) can't go there, ever. You won't find much mention of Graceland, either, since everybody goes there sooner or later.

What you *will* find on these pages is a potluck supper of all kinds of things weird enough to tempt you to get up and check them out for yourself. It may take a little practice to develop what Mark Moran and Mark Sceurman have identified as your "Weird Eye"—the ability to recognize real weirdness when you see it—but *Weird Tennessee* should help get you started. And once you've got your weird on, Tennessee will suddenly snap into focus. For, believe you me, it's been that way all along. —*Roger Manley*

Local Legends

Bring up the subject of Tennessee legends, and chances are that Davy Crockett will be at or near the top of anyone's list. After all, born on a mountaintop, killed a bear at age three, wore a coonskin cap, went to Texas to fight for independence—that's enough to make anyone legendary, right? The trouble is, not much of it is true. He was born in relatively flat country next to a river and went to Texas after he failed to get reelected to Congress. Walt Disney came up with the coonskin cap. Crockett didn't even call himself Davy. It's pretty likely that none of the other things attributed to him happened, either—like twisting the tail off Halley's Comet, using an alligator to power a boat up Niagara Falls, wading the Mississippi River, riding through a crab apple orchard on a streak of lightning, sliding down a thorn tree without a scratch, sleeping under a blanket of snow, or making love like a mad bull. The congressman from the Ninth and Twelfth districts of Tennessee was mighty nimble when it came to walking the thin line between fact and fiction, which is probably why he decided to go into politics in the first place.

That same thin line is where legends come from. There's always at least a kernel of truth—there were mountains within ten miles of David Crockett's birthplace; he probably was a pretty good shot, and he did fight at the Alamo (we can't vouch for how bovine his lovemaking was)—and the rest of the story usually boils down to a matter of "If that ain't how it was, it's at least how it should have been."

And then again, sometimes the truth is stranger than any fiction anyone could come up with.

The Witches That Weren't

Folklore is knowledge shared by a group. But as any folklorist can tell you, groups aren't just the handful of people you know. We each belong to many groups—defined by all kinds of things, such as age, gender, ethnic background, geographic location, social status—and so on. Each of us is located at the only place in the universe where all these different groups we belong to overlap.

When we don't quite understand why another group does what they do, we tend to make assumptions based on the way *we* think. What is "the truth" for one generation may just be "old superstitions" for their descendants. What is "practical problem solving" in one region may be considered "backward" by another. Old people don't always understand young people's music, so they assume it's satanic. City people don't understand how much skill it takes to run a farm, so they assume farmers are ignorant. And so on.

Tombstones in the Cumberlands provide a great example of how misunderstandings like this come about. In an area stretching from around Livingston in Overton County down to around Sparta in White County, there are some 257 small family cemeteries and churchyards with graves unlike almost any others in the world. The oldest and simplest graves here—dating to the early 1820s—are covered with four stones: two shaped like small triangles at the head and foot, with a "roof" of two more long flat slabs. Slightly later

graves have two larger trapezoid-shaped stones at the ends with epitaphs carved into them, and the same long slabs running the length of the graves.

Old-timers called them "comb" graves. The word *comb* comes from a very ancient word meaning "tooth" (as in "fine-toothed comb"). Certainly the big stones that form each end of these graves look a lot like teeth. But *comb* also means "to curl over," like ocean surf caused by big waves called "combers." No one now alive knows if the comb graves reminded their builders of teeth or of waves.

In either case, they probably originated in Overton County, because the local sandstone there could be easily split into flat slabs. But why those slabs were used to cover graves, no one knows: to keep out animals, say some; to keep the coffins dry, say others; while one old man said he wanted one for his wife's grave to prevent cows from "decorating" them.

One particularly evocative old cemetery full of such graves is the Stamps cemetery in Putnam County, at the junction of Brotherton Mountain Road and Stamps–Shady Grove Road. Designs on some of the stones have given rise to all kinds of conjecture by many who have seen them: Nearly every grave features a downward-pointing star or pentagram.

Every armchair occultist is aware that the inverted star is a symbol fraught with meanings for neopagans, witches, and Satanists, with the two upward points representing the horns of the goat Baphomet. Because of this, the Stamps cemetery has gained notoriety (especially among students at nearby Tennessee Tech in Cookeville) as a graveyard for witches. But it's awfully unlikely that the entire Stamps family was involved in Satan worship or witchcraft. Although the decorations on their graves are indeed unusual, downward-pointing stars are also a common Masonic symbol, and turn up in other places, such as on the Congressional Medal of Honor, the highest award given to military personnel, who seem unlikely Satanists, too.

Like grandma's secret pie recipes, decorative ideas and symbols tend to stay in small groups, but they are usually no more intended as carriers of sinister meanings than the patterns of old quilts or the ways flower beds are laid out. Designs run in families; they might favor roses, palm trees, asterisks, or geometric designs. In the days before widespread literacy, such symbols probably helped the illiterate find family members' graves. Perhaps the original patriarch of the Stamps family signed his name with something like a star instead of an X and it stuck.

While we don't think the Stamps family was comprised of Satan worshippers, we aren't saying the family graveyard isn't haunted. Like many others, it very well may be. It certainly *looks* creepy. The lonely, remote location, with its gathering of precisely sawn truncated triangles in dark stone, makes it look like what one reporter for the *Standing Stone Press* (in Monterey) called a "Tennessee Stonehenge."

Were they all witches? We don't think so. To us, that sounds an awful lot like folklore, even though their gravestones might seem quite weird by modern standards.

The Fain Witch

Atop a lone hill near the Bloomingdale Pike in Arcadia, Sullivan County, is the old Fain cemetery dating back to 1840. It may conceal an awful secret.

In the center of the small graveyard are more or less typical graves of early settlers in this part of the county, although their taste in biblical names was a bit unusual. More than one of the deceased was named Lot, for instance. Lot, as you may recall, appears in the book of Genesis. He escaped the destruction of Sodom and Gomorrah but then later got drunk and slept with his own daughters. His wife wasn't around to prevent this, since she had already been turned into a pillar of salt.

Surrounding the graves of the settlers is a row of slave graves marked with simple fieldstones. One grave, quite different from the rest, is rumored to contain a witch who can't quite seem to remain dead. In fact, he may never have been dead in the first place.

Residents had begun to notice strange maladies, first in their livestock. Cattle got the runs, warts, and lumpy jaws, and gave bloody milk. Horses had hoof problems. Goats rammed trees and fenceposts till their skulls cracked. Then when human infants died shortly after birth with strange deformities, the farmers began to wonder whether some kind of curse had been unleashed on them.

Two slaves, Beck and Jack, said they could solve the problem, in return for a promise that their children would never be enslaved.

Beck requested a dozen straight pins, saying they would reveal the witch who caused the abnormalities. The next day, a slave who had only recently been bought off a boat in Memphis doubled over with what looked at first like stomach cramps. As he vomited blood, a string of looped pins came out of his mouth. Unconscious, the man was crammed into inside a rock-lined hole and trapped by a heavy stone. In time, the strange diseases abated.

But things were never quite normal again. There are many stories about the haunted hill and a persistent thumping sound heard there. Some have compared it to the sound of someone "beating on the top of a coffin trying to escape"; others say it sounds like logs or wooden drums being pounded on rhythmically.

You can check it out, but our advice is to go there in the daytime. Whatever you do, don't sit on that big stone. It's not a bench.

Legend of the Bell Witch

The most famous haunting in all of Tennessee—perhaps even one of the most famous in the whole nation—is the Bell Witch of Adams. Dozens of books and Web sites are now dedicated to telling the story of the terrorizing of John Bell and his family by a witch or spirit called Kate. Between 1817 and 1820, there were dozens of documented sightings and encounters, supposedly even by future president Andrew Jackson, according to a historical marker along Highway 41.

In 1804 fifty-four-year-old John Bell uprooted his wife, Lucy, and their nine children and moved to Red River Station (later renamed Adams) in what is now northern Robertson County. Here he acquired a medium-sized plantation and established a farm, along with houses and outbuildings for about a dozen slaves.

In 1817 the local schoolteacher, Richard Powell, began taking a special interest in Betsy Bell, whom he had taught since the age of eight and who was now, at nearly twelve, "ripening into lovely girlhood" according to the oldest written account of the story. A boy in the school named Joshua Gardner also took a keen interest in Betsy, and was "as firmly impressed with her charms" as their teacher. (Keep reading to find out who got the girl.)

Also in 1817, very weird things started happening to John Bell and his family. Bell went out hunting in his cornfield one afternoon and encountered a "bizarre beast" that had the body of a dog and a rabbit-like head. But when the smoke cleared, the weird critter was nowhere to be seen. A few days later, his son Drewry Bell shot at "an unknown bird of extraordinary size" and it, too, vanished. Not long after this, twelve-year-old Betsy Bell saw a "little girl in a green dress" playing in the limbs of an old oak. She quickly disappeared as well. One of the house slaves then mentioned that he had seen a mysterious large black dog in the road at night. The dog had disappeared, too, he said.

Then young Betsy began having terrible nightmares and would wake the family with her screams. Knocking and gnawing sounds were heard at the doors. Mr. Bell began experiencing difficulty eating, with numbness and "stiffness of the tongue" making it impossible for him to chew and swallow. This continued for three years.

The family kept all these experiences secret for a while, afraid that their neighbors would think something was wrong with them. After a year or so, however, they could stand it no longer and told a trusted friend about the incidents. James Johnson

(a lay minister) and his wife came to the Bell house for a sleepover to see what was going on. Before bed, they conducted a short prayer service. After the candles were blown out, the noises began and the quilts were snatched off their bed in the dark. A mocking female voice mimicked Johnson's fervent prayers. The voice issued frank assessments of hypocrisies and misbehaviors such as drunkenness and marital infidelity. The witch called the praying Johnson "Old Sugar Mouth." John Bell was "Old Jack" and the witch threatened to kill him someday.

Over time, the Bells' place became "Entertainment Central" after dark. People came over to listen to the witch thumping on chairs and furniture while providing a nightly rundown of the local gossip. When cows stopped giving milk, it was the witch's fault. If well water ran brackish, it was her doing. If a white hen had brown chicks, it was because the witch made it happen. One night she talked about a buried treasure, saying, "I am the spirit of an early emigrant, who brought a large sum of money and buried my treasure for safekeeping until needed. In the meanwhile I died without divulging the secret, and I have returned in the spirit for the purpose of making known the hiding place, and I want Betsy Bell to have the money." The witch told them to dig under a huge boulder near a spring that everyone knew. The next day, a dozen people spent hours doing just that, but no treasure was found. That night's the witch laughed at how funny it had been to see everyone sweating so.

During one of the witch's disembodied "appearances" someone asked her what her name was. "Kate," she answered. Everyone remembered the dispute that John Bell had had with neighbor Kate Batts years before. Batts was an odd woman, hefty and strong, and many locals had long suspected her of being a witch anyway. People recalled strange events, like how a farmgirl could get her cream to churn into butter only when she put a hot poker in the milk. Kate Batts was seen with a burned hand later that same day. Was it mere coincidence?

Batts was understandably furious. It was a serious accusation back then and folks were still being tried for witchcraft in the courts. No one ever filed charges against Batts, but from then on the witch was known as Kate.

The witch made life unpleasant for the Bells and their houseguests, slapping them on their cheeks while they slept and hitting them with sticks in the dark, even beating one overnight guest nearly senseless. One young man convinced the witch to touch his hand in the dark and later reported that hers felt "soft and delicate like the hand of a lady." But most of the time people felt only slaps or punches.

After three years of near-constant torment and disruption, John Bell had been weakened as paralysis of his tongue had spread to other parts of his face. He fell prey to fits and spasms so violent that his shoes flew off his feet. "I cannot much longer survive the persecutions of this terrible thing," he allegedly said of Kate the witch. "It is killing me by slow tortures, and I feel that the end is nigh."

On December 19, 1820, John Bell lay in bed, unconscious and seriously ill. The witch cackled, "I have got him this time; he will never get up from that bed again." The next day John Bell was dead.

After that, the witch seemed greatly diminished though she continued to harass the Bell siblings from time to time, particularly Betsy. Despite the witch's admonitions that Betsy should never marry the Gardner boy, on Easter morning 1821 Betsy Bell (now age 15) accepted Josh Gardner's offer of marriage.

Inexplicably, Professor Powell showed up, saying, "That boy never could help loving you, and I never did blame him, as you were my little pet also, and I have waited almost as patiently as did Jacob for Rachel, hoping that you and Josh might forget that young school day love."

"Please Betsy Bell, don't have Joshua Gardner," said the witch again and again. Betsy broke the engagement, for she believed the witch would torment them for the rest of their lives if they married. Gardner moved away, never to return, and Betsy married Powell and moved to Mississippi, where she died at the age of eighty-six.

Such is the original legend of the Bell Witch, as related by Martin V. Ingram in 1894. His documentation of the story was allegedly based on a memoir written by Richard Bell, the second-youngest son in the Bell family, more than twenty-five years after the fact. Supposedly Richard Bell's son passed the memoir along to Ingram with the proviso that nothing be written until Betsy and her siblings were dead.

Before Ingram wrote his book, Albert Goodpasture mentioned her in passing in a chapter on Robertson County in his 1880 book, *History of Tennessee*, calling the Bell witch:

> *A remarkable occurrence . . . It would take the sugar from the bowls, spill the milk, take the quilts from the beds, slap and pinch the children, and then laugh at the discomfiture of its victims. At first it was supposed to be a good spirit, but its subsequent acts, together with the curses with which it supplemented its remarks, proved the contrary. A volume might be written concerning the performances of this wonderful being, as they are now described by contemporaries and their descendants. That all this actually occurred will not be disputed, nor will a rational explanation be attempted. It is merely introduced as an example of superstition, strong in the minds of all but a few in those times, and not yet wholly extinct.*

Goodpasture was only reporting what people told him had happened sixty years earlier.

A few facts are verifiable. John Bell did indeed live near what is now Adams. Court records show that he was sued for loan-sharking in Springfield (and lost) and then was kicked out of the Baptist Church in 1818. But there is no word about the witch in any early records, nor does there appear to be any evidence that Andrew Jackson ever visited.

To visit the original Bell family graves and homesite near Adams, drive east of the small town on Highway 41/11 past the Bellwood Cemetery and turn left (north) on Johnston Springs Road. Go seven-tenths of a mile and turn left on a private farm road to find the graves of most of Betsy Bell's siblings (36.585468, -87.049404 if you use satellite coordinates). To find the well of the old Bell place, which many people believe is haunted, go back to Johnston Springs Road and continue for another three-tenths of a mile. The ruins and well are next to lone trees in the middle of the field on your left (36.590639, -87.049021) while the graves of John Bell Sr. and his wife, Lucy, can be found in the woods to the north of the well (36.592122, -87.048810). These fields are private property and walking through growing crops can damage them, so winter is the best time to visit. Always be sure to ask permission of the owners and treat these historic sites with respect.

Weird Goings-on on Voodoo Hill

I've got a weird place for you. I'm from Murfreesboro, which is in Rutherford County. This weird place that I'm going to describe to you is called Voodoo Hill. I have heard about Voodoo Hill for quite a while, but me and four of my friends decided to go up there last Halloween and it was pretty scary. Voodoo Hill is supposedly a small community full of devil worshippers. It is actually pretty well known, because there is a shooting range approximately 10 miles away called Big Springs Target Sports, and quite a few famous people have been there including Charleton Heston, and the blond big-breasted policewoman from Police Academy.

There's a house that is the closest thing I have seen to the Leatherface house in my life—tin foil over every window and pots and pans and other contraptions hanging in the trees. You're going to think I'm crazy but I swore that I saw a couple of skeleton heads in the trees. In the back of this house is the supposed Devil worshipper church, which is a plain white barn. There are also usually two monstrous dogs chained to a tree and barking. There are bats and coyotes all over the place. There is also another church with a red crucifix in front of it.

We saw an antiques shop, which had a phone number on it, so I wrote that down. When we got home my friend called him and simply asked him if they were cannibals. The guy simply responded, "Why don't you come over and find out?" After that he hung up.

About a year before a couple of my friends went up there at 1:00 in the morning, and their car broke down. He said that a family gave them a ride with two little kids in the front seat with them. He told me they had to be on some kind of drug. He said the man did not say one word to him but the little girl said, "Look at my fingers, they move," over and over again.

My friend called me the other day and said that he did a dry run in the day to Voodoo Hill and he said he was more uncomfortable in the day than in the night. He saw the supposed devil church's windows were all blacked out. And there were two people sitting in the middle of the road in lawn chairs. When my friend went by he waved and they just stared at him. My friend's exact words were "There is something going on out there but I haven't put my finger on it."

I swear to you that all of this is true; it's pretty creepy going up there. —*Stuart Myatt*

The Witches That Weren't

An old man by the name of Ramsey and his wife lived near Allred in Overton County. Her grave in the Falling Springs graveyard was marked by large stones that formed a large box. He made a hole underneath the box and slept there at night, for years. Another grave in that cemetery is that of a young woman who died only a few years ago. Some people around here think she must have believed in witchcraft since her family erected a mausoleum of black marble, and it has some kind of markings all around it. Witchcraft symbols, they say. —*Paula*

I grew up in East Tennessee in a small city called Morristown. I spent several years of college in Cookeville, a town in middle Tennessee. There are some amazing places in Putnam County. The weirdest place that I visited during my stay in Cookeville was the Witches' Graveyard. The small graveyard rests on the side of a hill near the town. The graves are characterized by two stone slabs tilted against each other in an upside down "V" that run the length of the grave. At the foot and head of each grave is a marker that has an upside down pentagram.
—*David Freeman*

Hanging Rope, a Local Hangout

Projecting from a vertical roadside cliff that rises about two miles west of Center Hill Dam along Highway 141 (south of Lancaster, on the line between Smith and DeKalb Counties) is a short metal rod with a long length of rope dangling from it. It's been there for many years, long enough for a few legends to have grown up about it. But legends often have a core of truth, so there's no way of telling now if the "Hanging Rope" is about a death or only a description of how the rope now looks, hanging out of the cliff.

According to one of the legends, a man hanged himself here after his fiancée cheated on him. He knew that his unfaithful girlfriend and her illicit beau had driven up to the dam to spend the evening smooching. To get even, he ensured that his corpse, dangling above the road, would be illuminated by their headlights when they finally headed back to town. The body was recovered, but the rope was left hanging in the breeze, where it remains to this day.

The metal rod sticks out of such an awkward place that it's pretty hard to imagine either a lone nut or a group of crazed upholders of the local morality (such as it was) bothering to climb the sheer rock face to place it there. On the other hand, we can offer no counterexplanation for the rope or its original purpose. Witnesses have claimed that on moonless nights it is barely possible to make out the dim form of a limp and lifeless corpse swaying from its end, so the jury is still out. In any case, don't hang around gawking at it for long—the shoulders of the road are a little too narrow for safe parking along this stretch, and you won't want to end up permanently joining any other spirits that may already be haunting this neck of the woods.

Cursed Corner

On the west side of the square in the heart of Lebanon, Wilson County, is one of those buildings where no business ever seems to stay in business for very long. For decades people blamed the curse of Woolard's Corner on a large box elder in the square, a gaunt and ugly reminder of an act of violence from the early twentieth century.

As recounted in the *Mount Juliet Weekly News*, Lebanon Police Chief Robert Nolen and Officer Lynch Harris had gone to the house of Ned Whitley on the night of Sunday, March 5, 1916, intending to arrest Whitley's son Will, an employee of Martha White Mills, on a charge of bootlegging. According to the paper, Will Whitley asked if he could go get his hat before accompanying the two policemen down to the station. Instead he got a gun and shot Chief Nolen in the arm and abdomen. Officer Lynch returned fire, shooting Whitley in the hand and arm. Whitley was seized and an ambulance called for.

Chief Nolen was taken to Dr. McFarland's infirmary, where he lingered near death all the following day. As his condition worsened, a crowd gathered outside the clinic. By the time it was announced that the chief had passed away, it had just turned dark on Monday evening. A Cumberland University student named Pete Etheridge whipped the crowd into an angry mob. Etheridge led the crowd to the jail, where they forced open the doors and easily overpowered the police officers. The mob seized Whitley and carried him to the center of town—where a monument to Confederate veterans now stands—intending to hang him from a telephone cable that crossed the middle of the square.

When their rope proved to be too short to throw over the cable, they chose a lower limb of the old box elder. One of the crowd volunteered to climb the tree with the end of the rope between his teeth. He threw it over a limb and then, as the Mount Juliet paper reported, "willing hands soon hoisted [Whitley] into eternity." He remained hanging for over an hour, during which Abie Hobbs, Walter Carr, Reece Gibson, and other proud residents posed for photos of the grisly scene.

Perhaps this would be just another sad moment in history, much like the 250 other lynchings that took place in Tennessee, except that a little more is known about the leader of this lynch mob than is usually the case. After the killing of Will Whitley, Pete Etheridge quit Cumberland University and went to Texas to help round up draft evaders who didn't want to fight in the World War I. According to historical references, he helped send "train loads" of men to the front, although he himself never enlisted.

Instead, he came back to Lebanon in the 1920s to work as a roofer and preacher. In his spare time he hung out at the Westside Hotel, drinking and gambling. When nothing seemed to pan out back home, he returned to Texas once more. A few months later, in Orange County, Texas, he killed the chief of police.

Collinwood Hanging Tree

In the heart of Collinwood in Wayne County there's a small town park with a tree growing in it that many locals insist was used as the hanging tree back in the days when public executions were more common in Tennessee. On tempestuous nights when the elements are raging, all the trees in the park will sway and move in the wind, except that one. Its leaves remain still, as if the only thing that can stir them is the weight of a human body or the movement of a recently detached soul escaping through its branches.

The Hackberry and the Oak

Legends are born in all kinds of ways. Sometimes a real historical event happens, but then gets told and retold in such a way that gradually the details are refined or reemphasized (our delicate way of saying "forgotten" and "exaggerated") until it takes on a satisfying shape and is passed down for further embellishment by the next generation. At other times, a strange natural feature, such as a bottomless pit or a meteor shower, just begs for explanation, and the storytellers among us are always willing to supply one.

And then sometimes it's some combination of the two—a historical event is somehow reflected in a natural phenomenon because neither the event nor the phenomenon were quite weird enough to engender a legend on its own. The story of Connestoga and Nocatula seems to fall into this category.

In Athens, McMinn County, a huge oak and an almost equally large hackberry tree tower over the campus of Tennessee Wesleyan College, arching together with their leaves intermingled high above the ground. By itself, there's nothing particularly strange about this, but there's a legend attached to the trees nonetheless.

It dates back to the French and Indian War, which raged from 1754 to 1763. The war was mostly fought between the British and the French, with the different Indian groups taking sides as it best suited their interests. In this territory the Cherokees were at first allied with the English, who were stationed at Fort Loudoun, but after a few years the Cherokees switched alliances and began to help the French. In 1760 they attacked and destroyed Loudoun, then ambushed the English soldiers as they retreated toward South Carolina.

Though wounded, one of the English soldiers somehow managed to escape and staggered into a nearby Indian community, where he threw himself on the mercy of the elders. Not only did they admire him for this show of gall, but some of them could still recall the time just a few years before when the English had acted as friends. So they took pity on him and decided to nurse him back to recovery. A woman named Nocatula tended his wounds, and the officer fell in love with his nurse. Either his wounds took an awfully long time to heal, or he was in no hurry to leave, for eventually he was welcomed into the tribe and given the name Connestoga, meaning "oak."

However, the former soldier's living arrangement created friction within the village, and it threatened the Cherokee's relationships with the French, with whom they hoped to engage in trade. One man was especially put out at the presence of Connestoga, for he had hoped to become Nocatula's husband himself. In a fit of anger, he stabbed the Englishman in the chest, then dropped the knife and ran off into the woods.

According to the old legend, on seeing her dying lover, Nocatula then did the *Romeo & Juliet* thing and picked up the knife and plunged it into her own heart. To provide food in the afterlife for the two dead lovers, the grieving elders placed an acorn in Connetoga's hand and a hackberry in Nocatula's and buried them in adjacent graves. The two seeds sprouted and eventually grew into the two mighty trees that soar over the campus today.

Or maybe not. Other variants of the story say that the trees lasted about 150 years, and then died and were replaced. Either way, the college is committed to keeping the story going, for not only are there two large trees of the correct species on the site but a second (or third) new pair has already been planted and stands patiently waiting in the wings for the time when they, too, can take over the job of looming, intertwining, and proving that the legend is true.

The Lady of the Lake

Memphis's Overton Park is not the kind of place most people would find overly creepy. On any average afternoon it's filled with joggers and Frisbee throwers, picnickers and art students sketching away, and stroller-pushing couples on the way to the zoo—in other words, people just relaxing and enjoying themselves in a well-loved part of their city. But as darkness descends, the crowds dwindle down until it's virtually empty. A vaguely sinister ambience descends upon its 342 acres, and one gets the feeling that almost anything could happen.

Apparently something terrible did happen there fifty or sixty years ago that has left a lingering presence in the place. Just after dawn one morning, a contingent of bird-watchers found a woman in her midthirties, barefoot and wearing a blue dress, submerged in Rainbow Lake. Her mouth and eyes were still open in what looked like a stifled cry.

Although the "Lady in the Lake" was well dressed and showed no tattoos, scars, or needle tracks that might have suggested she had been a hooker, the body was never identified. There was no purse nor any jewelry or belongings—just the dress she wore—nor any sign of struggle to indicate what had happened. Even bloodhounds brought to the scene found nothing. It was almost as if the lady had been dropped into the water from a passing plane. After several months in the cooler at the county morgue, the corpse was quietly taken to the Memphis potter's field and buried under a numbered metal post, while the thin files of stapled police reports and autopsy paperwork were filed with the rest of the city's unsolved cases.

Within months of the death, park staff began hearing occasional reports from credible witnesses that a barefooted woman in a blue dress had approached them begging for help, but when they had tried to assist her, she vanished. Memphians are protective of their park—Overton has one of the few stands of old-growth forest left in the state, undisturbed since before the arrival of Europeans hundreds of years ago—and panhandlers are definitely frowned upon. But according to the witnesses, the woman in the blue dress seems far more distressed than someone merely asking for money. It's not, they've said, as if she wants something, but more as if she's frantically desperate to tell them something.

If you find yourself in that part of the park early in the morning or just at twilight when there are few other people about, and you happen to run into her, you could become the city's hero by being a good listener.

Boone's Buried Treasure

The town of Erin in Houston County takes great pride in its Irish heritage, so it's no wonder that some of the legends told thereabouts seem to have more to do with the Emerald Isle than with Tennessee. Maybe their ancestors brought some leprechauns with them. One local tale of buried treasure, however, seems to have nothing to do with the little people. In fact, enough folks believe the story to have invested a small fortune in shovels, metal detectors, and ground-penetrating radar in hopes that it would eventually pay off.

Old Man William Boone moved into the area in the 1830s and made quite a bit of money in the local industries. He built a house on Well's Creek at the Musterground near Erin, and even though his wife, Mary, had died shortly before the Civil War, he had somehow managed to make it through the Great Unpleasantness with his home and money intact. But in the summer of 1873 Boone came down with cholera, which was sweeping through that part of the country. Realizing he wasn't going to survive, he called his oldest son, thirty-four-year-old Ethelred, and asked him to dig a deep hole out in the orchard behind the house. He was

going to bury his money in a big cast-iron wash pot, he said, to prevent his lazy children from frittering away the money. Ethelred helped him bury the money.

A few hours later Boone was dead. Unfortunately, by the next morning Ethelred was sick, too. It hit him so hard and fast that he couldn't summon the strength to recover the pot of money and didn't even have time to do more than mumble something in his delirium about a treasure out in the orchard before he, too, passed away.

Ever since then, fortune hunters have dug through that orchard hunting Old Man Boone's gold, but as far as anyone ever heard, it was never recovered. The old Boone homestead still stands abandoned. Sometime in the 1940s the highway was rerouted and part of the area where the orchard once stood is paved now. Another part of it may be under the parking lot of the Deerfield Inn next door. But you have to ask yourself: How far could two men with cholera—one fully sick and the other coming down with it—lug a pot of money? Maybe someone will figure it out someday and strike it rich.

William Boone is buried less than a mile south of the homestead in the Lockhart graveyard on Coleman Loop off the Waverly Highway.

Green Is the Color of Revenge

Across the road from Greenwood Cemetery in Chattanooga is a small but deep lake where, according to Allan Mott, a murder took place many years ago.

At the far end of the lake there was once a large summer house belonging to a wealthy family. Around the turn of the last century the daughter of the family that owned it moved in with her new husband so he could finish writing a novel. For fun, the newlyweds sometimes rowed around the lake in a small boat, or went walking in the parklike cemetery, which had flowering shrubs and trees.

A few years later, the wife lost her baby during childbirth. It left her paralyzed from the waist down, but her doctors were optimistic for her recovery. She was bedridden for months, a shut-in in the upstairs bedroom, where her husband dutifully fed and bathed her. The two of them talked of future plans, but until she got better, things would follow the same seemingly endless routine, day after tiresome day.

When more than a year passed with no real signs of improvement, the husband started to lose interest in their shared future. He began entertaining the idea of having an affair. After so many months of sleeping alone, he wanted to feel good again—good enough to write again.

A woman he met in a bar and soon began seeing started dropping hints that if only his wife weren't around, he could have a normal, active life, free to create once again. In time, her subtle but relentless suggestions started to make sense. One evening, he told his wife that he wanted to take her down to the lake just like in the old times. He wrapped her in a heavy blanket, telling her he didn't want her to catch a chill.

But when they got down to the lake, he suddenly pulled the blanket over her face and gave the wheelchair a shove and watched it roll in. The soggy blanket muffled her screams. He wept bitterly as he lied to investigators, telling them that he'd gone back to the house for a second blanket. When he returned, he told them, he discovered that she had accidentally rolled in. He had jumped in to save her, but it was too late. They believed him, and even called him a hero.

The barfly moved in and eventually married. But once they'd tied the knot he discovered that his new wife was no match for the elegant woman he'd murdered. She drank, swore, and invited her "male friends" over. One of them threatened to kill him one night, chasing him with a knife down to the water's edge. To escape, the writer jumped in the boat and rowed it out into the middle of the lake.

As the writer rowed across the lake in the full moonlight, a greenish mist seemed to surge out of the water and swirl around him, momentarily obscuring him from view. When the mist cleared, the boat lay upside down, capsized in the water. The writer was nowhere to be seen.

Officials recovered his drowned body, burying him next to his first wife. It turned out that the house still belonged to her family, and without a new will, wife number two wound up with nothing.

Locals say the house mysteriously caught fire and burned not long afterward. And today, sometimes wheelchair tracks still reappear at the edge of the lake. If you see them, don't stand too close to the water, and beware of the mist.

Swift's Lost Treasure

After gold was discovered in 1799 near Concord, North Carolina, and in 1828 at Dahlonega, Georgia, the fate of the Cherokees was sealed. Rumor had it that the Indians had been mining gold and silver in the Appalachians. To get at the wealth of places like the lost silver mine of John Munday and George Swift, the English- and German-speaking settlers would have to send the Cherokees away.

According to a strange testament that Swift wrote shortly before his death, the two men had worked a rich lode, smelted it, and then left a load of coins and ingots hidden in the mountains. Swift had lost track of the cache; but he made a map based on his recollections, and people have been hunting for Swift's treasure ever since.

In 1718, as the testament describes, Swift headed to New Orleans. He gave up sailing and the buggy climate of Louisiana to try his luck in the English colony at Portsmouth, Virginia, changing his name to get out of his French navy contract. Here he met fellow renegade Leon Marquette, who told of a rich vein of silver. They agreed to become partners and planned to dig up the lode.

They headed west, crossing

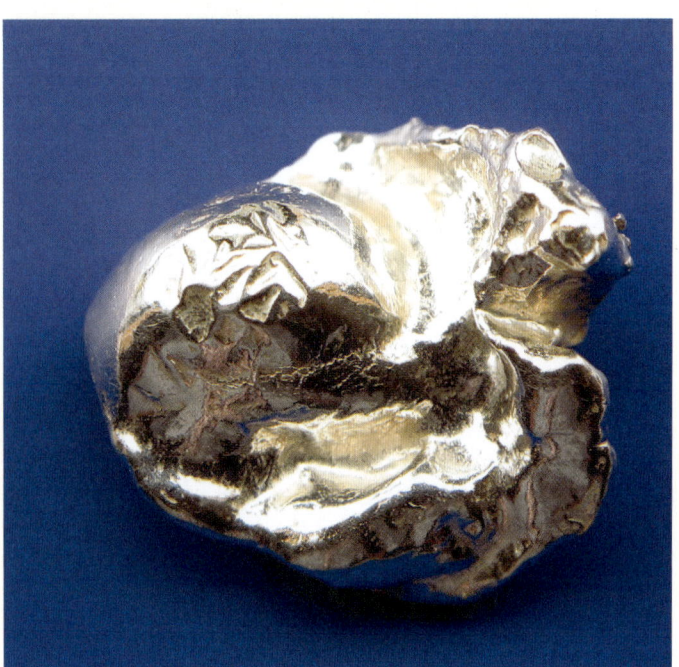

> . . . through several chains of Large Blue Mountains, then crossing a rolling limestone region 30 or 40 miles in a northern direction to a baron knob on a spruce-pine mountain, laying between the 36th and 37th degrees of north latitude. . . . We came through a large gap filled with spruce and cedar, in Indian language called Mocasona.

Swift described this location as being southwest of "Kent trading post." This, along with the latitude, narrows things down to roughly somewhere between Knoxville, Tennessee; Wytheville, Virginia; and North Corbin, Kentucky.

> Then [we headed] north across a bluffy region to an unknown river. Then up the river to a large bluff on the right hand side as you go up over, topped with cedars with [a] creek flowing in near opposite cliffs. Thence up said river about three miles to an old Indian graveyard. Thence up a small rush-filled branch flowing east through a bottom. Thence up said branch to a deer and buffalo lick basin and gap . . . filled with reeds and tall grass. Thence through this gap to a valley running east and west . . . Take notice to the ridge. Thence four or five miles to [a] half-mooned shaped rock house [a cavelike rock overhang] on a little creek filled with spruce and cedar.

After smelting the silver into two "pony loads" of French coins and returning to Portsmouth, they returned with third partner John Munday, and a female cook.

They make camp at a

> ... new place in a saddle gap on Long Blue Ridge, lying west. The ore being much richer and easier to work, carrying our ore over a large mountain to a little creek full of spruce and cedar where we smelted [it]. The smelter [was] hid near the forks of this little creek in a spruce pine cove surrounded by a horse shoe bend and wilderness. The creek being rough and full of large stones. Running south and flowing into the creek, near two peculiar rocks with the creek running between them, one facing eastward and the other westward.... The mine was bounded on the west by a creek and a big blue spring containing Indian beads in various shapes. Bound on the north by a long bald mountain, on the east by a creek and haystack nobs starting in a valley bottom
> ... On the south by a gap of haystack or potato knobs....

They stayed for almost a year, but Munday killed Marquette and the cook in a dispute. For reasons he didn't reveal, Swift helped Munday bury them in the "half-moon shaped rock house near the smelter."

They left, marking a large tree with the words SWIFT AND MUNDAY MINE carved in the bark. They left a pick, a couple of drills, and a hammer with "a French crown on face" in the mine; in the small overhang cave near the smelter they hid their coin molds and sheepskin smelters' aprons, then buried their crucibles in the sand. A load of coins was supposedly buried nearby.

Many years later Swift went looking for the mine one last time. By this time settlers had been chopping down trees, building cabins, and changing the landscape so that nothing looked the same. Now half blind and getting old, Swift no longer recognized the territory, either. Frustrated, he penned this testament, making an offer to anyone who would help him.

> I, George William Swift, being duly sworn, disposes and agrees that anyone finding my smelter and telling me, I will give them one half of the hidden treasure and one half of the mine.
> I dispose and sayeth that these directions and map of my smelter to any one that finds my smelter. This being given April 16, 1775. My age 86 years.

In case you feel like you haven't been socking away enough savings for your retirement, you can search for Swift's lost hoard. He's long dead, so you won't need to split the profits, but don't quit your day job—we'll say up front that lots of people have tried and failed.

Some of the locations that have been scrutinized are Newman's Ridge north of Sneedville, Holston Mountain north of Elizabethton, and in the Clinch range near Klondike in Hawkins County.

Effects of Moonshine

According to John Rice Irwin of Norris, when Harve Donahue of Powell, Knox County, took a straight stick of wood and stuck it into a barrel of moonshine, it came out so twisted it could never be straightened out again. Proof, as if anyone needed any, that moonshine can be bad for you. A hundred and eighty proof, in fact.

Whole Lotta Shakin' Goin' On

Two huge concrete heads fronting the parking lot across the way from the old homestead of legendary railroad martyr Casey Jones in Jackson represent the principal actors of another legendary drama, the fabled marriage of Princess Laughing Eyes and Chief Reelfoot. Reelfoot Lake, according to this dubious legend, was purported to have been created by the Great Spirit as a punishment inflicted on the clubfooted chief and his Chickasaw community for having stolen the maiden down in Choctaw country and making her his bride in northwest Tennessee.

Acting with a lack of surgical precision that will be familiar to readers of the Old Testament, the Great Spirit didn't just eliminate the disobedient Chief Reelfoot, but came down hard down on the entire area—flattening all the rest of the tribe along with whatever livestock they owned and, we can assume, Reelfoot's helpless, unwilling bride as well, even though she hadn't exactly gone along with the plan in the first place. The Great Spirit's foot stomp left a dent so deep that the waters of the Mississippi flowed in and formed the lake. The two big heads had been erected in the mid-1950s to mark the entrance to a recreational area beside the lake, then they were moved to Jackson in 1994.

Authors like Irvin S. Cobb say that the lake got its name because it is shaped like the splayed foot of a barefoot fieldhand. A number of historians, on the other hand, claim that it was named for one William "Reelfoot" Jones, a clubfooted local fellow who died in 1839 after he slipped off a log and drowned in one of the creeks that fed the lake. Both these arguments seem to hold a little more water than the Great Spirit legend.

But whatever the reason for the name, geologists point out that Reelfoot Lake formed during a series of truly major earthquakes that took place here between 1811 and 1812.

Collectively called the New Madrid Quakes (after the nearby Missouri town that was closest to the epicenter at the time), they rank among the most powerful tremors in recorded history. Although information is scant since so much of the country was sparsely populated then, the quakes would have registered more than 8.0 on the Richter scale, resulting in as many as 100,000 deaths, and were felt by people in an area of about a million square miles. (By comparison, the 1906 earthquake that destroyed San Francisco and left three thousand dead measured 7.9 and was felt over about six thousand square miles).

The New Madrid Quakes began around 2 A.M. on December 16, 1811, just across the Mississippi River west of present-day Dyersburg. More shocks occurred at 8 A.M. and 11 A.M. the same day. People living as far away as Savannah, Georgia, said the ground pitched like the deck of a ship tossing in the ocean. In Buffalo, New York, houses shook two feet in either direction for almost five minutes. As aftershocks continued over the next several weeks, entire towns along the river were quickly abandoned. When the next big quakes struck, on the morning of January 23, 1812, the entire towns of Little Prairie and Point Pleasant fell into the river and disappeared, fortunately with no loss of life.

The biggest quake of all hit two weeks later, on the morning of February 7. As far away as in Boston and New York church bells clanged on their own while President James Madison thought that intruders had broken into the White House. Meanwhile, waterfalls formed on the Mississippi as the land cracked and lifted. For a while the river ran backward; and where the land had subsided, it filled with water, drowning some 150,000 acres of trees to create Reelfoot Lake.

At the same time, parts of Tennessee wound up on the Arkansas and Missouri sides of the main current. Some towns still technically part of Tennessee (like Reverie) have

remained stranded west of the river ever since. Over the course of the next several months more than two thousand tremors continued to strike up and down the Mississippi River along Tennessee's western border.

Gradually the aftershocks subsided, although even today, almost two centuries later, they still occur several times a week. (Visit http://folkworm.ceri.memphis.edu/recenteqs/Maps/90-36.html to learn about recent tremors recorded here.)

Seismologists say that this means that really big quakes will happen again as soon as enough pressure has built up, but will be even more catastrophic next time since the fault falls along a major hub of U.S. commerce (between Memphis and St. Louis).

Until recently few officials have bothered to care. A major industrial complex with an aluminum refinery and a power station have been built next to the river just a mile and half from the Tennessee line and less than ten miles from Reelfoot Lake. According to the calculations of seismologists, the refinery is located almost exactly over the epicenter of the 1811–1812 quakes. If the story of Chief Reelfoot holds any truth at all, we may may find out that it's always a bad idea to buck the will of a higher power.

When the earthquake happens, as earthquake scientists assure us it will, they say, "Hurricane Katrina will look like a Sunday school picnic." For decades there had been plenty of forewarnings about that disaster waiting to happen, too.

LOCAL LEGENDS 35

Officers' Gate Post

A weatherbeaten and lichen-covered chunk of old split fence post in the Overton County Museum in Livingston offers stark, if somewhat confusing, evidence about an event that happened long ago in the Sinking Cane (now Rock Springs) community, about three miles north of Monterey.

William and Cynthia Officer were at home on the morning of Saturday, March 12, 1864, serving breakfast to some Confederate officers (including their nineteen-year-old son, John Officer). They were passing the biscuits and retelling the story of the Battle of Stones River that had ended on January 2 when a company of Union cavalry burst in and killed six of the Confederates in indoor combat. A seventh was dragged out of the house, stood in front of the fence post, and summarily executed by a firing squad. The dozens of bullet holes in the post are presented as evidence that this happened.

As the Yankees were preparing to burn the house, so the story goes, an elderly slave named Abe retrieved his personal belongings, including his old mattress. He came back out with his bedroll, having wrapped the still-alive John Officer inside.

It is a little hard to picture old Abe lugging a mattress containing a nearly grown man inside without raising suspicion. But oral history is, after all, the stuff from which legends are born.

In any case, as it turned out the house wasn't burned after all. After attempting to set fire to it, the Yankees grew impatient and left. The old Officer homeplace is still standing, two miles down Rock Springs Road off Highway 84, south of Livingston.

Ancient Mysteries

They are everywhere, and in plain sight. Hundreds of hulking mounds of earth. Thousands of gaping caves. Vine-covered ruins near every road and highway. Hieroglyphs from lost tongues on ordinary street corners. Bones and potsherds, strange symbols etched on outcrops, alignments of stones, lost temples to forgotten gods . . . each of them still asking questions: What are these things? What lies hidden inside? Where do they lead? What do they mean? Who made them, and why?

No need to go to Egypt, India, or Peru for a taste of the ancient and the mysterious. Expensive suburban houses in the Princeton Hills development near Cleveland, Bradley County, encircle the great Candies Creek Mound like a prehistoric village where thatched huts once stood eight hundred years ago.

Tennessee is crawling with mysteries. If we succeed in tempting you to go looking for them, bear in mind one of Oscar Wilde's famous lines: "The true mystery of the world is the visible, not the invisible," and keep your eyes wide open.

Mystery at Bat Creek

Mounted in a display case all by itself in the University of Tennessee at Knoxville's McClung Museum is a flat, dark reddish stone not quite five inches long. On its surface is a row of inscribed letters—neither pictographic hieroglyphs nor random natural markings, but some form of alphabetical writing. What this writing means, or why it was done, remains one of the unsolved mysteries of American archaeology.

The stone (see inverted image on facing page) was found in 1889 below a burial mound near the mouth of Bat Creek in Loudon County, on what is now a promontory jutting from the west side of the creek into Tellico Lake. Excavations in this area began in 1886 by John P. Rogan and John W. Emmert, two Tennessee archaeologists from the Bureau of Ethnology of the Smithsonian Institution. Their boss, Cyrus Thomas, assembled field expedition reports from Florida to North Dakota.

Three burial mounds were found where Bat Creek joins the Little Tennessee River. Excavations of the first mound revealed traditional burial goods associated with the Mississippian culture that had flourished in central and eastern North America (with huge temple complexes in places like Cahokia, Illinois, and Etowah, Georgia). When the second mound was excavated, a metal button and two metal buckles were found, suggesting that this burial had occurred after European arrival. However, since a large oak grew out of the mount, it probably hadn't been a very recent burial, either. (Mississippians were largely gone by around A.D. 1600, but some cultural rituals were still practiced among the many descended cultures, including the Cherokee.)

But when the third Bat Creek mound was excavated, the archaeologists stumbled upon a real mystery. They found nine skeletons, eight of which had been positioned with their heads to the north, and only one pointing south. They had been positioned directly on the ground, and then the burial mound—twenty-eight feet in diameter and five feet high—had been heaped over them.

In their field notes, the archaeologists numbered the nine skeletons with number 1 being the lone skeleton found with the skull toward the south. As Cyrus Thomas explained in his report:

> *No relics were found with any but No. 1, immediately under the skull of which were two copper bracelets, an engraved stone, a small drilled fossil, a copper bead, a bone implement, and some small pieces of polished wood. The earth about the skeletons was wet and the pieces of wood soft and colored green by contact with the copper bracelets. The bracelets had been rolled in something, probably bark, which crumbled away when they were taken out. The engraved stone lay partially under the back part of the skull and was struck by the steel prod used in probing.* [Cyrus Thomas, Twelfth Annual Report of the Bureau of Ethnology, 1894]

Thomas immediately identified the engravings on the stone as ". . . beyond question letters of the Cherokee

HOLINESS TO THE LORD. An inscription worn on the forehead of the High-Priest, as described in Exodus xxxix. 30: "And they made the plate of the holy crown of pure gold, and wrote upon it a writing like to the engraving of a signet, HOLINESS TO THE LORD."

alphabet invented . . . about 1821." For Thomas, that was the end of the story—he assumed this meant that the third mound dated sometime between 1821 and 1838, when most of the Cherokee had been forced out of Tennessee, Georgia, and the Carolinas and sent off to Indian Territory (a.k.a. Oklahoma) on the infamous "Trail of Tears" death march. The engraved stone and other items from the dig were illustrated in his *Report*, then relegated to the bottom of an artifact drawer at the Smithsonian where they would remain ignored and forgotten for the next seventy-five years.

Around 1970, Dr. Joseph Mahan Jr. of the Columbus (Georgia) Museum of Arts & Crafts happened to be reading Thomas's *Report* when he ran across the illustration of the strange stone. Mahan was familiar with the Cherokee alphabet, but couldn't see any relationship between the writing on the stone and the written Cherokee language. (See image on following page.) When he inverted the *Report*, however, the letters seemed to resemble more closely ancient writing from the Middle East. On a hunch, he requested a photo of the stone from the Smithsonian and sent it to Dr. Cyrus Gordon, an expert in ancient Mediterranean languages at Brandeis University. Gordon wrote back immediately that, ". . . there can be no doubt whatever. . . . five [of the] letters are definitely and unproblematically letters in the Old Hebrew [Phoenician] script." By looking at the stone upside down and reading the symbols from right to left (as one would read Hebrew), he translated part of the inscription as "L-YHW" and interpreted this as ancient Canaanite to mean "For Judea." In other words, this suggested that the one man who was buried backward from all the others might have been Jewish.

But this could be a perfect illustration of the old proverb, "To a hammer, everything looks like a nail." Dr. Gordon had long been a proponent of a theory that there had been Roman contact with the Americas as long ago as A.D. 200. He knew that Roman and Jewish coins had been found at several sites in Kentucky (although none of them had been excavated by trained archaeologists, which casts doubts on these "discoveries" today). Further study of the Bat Creek Stone (as it had come to be called) suggested

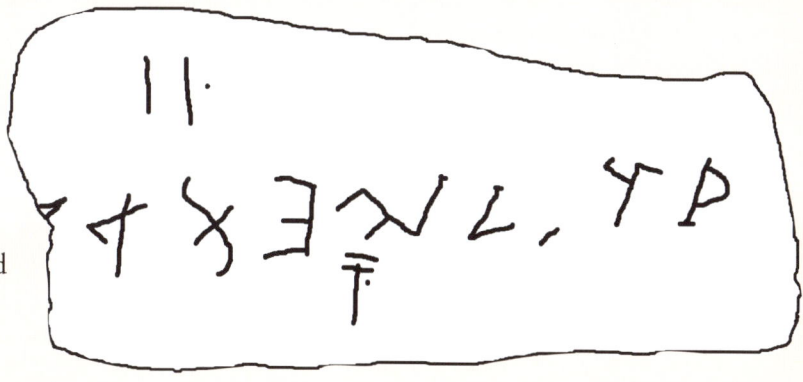

to Gordon that the fragment was part of a longer inscription, which could be translated as "Year 1 of the golden age for the Jews" or else, "Year 1: Comet [Messiah] of the Jews." If this interpretation is accurate, the stone might be evidence that around A.D. 135, Jewish refugees fleeing from the Romans after the Second Rebellion (A.D. 132–135) had made it across the ocean to found the Messianic Order in the New World in eastern Tennessee. Later researchers ratcheted up the date even earlier, proposing that a Judean ship may have escaped a Roman naval conflict and crossed the Atlantic as early as A.D. 68.

D a	R e	T i	&o	O'u	i v
S ga O ka	P ge	y gi	A go	J gu	E gv
T ha	P he	J hi	F ho	T hu	& hv
W la	O le	P li	G lo	M lu	A lv
& ma	A me	H mi	5 mo	Y mu	
O na t hna G nah	A ne	h ni	Z no	H nu	O nv
T qua	W que	P qui	V quo	W quu	E quv
U sa o& s	4 se	b si	t so	8 su	R sv
L da W ta	S de b te	J di J ti	V do	S du	O dv
& dla L tla	L tle	C tli	H tlo	W tlu	P tlv
G tsa	V tse	Ir tsi	K tso	J tsu	C tsv
G wa	W we	O wi	O wo	J wu	6 wv
&D ya	B ye	b yi	6 yo	G yu	B yv

The hypotheses soon began to sound like something from *The Da Vinci Code*, and other evidence has emerged to stick a few pins in them. Hiwassee College professor Lowell Kirk came to the conclusion that the "find" may instead have been a trick perpetrated by a man named Major Luther Blackman, a Republican tombstone carver who had moved to Tennessee from up North and opened a shop near Bat Creek.

Kirk pointed out that Cyrus Thomas had fired John Emmert in 1887 for public drunkenness, and only a few days after Emmert was reinstated in 1889, the mysterious stone was discovered. Kirk theorized that Blackman created the stone and then planted it, hoping it would be discovered as a fraud and thereby discredit both Emmert and the people who helped him get his job back. If that was Blackman's intent, however, it fizzled, for nothing came of the discovery at the time. Yet another theory has it that Emmert made the stone and submitted it with the other relics in hopes of getting even with his boss by making Thomas look like a fool.

One more piece of the puzzle emerged years later in a 2004 article by archaeologists Robert C. Mainfort Jr. and Mary L. Kwas, published in *American Antiquity*. They had discovered an illustration on page 134 of the *General History, Cyclopedia and Dictionary of Freemasonry* by Robert Macoy, published in 1868, which included symbols that looked an awful lot like many of the letters on the Bat Creek stone. Was the stonemason Blackman also a Freemason? Could he have copied the letters from his reference book?

Despite the incredible similarities, the jury is still out for those who support the "Jews beat Columbus" theory (notwithstanding the possibility that Columbus himself may have been Jewish; that's another story). They argue that both the Bat Creek inscription and the Masonic writing could have come from a similar ancient source. They point out that ancient Japanese pottery has been found in Peru, and that Zuñi Indians share Asian traits. If the Japanese could cross the Pacific, so this line of reasoning goes, then perhaps Jews crossing the Atlantic isn't so farfetched after all. Or maybe the inscription isn't Hebrew at all, but Old Welsh—that's yet another theory.

So for now, the little Bat Creek Stone represents a mysterious anomaly from the unrecorded past.

The Morristown Tablet

The Bat Creek Stone was hardly the last of the anachronistic inscriptions to have emerged from the soils of Tennessee. Although its current whereabouts is unknown, a flat rock was reportedly found near Morristown sometime in the twentieth century that was studied in 1981 in connection with another tablet said to be found in a mound near Grave Creek, West Virginia, in 1838. The Morristown Tablet (see image below) seemed uncannily similar to the Grave Creek Stone (see top image). In fact, it has been interpreted from "ancient Semetic" or "Iberian" to reveal exactly the same statement: "Mound in honor of Tadach. His wife caused this engraved stone to be inscribed." Finding two identical inscriptions three hundred miles apart has made some ancient inscription researchers doubtful. They ask, Could there really have been two guys named Tadach? We ask, Isn't it more likely that one or both of these rocks is a hoax? You be the judge.

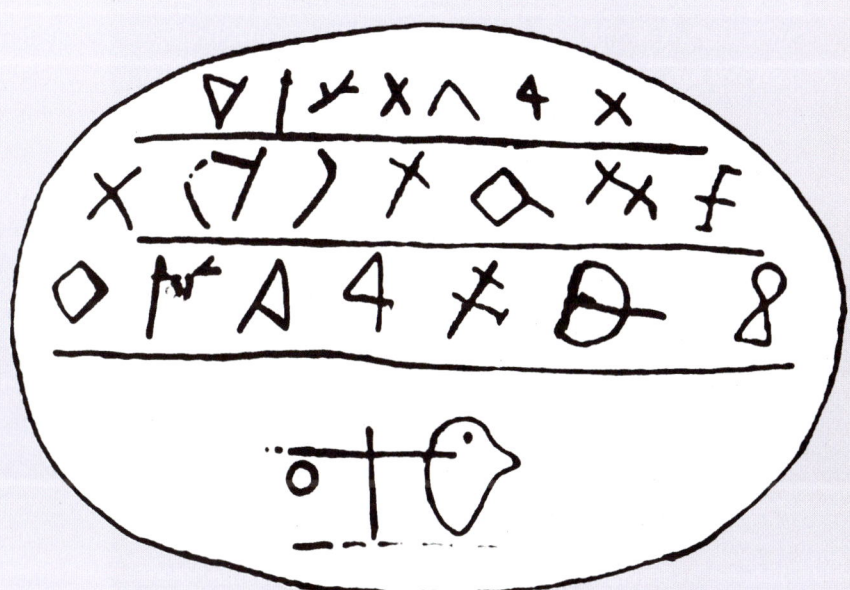

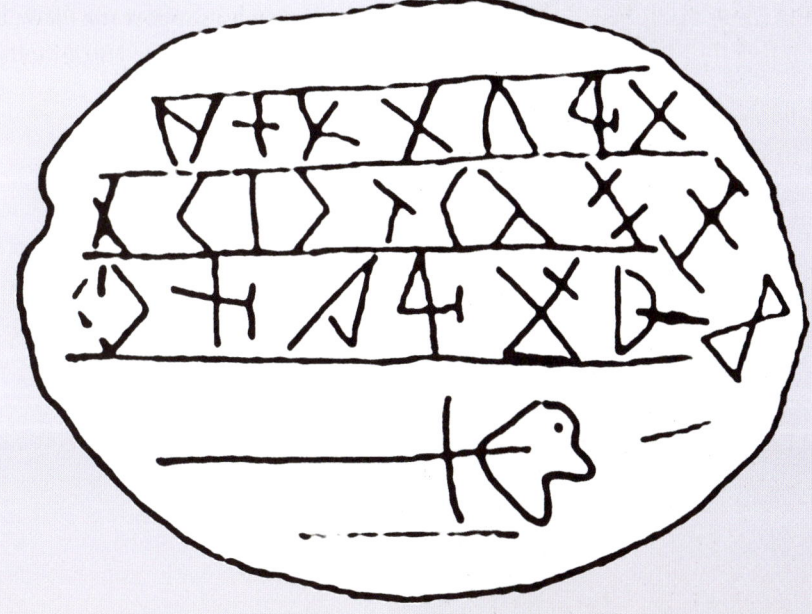

Holey Tennessee, Batman!

Tennessee has more known caves than any other state (nearly 8,500), and some of the most remarkable features of any caves in the country. These include the largest underground lake (at the Lost Sea, near Madisonville in Monroe County, which also contains a feature called "Hell Hole," as seen here), the second biggest underground room (the five-acre Rumble Room in Rumbling Falls Cave, near Spencer, Van Buren County), the ninth-longest cave (Blue Spring Cave in White County, with more than thirty-three miles mapped so far), caves with massive bat populations (Hubbard's Cave near McMinnville, Warren County, with more than 500,000 bats of six different species), and hundreds of rare and endangered species, as well as caves with famous fossil finds (Big Bone Cave in Van Buren County, where giant sloth bones were found in 1811, and Robertson Cave in Overton County, where two more giant sloths were discovered in 1962).

For thousands of years Native Americans used caves for refuge, mining delicate pre-Columbian "mud glyphs" (images scratched in mud) that have been found in a number of the underground shelters, some of them thousands of years old and others dating to around the time that Europeans began colonizing the Americas. Drawings of turtles, winged humanoids, owls, snakes, and turkeys intermingle with long wavy squiggles almost always made by using three fingers. The winged humanoid often turns up, but no one seems to know why. Figures farther away from the cave entrances show humans changing into snakes or underworld creatures.

Dunbar Cave

As whites settled Tennessee, caves saw other uses. During the war of 1812 and the Civil War, bat guano was mined from thick deposits on cave floors to be filtered through wood ashes and rendered into saltpeter. (Dunbar Cave in Clarksville, Montgomery County, was one of the guano suppliers.) Saltpeter mixed with sulfur and charcoal was used as gunpowder in early firearms and explosives. Caves were also used for making moonshine, storing food, and quick temporary shelter until houses could be built.

In more relaxed times, cool air made caves ideal for summertime entertainments. Bluegrass master Roy Acuff bought Dunbar Cave after the World War II and booked big band acts like Tommy Dorsey and Benny Goodman, as well as country and western shows, until television and electrical air conditioning brought the era of cave concerts to a close in the 1950s.

Ruskin Cave

In other colorful cave histories, Ruskin Cave in Dickson County was known for many years as the Great Cave, since it had a huge entrance fronting onto Yellow Creek that yawned open like an airplane hangar. In 1877 two men bought the cave and built a gristmill inside its entrance that became a tourist attraction. Less than ten years later an air-cooled dancehall inside the cave advertised the mill as an entertainment feature. Around the mouth of the cave a small community called Cave Mills provided housing for the people who worked in the cave industries.

In 1896 a utopian socialist group called the Ruskin Cooperative Association bought (and renamed) the cave, taking over most of the village to house its 240 commune members. The idea was that everyone would work together in Ruskin's small-scale industries and also share the profits while all decisions would be determined by group vote. Instead of money, they paid each other in scrip, which could only be used to buy things from other members of the colony. Ruskin Cave was an icehouse; a food warehouse; a meat locker (with a small railroad to haul the meat); a cannery; a mail-order business; and a water-powered factory for making things like chewing gum, caffeine-free coffee, pants, and suspenders. The socialist newspaper they printed on the premises, *The Coming Nation*, had sixty thousand subscribers around the country and generated a significant amount of income. Their big Fourth of July barbecue featured performances by the Ruskin Orchestra and Mandolin Club, with waltzes and polkas to bring in crowds of local farm families.

However, the Ruskinites quickly ran afoul of those same farm families and one another when it got out that they practiced polygamous "free love" in the darker back passages of the cave. Ongoing sex scandals and internal squabbles over property ownership and profit sharing eventually led them to move to Waycross, Georgia, and the colony disbanded shortly thereafter. The whole "socialist experiment" lasted only six years, and ended with the few remaining members in poverty and diseased. Tennessee still isn't a hotbed of socialism!

Meanwhile, in 1904 the Ruskin Cave College Preparatory School and Conservatory of Music took over the cave, specializing in military training and music. The cave's "natural auditorium" was 80 feet wide, 40 feet high, and 350 feet deep, so it was perfect for concerts and other performances. After that, various religious schools moved in to take advantage of the cave's natural amplification for preaching sermons in cool, comfortable surroundings. In 1925 it became the Ruskin Cave Resort with a trailer camp, tourist cottages, a swimming pool, and a seventy-five-room hotel. A concrete dance

floor and bleachers added in the 1930s turned it into the "world's largest underground ballroom." More than thirteen thousand people attended the first dance evening held there. The cave's big Saturday night events became a proving ground for country and bluegrass musicians who hoped to graduate to broadcast performances on the Grand Ole Opry in Nashville, while its "cave dances" lasted until the 1970s.

In the 1980s songwriter David Allan Coe, creator of such hits as "Would You Lay with Me (in a Field of Stone)" and "Take This Job and Shove It," bought the property for concerts and big July Fourth shindigs. Caught up in "theme park envy" inspired by Dolly Parton's 1986 purchase and renaming of Dollywood, Tammy Wynette reportedly wanted to buy the cave from Coe to set up her own theme park. Instead, after Coe's departure, Ruskin Cave was briefly used as a home for troubled teens but now it belongs to the Renaissance Center, a learning facility based in nearby Dickson.

Pot Cave

Not all of the uses to which caves have been put have been quite so public. The existence of one now-famous Tennessee cave, once called Cato Cave, was a virtual secret for years while it was transformed into one of the largest (known) illegal endeavors in the state's history. In December 2005, acting on suspicious spikes in electricity usage in eastern Trousdale County, law enforcement officers raided an A-frame house located at 2125 Dixon Creek Road, north of Dixon Springs, and discovered one of the most amazing criminal enterprises this side of a James Bond thriller. Now known as the Tennessee Pot Cave, the A-frame house concealed the entrance to an underground hydroponic marijuana farm.

To enter the secret complex, the operators could drive their vehicles down a ramp into a below-grade garage.

ANCIENT MYSTERIES 45

Once inside, a massive hydraulic steel door concealed a tunnel slanting some fifty feet below ground to a living area complete with office, bunkrooms, kitchen, pantry, bathroom, and recreation area for the crew of eight that ran the cannabis conglomerate. Most of the workers were out-of-state laborers who, blindfolded before their arrival, had no idea where in the country they were working or who paid them.

Beyond the living area was the first of two huge growing rooms, 20 feet high and 250 feet long, outfitted with intense thousand-watt growing lamps, chemical drip feeds, decked pathways for the workers, and an area for weighing and wrapping the handcrafted hemp. The air temperature was a constant 87° F to facilitate plant growth. At the back of the cave was a hidden escape route that emerged three hundred feet from the house, underneath a hydraulically lifted rock at the edge of the woods.

The operation was capable of producing up to fourteen crops of top-rank reefer every year, each crop valued at half a million dollars or more. During the nine years that the operation lasted, it made Brian Gibson, Greg Compton, and Floridian Fred Strunk very rich. Authorities have never described in detail how the fortress-like setup was seized and how the growers were captured despite all their elaborate escape mechanisms, for fear that other criminals might learn from their mistakes. In May 2006, Strunk, sixty-three years old, was sentenced to eighteen years in prison after a guilty plea.

The house was torched by an arsonist in November 2006. The property (including the cave, which survived the fire unscathed) was sold at auction anyway in December 2007 and purchased by a Wisconsin-based cheese company, which plans to use the Pot Cave to age its fermented but entirely legal dairy products.

Thunder Hole

Just about every town in eastern Tennessee has one: a cave where kids go looking for trouble. In Morristown, it's the Thunder Hole, so called because in bad weather, a frightening roaring or rumbling sound can be heard coming from its entrance shaft of fifty feet by twenty-five feet.

Local historian Howard Hill claimed that it has a Civil War legend attached to it. Back in the 1860s the Widow Cassidy drew her well water from a bucket that extended down into the cave's near-vertical entrance shaft. Her sixteen-year-old son, Massilon, at home on furlough from the Confederate Army, heard a detachment of Union soldiers heading their way. Widow Cassidy told Massilon to stand in the bucket and hold onto the rope as she lowered him down into the cave. When the Bluecoats showed up, their captain dismounted and approached the widow, who was still standing by the well.

"Could we have some water for ourselves and our horses?" he asked.

She replied, "You're welcome to it, but today's my washday, and I'm anxious to get all my washing done before sundown. So all I ask is that you let me have the first bucketful. After that you can have all the water you want."

The captain agreed and waved two of his men over. "Help this kind lady get her bucket up so we can get ours," he said. The men soon raised the bucket containing Private Cassidy. They jumped to grab him, but according to the Morristown *Daily Gazette-Mail,* the captain ordered them to back away, flourished his hat with a bow, and said to the widow, "Madam, the first bucketful is yours, just as I promised."

With that, the Union soldiers quenched their thirsts, watered their horses, then waved good-bye as they set off in the direction of Dandridge.

ANCIENT MYSTERIES 47

Mystery of the Old Stone Fort

Archaeology is a science in that it studies objects or phenomena, creates hypotheses or theories to explain them, and then attempts to support the educated guesses with experimenting and excavating. But interpretations of such studies depend largely on the personalities of the people running them. In other words, they often see what they want to see. For instance, two archaeologists can visit the same ruins or dig in the same places and come away with very different explanations of what happened there in the past. Sometimes one explanation holds for a while; then someone offers a completely different explanation, only to be replaced by yet another one as time goes on.

Take the old fort in Coffee County, for example. Almost two thousand years ago, some unknown people built an earth-and-stone embankment overlooking the confluence of the Duck and Little Duck Rivers, just west of Manchester. (On many old maps, the main channel is called the Barren Fork and the smaller river is called the Bark Camp Fork, until they converge at this point to form the Duck River.) The embankment encloses almost fifty acres of flat land inside low walls more than a mile long. The walls go almost all the way around the enclosure, except for a few places where sheer cliffs below the bluff made attack impractical, if not impossible. No one seems to know who built this bastion, and why they went to so much effort to do so.

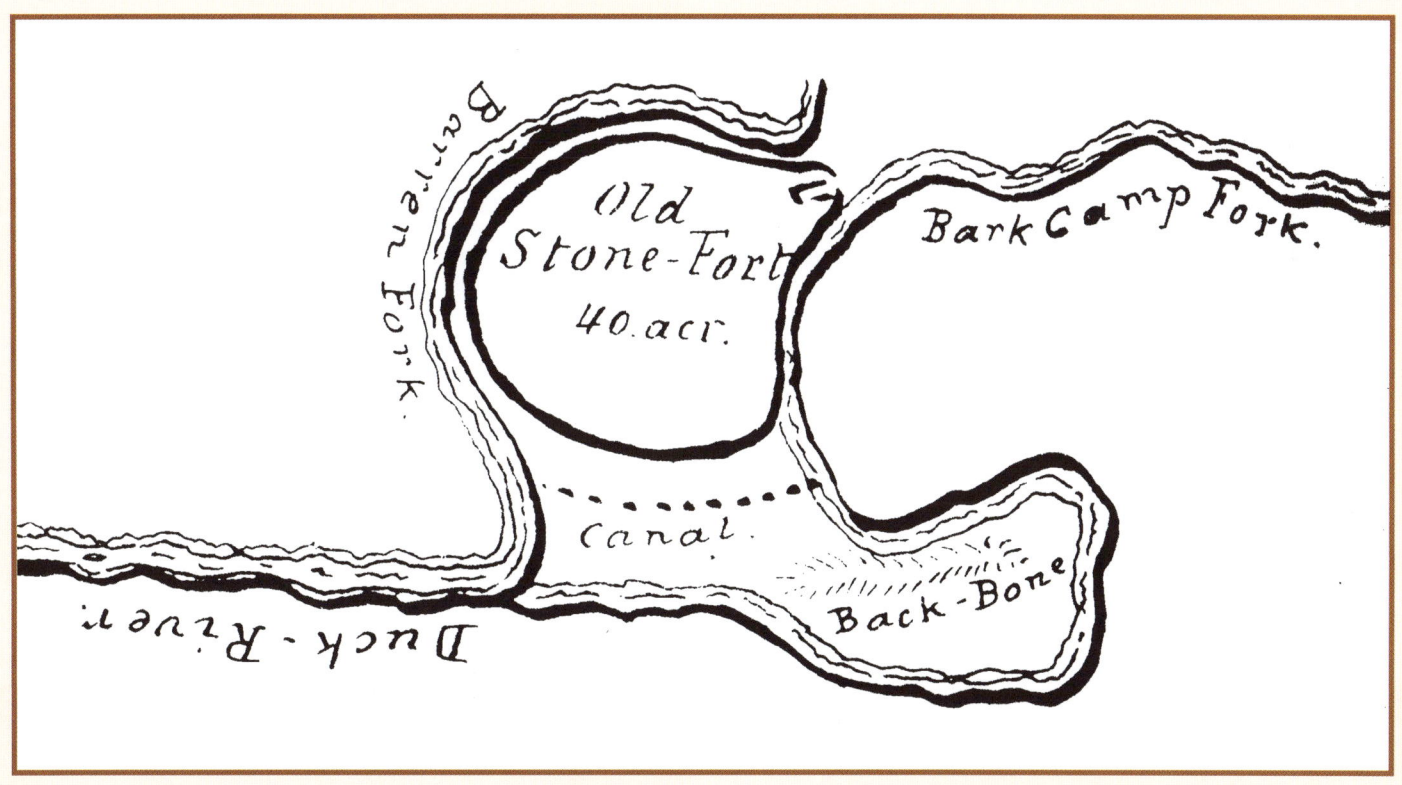

Settlers had trouble believing that Indians built this place, since typical villages were surrounded by wooden stockades or high fences made of pointed logs, not stone walls. Early maps of the region marked it only as the "Old Stone Fort" and the name stuck. In 1823, the Jackson (TN) *Pioneer* newspaper published a theory that it had been built in the sixteenth or seventeenth century by shipwrecked Spaniards, whose galleon had sunk off the coast of Florida, and who had made their way inland to get to Mexico.

As theories go, it's not as far-fetched as it may sound. Three conquistadors—Álvar Núñez Cabeza de Vaca, Hernando de Soto, and Juan Pardo—all led expeditions in the region, and both Cabeza de Vaca and Pardo built fortifications.

In 1827 John Neely Bryan explored the Old Stone Fort, looking for Spanish gold. He found only fool's gold. While he was there, he cut down a tree growing within the fort. Counting the tree's growth rings, Bryan estimated that the tree was at least 420 years old, meaning it was already an eighty-six-year-old tree when Columbus first saw America. (In case you didn't know: Columbus didn't discover the New World—nor was it new, since the Indians had been already here for thousands of years.) Since the fort seemed to predate the arrival of the Spanish, that theory fizzled out.

Over the next fifty-odd years, at least two top-notch archaeologists visited the site. Both Joseph Jones, hired by the Smithsonian in 1876, and Tennessee state archaeologist P. E. Cox in 1928 stuck with the prevailing belief that the place was an unusual example of a walled fortress built for defensive purposes. But built by whom and against whom, neither could guess.

In 1950, Chattanooga amateur archaeologist and local historian Zella Armstrong published a book entitled *Who Discovered America?* She noticed that walled enclosures in the South resembled similar structures in Wales.

She theorized that the Old Stone Fort had been built by Welshmen who had come to North America in the twelfth century with Prince Madoc of Wales. According to her theory, Welsh sailors had been blown off course and came ashore at Mobile, Alabama, about the year 1170, before making their way to Tennessee. She pointed out that the Dog River flows near Mobile, and that the river's name could be derived from the prince's name in old Welsh—Madog ap Owain Gwynedd. Not only that, but early English explorers compared some of the gutturals of certain Indian languages to the gagging sounds of Welsh. More than coincidence?

Probably not, according to most historians, who found Armstrong's theory a little too full of holes to hold much water. But then again, in 1960 ruins of a Norse village dating to around 1000 were discovered in Newfoundland, proving that Europeans had been in North America almost five hundred years before Columbus. In fact, more than a few people believed the Old Stone Fort had been built by Vikings.

Professional archaeologists continued to think it was made by Indians. Some thought it was an effigy mound, like the Great Serpent Mound in Ohio, but shaped like a turtle or a bear. (Aerial images reveal it is shaped more like a Christmas ham). Finally, in 1966 Charles Faulkner dug at the Old Stone Fort and came up with a new theory. Faulkner said that it, and perhaps other walled enclosures like it, were not forts at all but ceremonial places. The walls, he opined, were there to warn the uninitiated that what lay inside was sacred space, perhaps even a dangerous place to enter if one lacked the appropriate training or didn't belong to the group.

Faulkner had the advantage of new archaeological techniques such as radiocarbon dating, which enabled him to say that the structure had been built between roughly A.D. 30 and A.D. 430, and that at least two different peoples had worked on it slowly over hundreds of years. This seemed to rule out its use as a defense, since forts and castles tended to be erected as quickly as possible to defend against a threat of some sort.

He also argued that the walls were too low to have been much use as a defense, while the interior of the enclosure was too large to have been defended by the number of available warriors. By comparison, the Bastille fortress in Paris was only 90 feet by 220 feet and the Tower of London was 107 feet by 118 feet, with walls 90 feet high. For it to have been a truly functional "fort" like those were, the dimensions of the Old Stone Fort were all wrong.

Most telling of all: Almost no artifacts were found inside it, suggesting that the site had been kept as a "clean space." Civil War relic hunters know that even temporarily occupied camps often yield lost items, so the near-total absence of artifacts in the Old Stone Fort suggested that no one ever occupied the place.

In 1993, yet another theory popped up. Archaeologist Willard Bacon suggested that perhaps it was built as *both* a sacred space and a defensive site, but that its defenses were intended to repel supernatural entities or paranormal phenomena. It certainly feels like a spot where magical energies might be focused, and perhaps need to be harnessed and controlled. The only way in and out, without climbing a cliff or crossing a wall, is through a "spiritual airlock" located between two protective conical mounds that aligns with the sunrise on the summer solstice.

The jury is still out; theories and guesses are still coming in. Could it have been an astronomical observatory, like Stonehenge? Was it meant to keep ghosts out or to lock evil spirits in? Was it a UFO landing site? Since nothing has yet been "settled" for good or for sure, here's a chance to visit a real mystery and develop your own theory.

Fewkes Mounds

Where Moore's Lane crosses the Harpeth River in Brentwood, two relics of the past stand in close proximity to each other. The Boiling Springs Academy was built in 1832 as a private school for the sons of wealthy local landowners. It became a Williamson County public school in 1887, and was a church from about 1900 to 1918. After that it was used as a barn. Behind it are five Indian mounds. The tallest is nearly 25 feet high, and roughly 180 feet by 160 feet at the base, but the largest of the five was 240 feet by 162 feet. Several of the mounds were excavated in 1920, when the site was named for J. Walter Fewkes, chief of the Bureau of American Ethnology. Stone figures, tools, and skeletons were recovered in the excavation, suggesting it was a burial mound. The tallest mound (into which the academy was built) still holds its secrets.

Curiously, no bones or implements made of buffalo were found in the excavations, even though buffalo were plentiful in this part of Tennessee until white settlers eradicated them. Did this particular town—which had been occupied for about five hundred years—have some kind of taboo against killing or eating buffalo meat? By the time the first European settlers made it this far inland, their diseases had long since destroyed those who could have answered that question. The ancient community, surrounded by a palisade, had been burned, but no one knows if the fire was due to natural causes or set intentionally.

The mounds are now part of Brentwood's Primm Park, named for the family who used the academy as their hay barn.

Pinson Mounds

As high as a seven-story building, Sauls Mound is the second-tallest Indian mound in the nation. To create it, its builders dug, carried, and heaped up more than 127,000 tons of soil over a period of many decades. They did this with no metal tools and no draft animals, using only baskets to haul the dirt, probably balancing them on their heads or shoulders as they relentlessly piled it higher and higher. They must have been very determined.

Sauls Mound (named for John Sauls, the farmer who sold the property to the state) is one of seventeen large man-made mounds that together form the Pinson Mounds group in Madison County. As many as twenty more mounds in the same area may or may not be natural elevations that the ancient inhabitants built. This is the largest Middle Woodland Period (predating A.D. 500) mound complex in the southeastern United States. No one is completely sure why it was built, or for what it was intended, though it is widely held that the mounds were used for burial, residential, or ceremonial purposes.

The mounds were rediscovered in 1820 by surveyor Joel Pinson while mapping lands recently acquired from the Chickasaw people. Pinson noted the strange man-made hills on his charts but otherwise didn't pay much attention to them. Nor did anyone else until the late 1800s, when Jackson newspaper editor J. G. Cisco wrote a series of articles about them, drawing the attention of the Smithsonian Institution. In 1916, the first professional

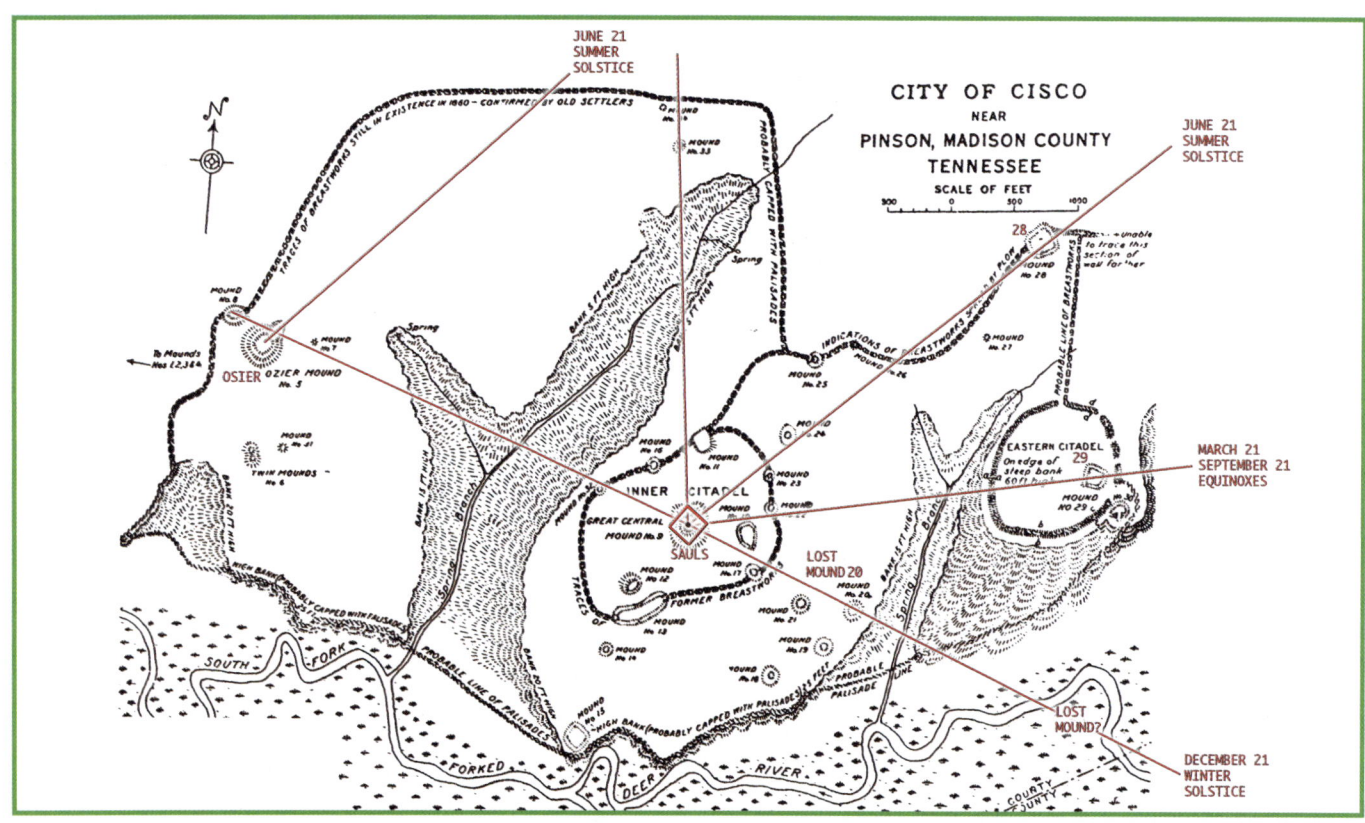

archaeologist visited the site. William Myer spent most of that year mapping the peculiar assembly, counting and numbering thirty-five mounds, measuring miles of earthworks and palisades, and describing at least three major clusters of structures.

Three of the mounds contained important tombs with elaborate burial ornaments made of mica, copper, crystals, and carefully knapped effigy flints. Engraved rattles made of human skull plates were buried in one tomb, possibly the final resting place of a spiritual leader. In another tomb, eight young women in their twenties, adorned with copper headdresses and necklaces of freshwater pearls, were buried together. Myer named the site Cisco City after the newspaperman who piqued his interest.

There were few surface artifacts and little evidence of cook fires or houses, and no sign that the site had been used for anything besides occasional ceremonial purposes. Myers thought he could discern some kind of master plan—the place seemed to be organized according to some overarching scheme, and he noticed that the tallest mound's corners were aligned exactly with the cardinal directions—but what plan could possibly reveal the purpose behind all that enormous effort?

In 1979 an artist studying petroglyphs in New Mexico's Chaco Canyon made a chance discovery that at exactly the moment of the summer solstice, a narrow beam of sunlight passing through a crack between two boulders seemed to "stab" an ancient spiral image that had been pecked into the wall of an underhang. At first, professional archaeologists thought it was a mere coincidence. But then they found that at the winter solstice, the same beam of light penetrated the center of another nearby spiral, also carved eight hundred years ago.

Similar events took place at the equinoxes, too. This touched off a sudden widespread interest among archaeologists in finding out if astronomical alignments occurred at other ancient sites. A new field, archaeoastronomy, was born.

In the late 1980s, archaeologists at Pinson Mounds began to suspect that the earthen ramp leading up the front of Ozier Mound, the second-largest mound at the site, was aligned exactly with the summer solstice. Further analysis of the other mounds revealed that from the top of Sauls Mound (which had been built high enough to permit a clear view of the horizon above the surrounding trees), the rising sun would come up directly behind a large mound called Mound 29 on the mornings of the spring and fall equinoxes. Suddenly it seemed possible that Pinson Mounds might have been built as a huge astronomical observatory. But again, for what gain? What were the people trying to achieve?

The middle alignment—with Mound 29 and both equinoxes—leads to a vast enclosure, 1,200 feet in diameter and forming a near-perfect circle (it *was* perfect when it was first built, but encroaching erosion from the river bank side forced them to rebuild part of the wall on the east side slightly closer to the center). Though it was called a "citadel" on Myer's map, the walls are too low for that purpose. Was it another part of the observatory? A ritual space? A water reservoir? A landing site for winged humanoids? These are only some of the interpretations that have been offered.

Future studies may reveal still more alignments of other mounds with stars, constellations, and planetary movements. See for yourself and come up with an explanation all your own. To get there, take Highway 45 south from Jackson eleven miles to Pinson. Turn left (east) at the park sign, onto Ozier Road/Highway 197 and go two and a half miles. The mounds are managed by the Tennessee Department of Environment and Conservation and close at 4:30 P.M. each day.

De Soto Was Here

Just across the street from the now-defunct Marine Hospital on Metal Museum Drive in Memphis are two ancient earthworks, now called the Desoto Mounds, that may have been used as temples honoring the river or the sun. According to legend, the largest (Chisca Mound) is said to be the place from which Spanish explorer Hernando De Soto and his men first laid eyes on the Mississippi River in 1541.

The Spaniards didn't stay for long. As soon as they could build rafts and float across the river, they left. De Soto died of a fever the following year without ever having found what he was looking for: gold.

More than two and a half centuries later, Fort Pike was built here, taking advantage of the mounds' elevation for observation posts. From 1814 to 1818 they were the site of the Chickasaw Indian Agency, and during the Civil War they were incorporated into Fort Pickering and used as Confederate cannon emplacements. Chisca Mound was hollowed out and used to store gunpowder in 1863.

Ancient IOU?

While digging around on the Noel family farm near Nashville in the early 1890s George Wood unearthed a stone box containing a skeleton clutching a small stone disk (or, in archaeologists' terminology, a "lithic discoidal"). The discovery has puzzled scholars ever since. The artifact—slightly concave on the back and about the same size, shape, and general appearance of an ordinary peanut butter cookie—is inscribed with six to ten marks (depending on how you count them) that render it unlike almost any other artifact recovered from ancient America.

Eccentric Harvard zoologist Howard Barraclough Fell examined the disk in the 1970s. Though he'd been trained in the study of oceanic creatures, Professor Fell spent much of his tenured career trying to prove that the ancient Egyptians had colonized parts of the New World, teaching locals how to build pyramids and passing along the mythology of the ancients. According to Fell, the symbols could be translated as "The colonists pledge to redeem." In other words, it was a kind of ancient IOU.

This makes us wonder: Did the poor fellow that George Wood dug up grip a kind of blank check in his hand? The Tennessee State Museum, however, has elected not to cash it in, so instead the discovery remains tantalizingly on display, ever tempting the legislators working just across the street in their never-ending hunt for new sources of revenue.

Inscribed Wall of Chatata

One of the greatest mysteries of the ancient Americas may now lie forgotten near the top of a ridge overlooking the No-Pone Valley in northwestern Bradley County. In 1891 Isaac Hooston Hooper began removing stones from a wooded portion of his land near Eads Bluff. He found a row of what he later described as "marker stones" projecting from the soil every ten paces, along a curved arc about three hundred yards long.

One of the stones near the middle was pointed like a flatiron. Etched into it was what looked like writing in an ancient script. When he dug beneath this stone, Hooper discovered a strange wall covered with more mysterious inscriptions—long sentences interspersed with pictograms of exotic animals, sun symbols, and other images. In time, about seven hundred feet of the wall was exposed to a depth of about eight feet, all of it inscribed.

Among the hieroglyphs on the Inscribed Wall of Chatata were a number of peculiar images, including one that looked something like a kangaroo, but with a projection below its mouth that could be a leaf or perhaps big fangs. The image has yet to be identified.

Visitors and curiosity seekers flooded in from across the region to see the peculiar structure, said to be about two and a half feet thick and made of stones two feet square and almost a foot deep. The *Cleveland* (Tennessee) *Herald* ran an article a few weeks after the discovery, surmising that the glyphs had been cut "by some lost race who built the wall

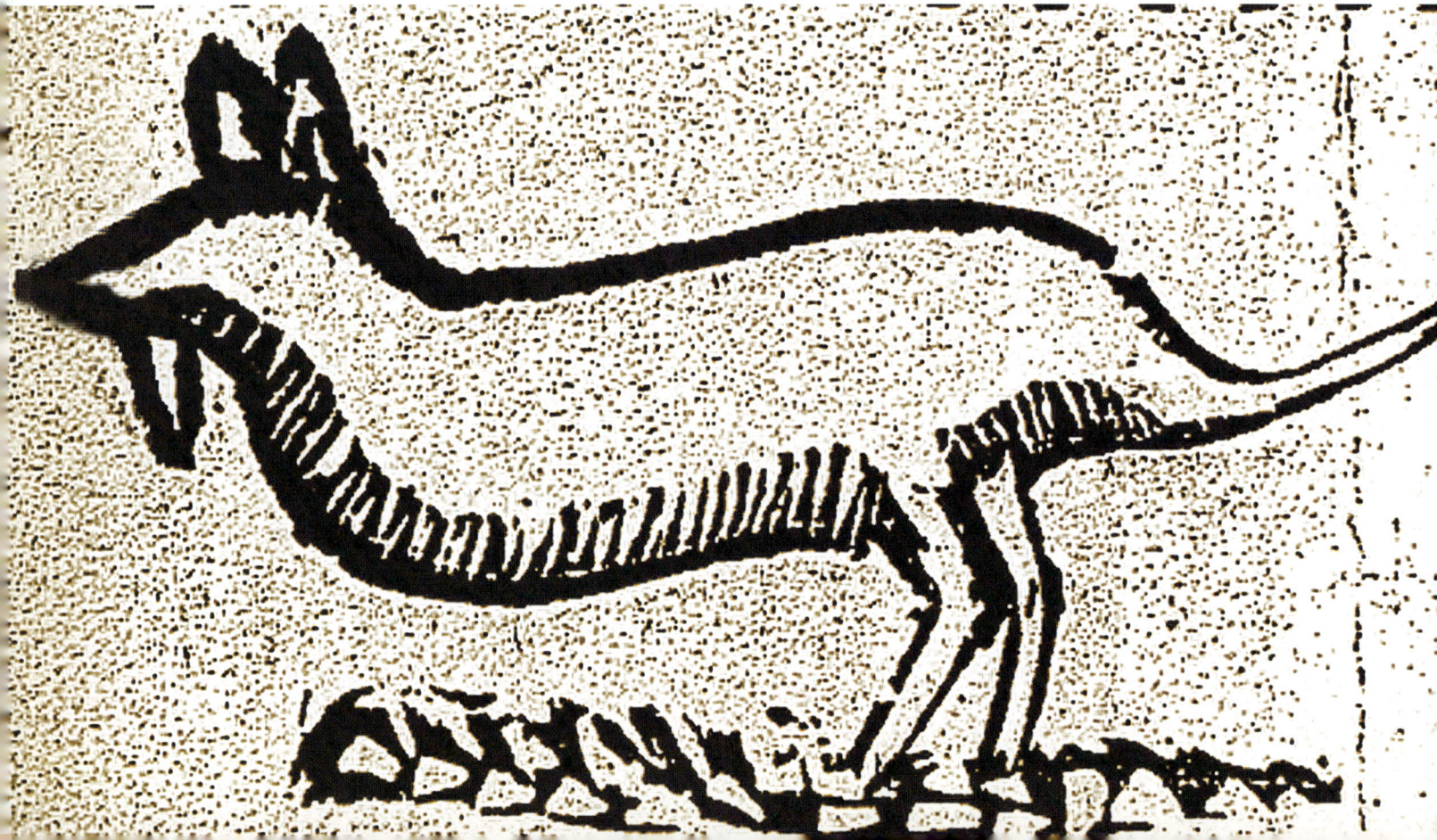

long before any white man lived." Observations suggested that the writing had been carefully masked to hide or preserve it for some unknown reason.

A Smithsonian Institution paleontologist hypothesized that the writings were only trails left by ancient insects, worms, or mollusks or else the fossilized remnants of leafless seaweed vines. But an artist/archaeologist on the same Smithsonian team, A. L. Ralston, proposed a more intriguing theory: that the writing was a dire warning. Ralston was so convinced that he made detailed copies of the writings and, according to local stories, hired a team of "cipher experts" to translate them on his own dime.

The experts determined that the writings were a form of "old Hebrew" written by scribes from an ancient culture that had been faced with some kind of calamity and was about to be wiped out at the time the inscriptions were carved. The giant stone document had been created in a desperate attempt to preserve their cultural knowledge and history for future generations to rediscover. The hieroglyphs had then been disguised under layers of ordinary stone laid in clay and the whole wall buried to keep it from falling into the hands of their enemies.

Ralston posited that the wall was between 4,000 and 4,500 years old, constructed by one of the "lost tribes of Israel" according to Moses' command. To corroborate this theory, Ralston cited similar mysterious inscriptions found in Massachusetts and in Palmyra, New York, by Mormon founder Joseph Smith some sixty-three years earlier. He saw particular parallels with the biblical story of the stones erected on Mount Ebal in the Holy Land as described in Joshua 8:32. This may have given the onlookers pause, for the structure on the original Mount Ebal had been used for the chanting of curses.

The Smithsonian team hauled some of the mysterious rocks back to Washington and urged Hooper to be patient, since the process of translation might take five years or more. Meanwhile Hooper attempted to capitalize on his discovery by commissioning an illustrated book. On October 13, 1893, Hooper obtained Library of Congress copyright number 45897r for a manuscript entitled *The Wonder of the World, America's Mount Ebal, or the Hand Writing on the Buried Wall* by R. J. M. Only. The Smithsonian put some of the inscribed rocks on exhibit in the national museum from 1900 to 1902, but the promised translations never materialized. When no further credible archaeological interpretations seemed forthcoming, locals around Bradley County gradually lost interest. Except for a mention in the *Cleveland Herald* in 1920 that a group of picnickers had revisited the site of the great wall, it slipped back into oblivion.

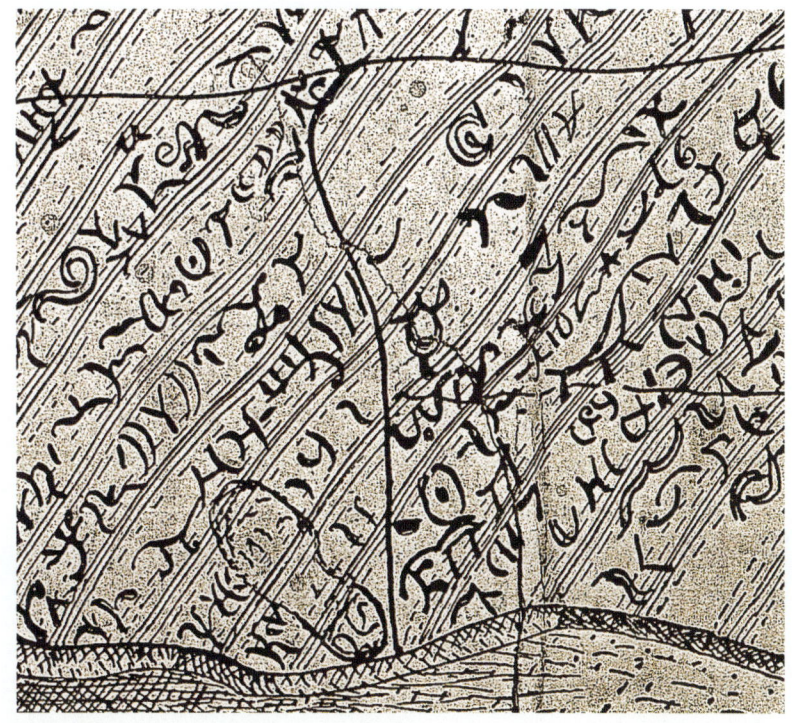

Standing Stone

The Standing Stone monolith in what is now Monterey, in eastern Putnam County, remains the proud symbol of what has been called (by one person, at least) "Tennessee's greatest mystery." In fact, it's largely a disrespected structure, comparable to a hitching post, though people say it really *used* to be something amazing.

As early as 1788 settlers described a ten-foot-tall monolith looking like a huge gray dog sitting on its hind feet. It marked an ancient Cherokee trading path now known as Walton Road. But whether it was a natural formation or had been hewn to that shape by human hands, and whether it was a vertical outcropping of "living rock" or had been dragged to that site with tremendous effort and purpose, no one can say. The monolith may have had nothing to do with Native Americans at all.

The builders of the Nashville & Knoxville Railroad blasted the giant statue so they could lay train tracks. Souvenir hunters made off with all but two pieces that were erected in town. A local chapter of an all-white fraternal society that called itself "The Narragansett Tribe of the Improved Order of Red Men" built a pedestal to elevate a tiny piece of the former landmark. The Improved Red Men named the rock Nee-Yah-Kah-Toh-Kee (which they said meant "standing stone"), carving this and other words on the front of the relic.

The incredible shrinkage of the monolith was offset by a growth industry in legends that sprang up in creative attempts to explain it, or at least try to make it a little more interesting. Some claimed that it had once marked the location of buried treasure, or that it was a Sphinx. Though many have accepted these tales as gospel, archaeologists and geologists discount the likelihood of any of those "explanations."

Think Brick

Perhaps the General Shale Museum of Ancient Brick in Johnson City is an attraction that only a mason could love. The display presents a cavalcade of brick through the annals of human history. It's a rather sedate parade, since there were only rare and incremental improvements from one civilization to the next.

But if you're in the right frame of mind (i.e., if you're looking at the world with your Weird Eye) or you are easily amused, it could be interesting to see just how much the bricks of today resemble those of, say, ancient Egypt or Tibet.

The brick museum was General Shale CEO George Sells's brainchild. In 1964 Sells assigned English amateur archaeologist and former merchant seaman Basil Shaffer the task of gathering historical bricks from the farthest corners of the earth. Shaffer set off in pursuit of his quarry by boat, car, foot, and camel to bring back the bricks, which include pieces of the walls of ancient Ur, Anuradhapura (in Sri Lanka), and the Great Wall of China; bits of the palaces of Nero and Nebuchadnezzar; and pieces from the birthplaces of presidents Washington and Lincoln and Babe Ruth. The sources of the collection are eclectic, even if the items betray a marked tendency toward reddish oblongularity.

In a 1982 article in the *Ocala Star-Banner*, Shaffer proudly discussed the collection and his role in assembling it. "Apparently I'm the only brickologist in existence. . . . Nobody else studies just brick." He assessed the collection as "irreplaceable."

The museum is located at General Shale's corporate office building at 3015 Bristol Highway, Johnson City, and is open free to the public during weekday business hours.

Fabled People and Places

A *legend is supposed to be fact or history,* even if it's been "improved upon," while a fable is always completely made up, right? And isn't it true that a legend offers an example to be aspired to (or else avoided), while a fable is supposed to teach you some kind of moral or lesson? It might be nice to think so, but it's rarely that easy to sort things out, especially not in a place like Tennessee, where all kinds of odd things not only have happened, but are happening **right now**.

Once you take a look at just a small sampling of the fabled happenings here, a few of the hard-to-believe people involved, and a handful of the mind-boggling places that have hosted such events, we think you'll begin to see what we mean.

Devil's Looking Glass

A few miles west of Erwin, and across the Nolichucky River from the River's Edge Restaurant on Highway 81 is an outcropping of rough, vertical rock that juts three hundred feet above the water. It's been called the Devil's Looking Glass for as long as anyone can remember. Even the Cherokee regarded the site with dread and hurried past the riverbend below the cliffs . . . and completely avoided the site at night, when it's easiest to make out the profile that earned the place its name. A huge face (with a rather big nose) seems to be looking at a broken and distorted reflection of itself in a cracked mirror.

American Indian legends maintain that it wasn't just scary-looking, but haunted too. The ghost of a Cherokee woman who committed suicide by jumping off the precipice after her husband was killed in battle is thought to linger near the cliff's base. Hidden in a deep crevice in the flaking rock, it's said, is a demon who lies in wait to attack idlers who pause while paddling their canoes along the river.

White settlers reported hearing a girl's screams or seeing streaks of glowing light near an alleged witch's shack. One night, they said, a traveler looking to escape a thunderstorm stumbled upon her shack and was never seen again.

Seeing Satan in the Pale Moonlight

I live in east TN, in the city of Jonesborough. There is a place not far from here that is called the Devil's Looking Glass. It's located in the mountains next to a small river and is recognizable because it is a large patch of rocks in the side of a mountain. You're supposed to be able to see the devil's face in it. It doesn't work very well at all in the daytime, but if you go there at night, with the moon shining on it a little bit, you can see the face of Satan, or what looks like the devil. —*Letter via e-mail*

Booger Swamp

Booger Swamp in Cookeville consists of only a few acres of low-lying land east of town along Burton's Branch.

In the early 1850s a Baptist preacher was heading home on horseback from a revival meeting, perhaps humming "Rock of Ages" while looking forward to a late supper and a soft bed. At a turn in the road the horse shied and he turned to see a most unusual sight.

"The apparition was a pure white body," he later recounted, "floating about a yard above the ground [and] about the size and length of a weaver's beam."

Vaguely female in shape and demeanor, it seemed to reach out and beckon him closer, but his horse was thoroughly spooked and dashed past the haint.

To his church deacons, the preacher's vision didn't sound like a blessing of the Holy Spirit. If he hadn't already been thinking temptatious thoughts, they reasoned, then why would such a sight have appeared to him? Shortly therafter the poor pastor was ousted by his congregation.

Ever since then, witnesses from hunters to lovers have told of seeing strange lights or wispy glowing forms hovering over the swamp and along the road.

The spot where the preacher made his sighting is on Dry Valley Road (formerly the Old Sparta–Livingston Road), roughly a half mile north of the intersection with Buck Mountain Road. This is a part of the swamp that has since been cleared, but a pair of ponds on either side of the road remains to indicate the low ground where the supernatural encounter took place.

The Dashing Assassin's Mummy

Until 1923, the garage behind a house located at 1234 Harbert Street in Memphis sheltered a mysterious lodger who, in fact, had been dead for some twenty years. The house's owner, prominent Memphis attorney Finis L. Bates, decided not to bury the poor fellow because he needed him as a witness. Only he, Bates believed, could substantiate a strange claim that he was none other than John Wilkes Booth (shown here), the actor who assassinated President Abraham Lincoln on April 14, 1865.

On April 26, twelve days after the assassination, Union cavalry tracked Booth and a fellow conspirator to a farm near Port Royal Crossroads where they holed up in a tobacco barn. Booth's comrade surrendered, but he refused to come out, so the soldiers set fire to the barn. Booth was shot in the neck, and soldiers dragged him from the burning building. They laid him on the farmhouse porch, where he died three hours later.

The corpse was taken back to Washington for autopsy and identification and then buried inside a warehouse storage room. Several years later the bones were moved to an unmarked grave in Baltimore.

All of this was smoke and mirrors, according to Bates, who claimed that a man who looked similar to Booth was killed at that northern Virginia farm. Bates held that Booth had escaped and made his way to Texas, where he spent the next thirty-five years living under the adopted name of John St. Helen, then David George. According to Bates, the real John Wilkes Booth died of arsenic poisoning after a drinking binge in Enid, Oklahoma, in 1903.

Bates befriended John St. Helen in 1872, when Bates had a law practice in the same town where St. Helen established a reputation as a gifted speaker. Following an 1876 incident, St. Helen thought he was dying and confessed to Bates that he was really John Wilkes Booth. He told Bates how he escaped, and how the soldiers killed the wrong man. Then he handed the lawyer a photo of himself, asking Bates to send it to his brother, the actor Edwin Booth, who would want to know of his death. St. Helen recovered, but Bates never forgot the confession. He kept in touch with St. Helen and years later, when he learned his old friend had really died, he went to Enid to claim the body.

When he arrived, he found that the undertaker had embalmed but not buried the corpse, since St. Helen died without leaving a will or money for a funeral. Bates paid the embalming bill and took the corpse of his old pal back to Memphis. Meanwhile,

the arsenic that St. Helen swallowed combined with the embalming fluid and the hot dry air of central Oklahoma to mummify the body.

After spending much time and money trying to prove that St. Helen was indeed Booth, Bates published *The Escape and Suicide of John Wilkes Booth, or The First True Account of Lincoln's Assassination, Containing a Complete Confession by Booth Many Years After His Crime* in 1907. To promote the book's release, Bates took the mummy on tour (shown here), and it became a grisly sideshow feature at carnivals and fairs for several years. The book went through multiple printings before the sensation died down.

Bates hoped that the book and the mummy exhibition would encourage the Army to reopen the case, but it never happened. After Bates's death, a 1924 *Harper's Magazine* article created a national sensation, and the mummy went back on the sideshow circuit. After that, the corpse was bought and sold by several amusement operators, kidnapped and held for ransom, seized as collateral for a bad debt, and featured in Jay Gould's Million-Dollar Circus in the late 1930s before appearing in *Life* magazine in 1944.

In 1931 Chicago radiologist Orlando Scott x-rayed the mummy. The corpse had a fractured left fibula, a disjointed right thumb, a scarred eyebrow, and a scarred neck—all of which matched descriptions of Booth's injuries. The X-rays also revealed an object in the mummy's stomach which, when they cut into the body to retrieve it, turned out to be a signet ring with the letter "B." This gave rise to a theory that Booth swallowed his ring during his escape to destroy evidence of his identity.

Did John Wilkes Booth ever reside in Memphis? All anyone can say for sure is that *some* mummy did, for the evidence seems to have vanished. The last time the location of mummy was officially documented was in 1942, when it belonged to John Harkin, the Tattooed Man in the Hagenbeck-Wallace Circus.

Horseplay

If anyone tries to tell you that centaurs never existed, tell them they are sadly myth-taken. Proof may be found in the John C. Hodges Library at the University of Tennessee in Knoxville (UTK). Here, in a deep display case, are the skeletal remains of one of the half-human horses that trampled the Greek countryside in days of yore. The archaeological discovery is attributed to Bill Willers of Wisconsin, who found the creature near Volos, the capital city of Magnesia (a region of central Greece).

In 1980 Willers was participating in a dig sponsored by the Archaeological Society of Argos Orestiko eight kilometers north of the city when the first of three centaur burials was discovered. In an agreement worked out with the Greek government, the University of Wisconsin–Oshkosh biology professor was allowed to bring one of the compound skeletons back to the United States, where it was cleaned and mounted for exhibition in Madison.

After several years, it was taken off display and stored in a barn. It hardly seems a fitting end for kin of Cheiron, the half-horse mentor of such brainy musclemen as Achilles, Aeneas, Ajax, Jason, Heracles (Hercules), and Theseus. Luckily, Professor Neil Greenberg of UTK's Department of Ecology and Evolutionary Biology and Beauvais Lyons, director of the university's Hokes Archives, offered the bones a more suitable resting place in the Hodges Library. A few centaur artifacts found with the burial round out the display.

Whatever happened to the centaurs? Sociologists point out that passages from ancient Greek history are filled with stories of their Dionysian excess and debauchery, which suggests that alcoholism and too much partying may have been contributing factors in their decline and disappearance. Other researchers aren't so sure: UTK's Center for Genomics and Bioinformatics and its Joint Institute for Computational Science has proposed a project to sequence the centaur genome to see if there were genetic factors as well, since the university now owns the United States' only known skeletal remains and tissue samples. The geneticists argue that centaurs could perhaps have been prey to both human and equine maladies. The project awaits federal funding.

For now the bones rest in their case, where they inspire each year's incoming students to wonder if everything their professors tell them is true.

Spring of Blue Tears

Eladwadiyi, the Cherokee called it, meaning "red earth place." A striking natural phenomenon called the Blue Hole marks this spot. A deep and legendary spring, it emerges as an iridescent blue and forms the headwaters of a clear, cold creek. It also marks the where the Cherokees desperately tried to negotiate their way out of the federal government's plan to tear them away from their ancient lands and send them to Oklahoma. The Blue Hole—or Council Spring, as it is now sometimes known—was the beginning point of the Trail of Tears.

Although by 1838 the Cherokee had developed their own alphabet and adopted enough European culture to be counted as friendly, it wasn't enough. White farmers wanted their land, and prospectors believed the Cherokees were hiding vast deposits of gold and other precious metals. The Blue Hole itself was believed to lead to a secret cave filled with Cherokee gold. But for the whites to get at it, the Cherokee had to leave.

On May 10, 1838, Gen. Winfield Scott announced the terrible orders at the last Cherokee Nation council meeting (basically, leave this land, or "spare me, I beseech you, the horror of witnessing the destruction of the Cherokees"), which took place under a simple log shelter just a hundred yards from the blue waters of the spring.

Several months later the Cherokees gathered here to begin the long march to Oklahoma. Some four thousand—one in three—died along the way. If you ever wonder where the homesick blues come from, this blue spring of tears would be as likely a spot to point to as any.

The Real Indiana Jones?

Although neither George Lucas nor Steven Spielberg ever affirmed that any real-life archaeologist-adventurers were inspirations for their Indiana Jones character, many have speculated on possibilities. It could it have been Hiram Bingham, the American discoverer of the "lost city of the Incas," Machu Picchu. Or perhaps F. A. Mitchell-Hedges, the Briton who claimed to have found remnants of the "lost continent of Atlantis" in the islands off Honduras. Or how about Otto Rahn, the German Nazi archaeologist who tried to find the Holy Grail and the Ark of the Covenant?

Little of this ongoing speculation seems to have included Tennessean Ron Wyatt (shown here), the late founder of the Wyatt Archaeological Museum near Cornersville. Trained as a nurse-anesthesiologist, this Seventh Day Adventist autodidact claimed not only to have found Noah's Ark (along with Noah's House and Noah's Grave), but also the Tower of Babel, Sodom and Gomorrah, the cavern that contains the essential building blocks of Solomon's Temple, the original Mount Sinai, the altar of the Golden Calf, the second set of the Ten Commandments (engraved in stone), the hole in the ground where the cross had been planted to crucify Jesus, and even some of the Lord's dried blood. What's more, he claimed he also glimpsed the Ark of the Covenant itself, glowing through a crack in an excavated cave near Jesus's temporary tomb. And as if these accomplishments weren't enough, Wyatt also figured out how the pyramids were built and how Noah's Ark was stabilized to be manageable in rough seas.

Quite a bit of physical evidence is on display in a converted former gas station located on Highway 129 just west of I-65 at exit 27 in Marshall County. Here, for a small voluntary donation, anyone can gaze upon what are surely some of the most remarkable artifacts in the world. Wyatt's museum displays bits of glass, nails, and pottery along with pieces of the chariots and desiccated hooves

from the Egyptian horses that pulled them (left submerged at the place where the Israelites crossed the Red Sea and where the pharaoh's army subsequently drowned). The hooves are tiny, but as one label explains, that's because they shrank from the central heating and air-conditioning used in transporting them to Tennessee, after spending several millennia at the bottom of the Gulf of Aqaba. That's where Wyatt calculated the famous Red Sea crossing in Exodus 14 actually took place (with the aid of a "molecular frequency generator" attached to a boat), and where he went and easily retrieved them.

Other cases hold not only a number of petrified planks from Noah's Ark (along with a scale model of the ark to show exactly how it originally looked when it was still a seaworthy vessel). Not to be missed is the petrified dung left in the cages by some of the animals that took that fateful voyage.

Other wall panels and videos explain the current condition and location of the landlocked shipwreck, which anyone with access to Google Earth can easily see by entering the proper coordinates (39.440559, 44.234522). Richard Rives, an Indiana Jones type himself, maintains the amazing collection, since Wyatt passed away in 1999.

The jury's still out as to whether or not any of Wyatt's claims is true. We urge readers to maintain an open mind and stop by to check out the exhibits. They're nothing if not educational.

The Petrified Soldier

Of all the graves in the little churchyard that extends to the east of Grassy Cove United Methodist Church, there is one that stands out: a huge, unmarked stone slab resting on a low wall of smaller hewn stones. (All the other burial sites are below ground.) Legend has it that this particular slab once held down the restless remains of what locals called the Petrified Soldier.

He was discovered in a saltpeter cave. Such caves are frequently inhabited by a large colony of bats, whose guano is the source of saltpeter. Saltpeter was used by Native Americans to fertilize their fields and by settlers to make gunpowder. Saltpeter caves traditionally emit a powerful attraction to foolhardy young boys, because there is always the chance of finding old artifacts left behind by Indians, early pioneers, or Civil War soldiers.

A few years after the Civil War ended, local kids ventured into the Grassy Cove Saltpeter Cave, which both Union and Confederate forces had occupied at different points. Lighting their way with pinewood-knot torches, they made their way through the cave's front chambers until they came upon a sight that far exceeded their hopes for cool abandoned booty. On a low platform created by a naturally flat-topped boulder they discovered a crude stretcher made of hickory bark strips. Upon it lay a soldier in a remarkable state of preservation, fully attired in his gray Confederate uniform. A hat hid his face, but there was no doubt that the man was quite horrifyingly dead. The adventurers scrambled out of the cave as quickly as they could and ran to tell some adults about it. One sent word to the county coroner, James W. "Soup" Matthews.

Matthews and a group of older men reentered the cave and made their way to the primitive bier where they found the dead man. They lifted off the hat and gazed upon a face with eyes closed, as if the man were asleep. He looked to be in his midthirties and had mummified to the hardness of rock. There were no visible wounds, lesions, or bruises, and almost no wear on the boots or clothing. It was as if the man had died within days of first putting on his uniform. No autopsy was performed since at that time the law forbade autopsies unless there was sufficient evidence of foul play. In this case there was none.

Eventually he was taken to the old Methodist church in Grassy Cove and lowered into a hole dug in the third grave space to the left of the huge stone slab. Contrary to the legend that grew up later, the unknown soldier's grave was never marked and never under the slab itself.

Within days, people living within earshot of the church began to hear screams at night coming from the churchyard. The doors of the church began slamming repeatedly, and sacramental objects left on the altar would be found dashed to the floor. Then, loud noises began to be heard in the vicinity of the saltpeter cave as well. Children refused to attend the local school since it was so close to the creepy grave. Adults were terrified to walk along Kemmer Road in front of the cemetery after dark.

The soldier was exhumed and moved to an undisclosed cave. Given that caves stay at the same temperature and humidity year-round and that the Petrified Soldier had already mummified, it's likely he's still there today, waiting out eternity in his own private hideaway.

Secrets in Plain Sight

A strangely blank plaque on the wall of the Trial Lawyers Building at 207 W. Madison Street in Pulaski marks a place where history took a sudden turn, and not for the better. In fact, the plaque is not blank, but is turned toward the wall and the bolts holding it there are welded shut to prevent them from ever being loosened again. If you could see the other side, you would discover the names of several men who met here at the law office of Judge Thomas Jones on Christmas Eve 1865 to form what they claimed was just another men's social club: the Ku Klux Klan.

Perhaps that's all it was at first. America had long been fascinated with fraternal organizations and secret societies, and participation in them was considered not only normal but useful, especially in business or politics. Many of the Founding Fathers belonged to the Freemasons, while the Odd Fellows, Rosicrucians, Red Men, and other brotherhoods and organizations were already well established before the Civil War. But that war touched off a massive increase in secret societies, with hundreds of new organizations forming soon afterward.

Some war veterans found it hard to resume ordinary domestic life and wanted to be back with their buddies without their wives keeping tabs on them.

Other groups formed to reinforce ethnic and religious identities (like the German Catholic Union or the Irish Protestant Association), or share trade secrets (like the Railway Accounting Officers Association, or the Exalted Society of Order Hounds, for salesmen), or else to fight alcohol (the Cold Water Army) or encourage more liquor consumption (the Royal Fellows of Bagdad). Many were created to pool money to provide mutual life insurance, at a time when few real insurance companies existed.

But the vast majority of fraternal clubs had mostly to do with having fun during a grim period in the nation's history. The Klan was first created, so its founding members later insisted, only for the purpose of having ". . . fun by means of farsical initiations and ceremonies." The club's name came from the Greek word *kyklos*, meaning "circle," with *clan* purposely misspelled with a *k*.

Its first secret meetings were held in the basement of a storm-wrecked house in Pulaski. Dressing up in masks and robes with mystical symbols sewn on added to the spooky ambience of their get-togethers, most of which involved hazing new initiates. Incoming candidates were blindfolded, dressed in donkey costumes, and put to what now seem like drastic tests of their ability to trust and obey (such as being rolled down a hill in a barrel or ordered to jump down a well). Still, the rituals are nothing unfamiliar to anyone who has joined a college fraternity or a military unit.

According to an old pamphlet (written by Klan sympathizers many years later), a black man accidentally came upon one of their meetings shortly after the group's founding, mistook them for ghosts, and ran away screaming. It dawned on the assembled Ghouls (as they called themselves) that their masks and secrecy gave them a terrifying power. The organization's focus shifted from foolhardy amusement to things far more ominous and sinister. The KKK was not the first domestic American terrorist organization, but it quickly became one of the worst and most virulent. Dens formed in nearby communities, and, at its peak the KKK probably had more than a half million members.

Klansmen dressed in masks and robes to hide their clothes and faces, and rode horses draped with sheets (to disguise them). They began paying midnight visits to frighten people they wanted to punish. They could get away with this with impunity—many law enforcers had also joined—and the terror increased. Whippings, lynchings, and murders of blacks, as well as whites who sympathized with blacks or were seen as aiding the postwar federal military occupation, became commonplace.

So many excessive acts of post–Civil War violence were committed that martial law was declared in several Tennessee counties. Finally Congress enacted the Civil Rights Act of 1871 and federal officers began prosecuting Klan members. With such pressure increasing and eroded local support, Klan officers under the leadership of Grand Wizard Nathan Bedford Forrest decided to disband their national organization. In elaborate rituals, robes and regalia were ceremonially burned, and by 1874 the Klan was essentially shut down. Acts of terror continued, though—in 1892 there were 230 lynchings—with crowds of grinning citizens allowing themselves to be photographed next to the dangling corpses of their victims for their local newspapers.

Like a horror movie monster that gets killed only to come ripping up out of the ground again, mutated into something even more horrible for the equally horrific sequel, the KKK reemerged in Georgia. Borrowing a lot of ritual mumbo-jumbo from the original Klan, the second Klan venerated many of the sites associated with it, including the founders' gathering place in downtown Pulaski. The plaque on Madison Street was hung in 1917 to commemorate the spot.

This second manifestation was much larger (as many as six million paying members by 1924) and far more widespread, with large memberships in Midwestern states like Michigan, Ohio, and Indiana. Many new members were factory workers afraid of losing their jobs to blacks migrating to the North. This second Klan operated as a network marketing business, making millions of dollars for its elite leadership. The cash, however, led to its eventual undoing in 1944, when the IRS shut it down for failure to pay some $685,000 in back taxes.

After this, dozens of splinter groups continued to use variations on the name (like Knights of the KKK or United Klans of America), wear the infamous pointy-hooded outfits, and speak in Klan jargon while planning acts of homegrown terrorism. There was a resurgence of activity in the 1960s and 1970s in response to the Civil Rights Movement, but most experts think there are fewer than three thousand active members now.

Even so, hate groups' ongoing efforts to perform ceremonies and demonstrations in Pulaski have finally worn thin with locals. When the old building changed hands in 1990, the new owner reversed the plaque and welded it in place with the blank side out. Maybe it's an elegant way of saying, "We can't pretend that the past didn't happen, but can we please move on?"

Love Potion

Every two hours and forty-seven minutes the Ebbing and Flowing Spring in Hawkins County diverges from its usual trickle, gushing more than five hundred gallons a minute. The water comes out at a constant 34°F year-round, just barely above freezing.

The spring was discovered before the American Revolution by Col. Thomas Amis, who settled nearby and whose descendants still own it, but the waters' now legendary properties weren't fully understood in the early years. When Joseph Rogers shared a cup of the spring water with Mary Amis, the colonel's daughter, they fell helplessly in love despite the old officer's disapproval. They married and Rogers went on to found the town that bears his name. According to local beliefs, other couples who share the water also firm up their own relationships.

The Ebbing and Flowing Spring is one of only two known examples of cyclical (or tidal) springs in the world. The spring's underground channel makes an s-bend, which causes its underground reservoir to "flush" like a toilet every time it refills. But why it refills on such an exact schedule, no one really knows.

To find it, head east from Rogersville on Secondary Road 347 (Burem Pike) about three miles and turn left (north) on the road named for the spring for another mile or so.

Minié Ball Miracle

The American Civil War has often been called the "first modern war" in part because of the technological advances in warfare—mines, machine guns, submarines, torpedoes, gun turrets, balloons, hand grenades. Despite the advances, the war was wasteful and costly in terms of matériel. For every soldier who was actually hit by a bullet, historians estimate, 240 pounds of gunpowder and 900 pounds of small lead projectiles were used.

The vast majority of those bullets were "minie balls," named for their French inventor, Claude-Etienne Minié. These chunks of molded lead weren't round, but pointed on the front end and hollowed out in the rear so they expanded when the rifle was fired and came spinning out of the barrel like a well-thrown football. Although most missed their target and their range wasn't great, a successful hit was likely to be devastating. The bullets were so big and heavy they left gory, easily infected wounds. They caused more than 90 percent of Civil War battlefield casualties.

It was considered a miracle of the Battle of Chickamauga when Pvt. Edmund Tate survived a shot through the left nipple that went clear through his back. After his companions saw the exit wound, they abandoned him for dead. Lucky for the young private, his brothers returned after the battle subsided to collect his body for burial. The field surgeon was equally astonished: Tate was clearly alive, but the doctor could detect no heartbeat.

The minié ball had created such an intense internal shockwave in Tate's body that it had knocked the heart to the far right side of Tate's chest, where it remained pumping away for the rest of his long life.

Meriwether's Mystery

In a clearing in the woods a few miles south east of Hohenwald in Lewis County, Meriwether Lewis, the county's namesake, lies buried beneath a stark stone monument, erected in the shape of a broken column, symbolic of a life ended too soon. Meriwether Lewis was only thirty-five when he died. But his life did not end before he'd already made his mark on history. Along with William Clark, six years earlier (in 1803) he led the Corps of Discovery (the Lewis and Clark Expedition) on a three-year, 7,700-mile journey from Pittsburgh, Pennsylvania, to the present site of Astoria, Oregon, and back. Along the way, they mapped the continent's interior, collected mineral specimens, and identified hundreds of new species of animals and plants, while making contact with numerous Indian tribes, many of whom had never before encountered white men. Lewis and Clark's crew was only the second group of non–Native Americans to make it from one side of the continent to the other, during a time when the territory they explored must have seemed as remote, unfamiliar, and difficult to access as the surface of Mars does today.

As a reward for his accomplishments, Lewis was granted a large estate near St. Louis and was appointed by President Thomas Jefferson as governor of the Louisiana Territory, an area about a third the size of the continental United States that included all or parts of fourteen future states.

Despite his many successes, a deep depression seems to have settled over Lewis. The daily chores of running a bureaucracy held little interest for him and soon he became known as an inept if not corrupt administrator. After failing to keep his superiors adequately informed of gubernatorial matters and being accused of financial indiscretions, he was recalled to Washington to face complaints about his performance. Setting off in September 1809, he took along the journals of his famous expedition, which he had yet to formally finish editing for publication.

But Lewis never made it to Washington, and what happened along the way remains a mystery to this day. The known facts are scant. On October 10, 1809, Lewis arrived alone and stopped for the evening at a remote inn along the Natchez Trace, one of the major roads traversing Tennessee. Grinder's Stand, the inn owned by Robert and Priscilla Grinder, stood next to a small tavern and way station some seventy-two miles southwest of Nashville. Mr. Grinder was away for the evening, so only Mrs. Grinder and her children were on hand to prepare Lewis's dinner and a place for him to stay.

Around 3 A.M., two gunshots were heard. Just before sunrise the next morning, Lewis's personal slave, Captain Tom, and a Creole servant named John Pernier (or Pernia, in some accounts) discovered him barely alive in a pool of blood from wounds in his chest and forehead. In a matter of hours he was dead, and he was hastily buried with little ceremony a few hundred yards west of the tavern.

Scholars and historians have argued about Lewis's demise ever since. Was it a murder, or a suicide? Lewis was depressed and moody. He'd attempted suicide several times, perhaps even a few weeks prior to his death. His problems as governor, his ongoing fears of financial ruin, a growing controversy over his handling of government vouchers and expense accounts, and the subsequent loss of Jefferson's respect and friendship have all been tagged as possible and compelling reasons. Indeed, when news of Lewis's death reached Jefferson, the president quickly accepted it as a simple, if sad, case of suicide.

Murder, however, can't easily be ruled out. He'd been shot in the head (which blew away part of his forehead) and chest with his own pistols. It's hard to picture how anyone could have fired one weapon, put it down, then picked up the other for the second shot.

Mrs. Grinder claimed that Lewis behaved erratically that evening, intermittently smoking his pipe quietly and then raving to himself until he was red in the face. But in subsequent testimony given during the course of three separate inquiries into the incident, she changed key details of her story. She never adequately explained why Lewis wasn't discovered earlier when his weapons had been fired within earshot of the inn. She claimed she had heard the shots but didn't help out of fear, but many locals came to believe that she killed Lewis for his money, since shortly after the incident she and her husband purchased a prosperous farm along with a number of slaves. Their neighbors also found it strange that Lewis had only twenty-five cents in his pocket—an unbelievably small amount for an experienced traveler and territorial governor to possess during a long, cross-country trip.

Lewis's servant, Pernier, has also been tagged with the possible crime. According to this theory, Pernier—who has sometimes been described as a ne'er-do-well drifter—made off with Lewis's money, papers, and gold watch, and headed home to New Orleans. Supposedly he later killed himself when he was accused of the murder. Both the gold watch and papers mysteriously resurfaced, years later.

Still other historians think Lewis may have been murdered by a renegade federal agent named James Wilkinson, who may have had reasons to want Lewis dead. Wilkinson, in charge of the district where Lewis died, had allegedly been in league with Aaron Burr. Burr, who was tried for treason in 1807, encouraged newly acquired Louisiana territories to secede from the United States and ally with Spain. Lewis was President Jefferson's representative at Burr's trial, and Lewis took over Wilkinson's job as governor of the Upper Louisiana territory.

Other accounts say Lewis was found with his throat slashed, or shot in the back and dragged off into the woods. The great explorer's grave remained unmarked and forgotten for almost forty years. Finally the area was excavated for Lewis's body, then a monument erected to mark the site and the county named after him.

We'll probably never know who killed Meriwether Lewis. Many say his spirit still haunts the place, seeking justice from beyond his restless grave. On dark nights, people claim, his last words can still be heard exactly as Mrs. Grinder reported them: "So hard to die . . . so hard to die."

Oak Ridge–The Weirdest Town in Tennessee

Homespun Tennessee mystic John Hendrix, in an attempt to mimic Jesus' forty-day vigil in the Judean desert, spent forty days and nights in the backwoods of Anderson County. When he stumbled half-starved and wild-eyed out of the forest he shared a vivid supernatural vision he'd had of buildings and factories and people all working to win a great war.

When Hendrix died in 1915 at the age of 49, he was still considered a nutcase, but when the "secret city" of Oak Ridge came into being in the early 1940s, people recalled his raving vision. Federal agents commandeered sixty thousand acres of Roane and Anderson counties for what was to become the biggest industrial complex in history. Three thousand inhabitants swelled to seventy-five thousand in what was referred to as the "Clinton Engineering Works."

Scientists settled on three ways to refine uranium ore to make atomic bombs, but weren't sure which would work best, or at all, so all three were tried. The Y-12 facility (shown in image), refined the uranium used in the Little Boy atomic bomb that was dropped on Hiroshima, Japan, on August 6, 1945. The world's first operable nuclear reactor was built in the Secret City.

For the workers, what went on in Oak Ridge (named for Black Oak Ridge, just as John Hendrix had predicted) was often a puzzle. The town grew at a rate of one new dwelling every thirty minutes—so rapidly that people coming off shift sometimes had difficulty locating the homes they had left that morning. Oak Ridge became the fifth largest city in Tennessee and had the sixth largest bus system in the entire nation, yet there were no paved roads.

There was other weirdness. The high school sports teams, for instance, never played home games, since outsiders weren't permitted here, and only numbers were used on sports jerseys, never names.

One-eighth of the nation's electricity was channeled into Oak Ridge and an average seventy trainloads of materials arrived every day to make blue-green powder called U-235 tetrafluoride. It was valued at $250,000 an ounce, making it the most expensive product ever made, and up till then, the most deadly. A military security lieutenant in civilian clothes transported the powder from Knoxville to New Mexico.

Even after the bombing of Hiroshima and Nagasaki and the surrender of Japan, Oak Ridge remained guarded. In 1949 the community finally appeared on road maps, and in the early 1950s residents could purchase houses. Even so, the place is still patrolled, some roads remain closed, and unaware hikers wander into places that are verboten.

John Hendrix, meanwhile, went from local lunatic to revered prophet. His grave at 123 Hendrix Drive in Oak Ridge's Hendrix Creek subdivision has become something of a local shrine. It's on private property, but you can visit it if you ask permission.

Atomic Guest House

The Guest House, a.k.a. the Alexander Inn, opened in 1943 and housed nuclear scientists Enrico Fermi and J. Robert Oppenheimer, government officials, and Manhattan Project administrators.

The seventy-eight-room hotel closed its doors for good in 1993, though there are groups that want to either restore it or tear it down.

If the hotel is haunted—and many people claim that it is—it is probably the ghosts of the 220,000 people who died as a result of the work of Fermi, Oppenheimer, and their cohorts.

Katy's Kitchen

During World War II, Manhattan Project facilities at Oak Ridge were so ultra-secret that not even members of Congress knew of its existence. After the atomic bombs were dropped on Hiroshima and Nagasaki, the government needed a new place to hide its stockpile of enriched uranium. The solution: a highly fortified and reinforced underground bunker, codenamed Installation Dog but often referred to as 9214, cleverly camouflaged to appear as an old barn and silo. Security personnel dressed in bib overalls swung open the barn doors to allow the unloading of radiation-shielded vehicles disguised as farm trucks.

During the 1950s the barn was used for studies of radioactive samples of fallout, like the drifting dust from the Nevada atomic test site that farmers in southern Utah claimed had killed thousands of their sheep. The barn was nicknamed Katy's Kitchen after division secretary Kathryn Odom, who often worked there and brought lunch to the scientists. The name stuck.

The barn sports blue metal siding and its old vault holds samples of radiation-contaminated tissues, skins, and other biological materials. It's still off-limits and only one regular employee has the key, but Katy's Kitchen remains a strange monument to the outset of the Cold War.

Eeph Meisters

Tennessee's contribution to vocal noisemaking and percussive singing lies with eephing, a "kind of hiccupping, rhythmic wheezing." Eephers imitate coonhunts, birds, barnyard animals, common musical instruments like banjos and Jew's harps, and even the sounds of steam locomotives, Model-T Fords, and flushing toilets. Sounds made with the mouth alone, or by slapping cheeks or tapping teeth, are often accompanied by flatulent sounds made with greased palms, tire pumps, or blown-up rubber gloves. Like a lot of the other vocal acrobatics that humans have come up with, the invention of eephing probably owed a lot to poverty, isolation, and boredom, but the effect is still pretty funny. In fact, we're sure that it mostly came about because it was fun.

Unexplained Phenomena

A *glowing ball hovering in the sky* may be "an anomalous aerial phenomenon" or an "unidentified flying object." A glowing orb drifting through a cemetery at night may be a "paranormal event" or a "supernatural singularity." All weird stuff.

But what if the ground shakes, drops, and splits open, and water rushes in to form a lake (as happened in northwest Tennessee in 1812, when Reelfoot Lake came into being)? Is it only due to "natural causes," like stressed underground geological faults, or can it be attributed to the angry wrath of the Great Spirit stamping his feet, as the Chickasaws were said to believe? Is only one explanation a true scientific fact, while the other is only a "primitive legend"? What if the same thing had happened in Egypt thousands of years ago, with the water rushing in and drowning a pharaoh's army? Was that "just a legend," too?

Our point: Strange and amazing things do happen from time to time, but how we interpret them and what we make of them has to do with how we think, what we believe, and whether we witnessed such things for ourselves or only heard about them.

You may or may not believe in all the things that follow, but others who saw them came face-to-face with things they could not explain. If you think such things are impossible, keep in mind the ancient Greek proverb "One who does not expect the unexpected will never find it." There are far more strange and amazing things in the world than you might think.

A Dark Day in Memphis

Anomalist Charles Hoy Fort specialized in the compiling and cataloging of strange and unusual phenomena and events. He is regarded as a pioneer in an odd field. One of the events Fort "collected" was a "faux eclipse" that happened in Memphis between 10 and 10:15 A.M. on the morning of Friday, December 2, 1904. For no known astronomical reason, the city was suddenly blanketed in complete darkness for fifteen minutes. Fort quoted local newspapers as saying, "We are told that in some quarters a panic prevailed, and that some were shouting and praying and imagining that the end of the world had come." The mysterious and terrifying (if brief) spell of darkness has never been explained.

The Dark Day of Memphis was never taken quite as seriously as the "Black Friday" of May 19, 1780, that sent waves of terror through New England. It was commemorated in a poem entitled "Abraham Davenport" by John Greenleaf Whittier, which describes how the Connecticut legislature moved to adjourn because lawmakers were convinced that the world was about to end. However, House Speaker Davenport refused to go along with the motion, saying, "Let God do his work, we will see to ours. Bring in the candles." Davenport became a hero for continuing to serve the public, no matter what.

The Chapel Hill Light

It was a dark and stormy night. A signalman with the Louisville & Nashville Railroad was out near Winns Crossing with his lantern, ambling along what for Tennessee is an unusually straight and level section of track, when he somehow tripped and fell, knocking himself unconscious and falling with his neck on a rail.

You can guess what happened next. Yep, one of the locomotives came speeding down the tracks with a load of Birmingham steel, and pop went the poor fellow's noggin.

When the signalman went missing, his coworkers found the body, minus the portion normally featured in portraiture. Ever since then, most local folks say, the poor signalman has had to go headhunting for himself. On dark, misty nights, a light appears along the tracks and comes toward the crossing with extreme rapidity. It bobs from side to side like a lantern held by someone looking for something. As it gets ever closer, it gets brighter and brighter, glowing and bobbing, seeming to get larger and larger, till suddenly . . . nothing. The light just vanishes, and the whole thing starts over.

We're told that damp summer nights between twilight and midnight are the best times to see the light, though sometimes it reappears and other times not at all. Despite its occasional frustrating failure to perform, the Chapel Hill Light is one of the most reliable paranormal marvels in the state.

There is another local explanation of the Chapel Hill Light, though few folks now recall it and even fewer mention it anymore. Many years ago

WINNS CROSSING

an area man by the name of Skip Adgent was found dead on the tracks, minus the body parts above the collar. Some say he was murdered first and then left on the rails to conceal the evidence, and others insist he was murdered by being placed on the rails, but in either case the outcome was the same. According to this version of the story, Adgent is out there with a light not only trying to save face (along with scalp, ears, and upper vertebrae) but looking for revenge against those who killed him.

But we'll be upfront with you: We don't recommend visiting this place. Local law officers are quick to issue tickets or worse— and the fines and bailouts really do help the local economy. But even more important, it's incredibly dangerous, because the track is still in use. You might think you see Chapel Hill Light when in fact it could be a very real CSX freight locomotive speeding your way.

Fires of Dyer

South of Windrow, in Rutherford County, is a rise called Red Hill, and just beyond it, a dead-end lane called Dyer Road. The road terminates at the Dyer Cemetery, a stand of old cedar trees surrounded by a cluster of graves, lost by itself in the middle of a big empty field. No dwellings are in sight. According to a legend we heard, sometime in the nineteenth century, when people still thought all witches were evil, several women accused of witchcraft were taken to this spot to be killed and buried. Ever since then, the place has been considered cursed.

Phenomena do occur here, we were told. Reddish glowing balls of light drift across the area just barely above the ground but fade out as they approach the cedars. Voices can often be heard if the wind is blowing, and once in a while a figure may be seen flitting around the edges of the site, particularly near a heap of weedy growth at the southeast corner. We were told that the "changing seasons" of spring and fall, particularly around the vernal and autumnal equinoxes, are the most likely times to experience paranormal activities. Since these were times of year when ancient pagan or Wiccan practitioners often held rituals to celebrate the cyclical wheel of the seasons, it makes sense that any spirits in residence might make appearances at this time. But if any of the poor women had been subjected to some of the old methods for eradicating witches—pouring boiling water over them, shooting them with silver bullets made from melted dimes, pouring hot lead in their ears, and so on—they might not be all that cordial if you were to encounter them.

No need to bring guns or silver bullets with you—chances are you'd only end up shooting another researcher like yourself—but a bit of silver is never a bad idea. One traditional hex repellent, though technically a federal offense, was to punch a hole in a dime, run a string through it, and then tie it around your ankle. Be sure to use a dime with a date of 1964 or earlier, since dimes made after that year don't contain silver. Best are old "Mercury" dimes, which you can get from any coin dealer for about a dollar. Pretty cheap protection, we say!

In any case, be careful if you decide to check it out. As one person pointed out, "It's so far from the nearest houses that no one would even hear your screams."

Pillar of Fire

More than two hundred citizens of Cheatham County once witnessed what many thought was a biblical omen. According to an 1869 issue of *Symon's Monthly Meteorological Magazine*, a whirlwind passed over a small woods fire and then somehow turned into a flaming tornado that seemed reminiscent of the Pillar of Fire the Israelites followed out of Egypt toward the Promised Land, as described in Exodus. Moving at about five miles an hour, the towering wind inferno swept over a team of horses grazing in a field and immediately scorched their manes and tails "to the roots" (the horses presumably survived), then over a haystack and a farmhouse, burning them both to cinders.

With each combustible object it consumed, it gained still more size and power. After destroying the farm buildings, it headed on toward a wheat field, charring all the stacks of recently mown wheat. From there it set fire to all the trees in a sixty-foot swath before speeding up to make a beeline for the Cumberland River near Ashland City, as if it needed to cool off. When it reached the river, it turned and began following the watercourse downstream. With a tremendous hissing sound its smoke and flames turned to steam. Billows of steam rose several thousand feet in the air before the frightening spectacle finally flamed out and vanished. A blackened path of destruction several miles long was all that remained to mark the occurrence of the weird event.

Hounds of Helios

In the late spring of 1977, so many people were stunned by an amazing sight on Highway 25E near Harrogate, Claiborne County, that traffic was stopped for miles while everyone got out of their vehicles and gawked at it. A giant silver ring hovered over the highway like a signal of the End Times. Darrell Dickens, a truck driver staying at the Wilderness Road Inn, said, "It changed colors and gave off rays of light. It just hung up there till it kind of floated away." UFOlogists chalked it up to yet another bit of evidence that, as jazz master Sun Ra liked to say, "Space is the place, man."

Many unidentified things in the sky indeed are inexplicable, but this is one of those cases where there's probably a reasonable scientific explanation. When dustlike ice crystals float in freezing-cold layers of air in the upper atmosphere, they can act like tiny prisms and bend light to make what is called a solar halo. Such halos often include a parhelion, or what airline pilots call "sun dogs." Indians often knew them as "the sun's earrings," because they can form bright dots or rings that are even with the height of the sun. Because of the way light bends through frozen water, the earrings are always 22° from either side of the bright sun.

That, at least, is what a scientist would guess this probably was. Just because there happens to be a *possible* explanation for something doesn't always mean that it's the *right* explanation. After all, for thousands of years people thought the sun went around the earth because it made sense, based on what they saw. They turned out to be wrong.

So always keep an open mind—you'll see more weird and amazing stuff that way.

Flesh and Blood from Above

What happened in a field in central Tennessee in 1841 would be considered shocking even to today's jaded observers.

The Nashville *Daily Republican Banner* reported on Friday, August 20, 1841, that a "shower, apparently of flesh and blood" a mile in length and seventy-five yards wide, fell in Wilson County, near Lebanon.

According to W. P. Sayle, a local physician who arrived on the scene as soon as he heard about it, the shower occurred between 11 A.M. and noon on Friday, August 13. A small red cloud had passed in an otherwise blue sky not far above the ground. Out of it, according to Sayle, had fallen "animal matter, blood, muscular fibre, [and] adipose matter [fatty tissue]," though most of what fell was blood. Sayle wrote that ". . . the extent of surface over which it has spread, and the regular manner it exhibited on some green tobacco leaves, leaves very little or no doubt of its having fallen like a shower of rain. . . ."

Sayle sent samples to Dr. Gerard Troost, a major scientist in nineteenth-century America, and an expert in several disciplines. In August 1841 he was the state geologist and professor of chemistry at the University of Nashville. Troost was convinced that the samples were indeed chunks of meat and blood. A visit to the site further confirmed his assessment, although he was still at a loss to explain how it could have happened.

In an article for the *American Journal of Science*, Troost later hypothesized that, though unlikely, a tornado could have passed over a slaughteryard or inhaled a flock of birds and somehow ripped the meat into unidentifiable bits. (No hair, bones, or feathers were found.)

Bible Belt newspaper editors suggested that this and other recorded instances of "bloodfalls" in Kentucky, North Carolina, and other parts of the South in the nineteenth century were a result of heavenly displeasure with slavery. However, the last major bloodfall in the United States took place in 1884, well after legalized slavery had ended. Francis Preston Venable, one of the foremost chemists in the world, analyzed it and confirmed that hemoglobin (the main component of blood) had in fact fallen from the sky, though he couldn't explain why.

So the mystery remains a double puzzle: Why did blood and tissue fall from the sky and then stop? Was the cause supernatural, paranormal, or extraterrestrial in origin? Whatever the case, it was definitely weird.

Cloudy, with a Chance of Angel Hair

The moon and stars must have been in the astrological sign for "strange" in October 1966. Just after 7 P.M. on Tuesday, October 11 people in Jonesborough, Washington County, saw a "cigar-shaped object" hovering over the town for a few minutes, before it lit up brightly and sped off in a northerly direction. Then two disc-like objects arrived on the scene, with "bulges" on top and bright beams of light or energy projecting underneath.

Beginning around noon the following day and lasting for almost five hours, many witnesses saw many flying discs accompanied by sticky airborne filaments called "angel's hair." People who came in contact with the substance reported itching, nausea, and a burning sensation. Even farm animals seemed to be affected by it.

"Angel hair" has been associated with UFO sightings for centuries, as well as with religious apparitions. Theories suggest it is a form of exhaust or a byproduct of propulsion systems of UFOs, part of an alien probe or intelligence-gathering procedure, or atmospheric dust ionized by static electricity as space vehicles enter or navigate through the upper atmosphere.

Snakes Alive

According to the Memphis weather observer, on the morning of January 15, 1877, the day began with southwesterly winds and a light rain. Heavier torrents started around 10:20 A.M. and lasted for about fifteen minutes. As soon as the rain let up, startled residents living near today's FedEx Forum stadium witnessed millions of snakes carpeting the landscape in a writhing, teeming tangle. They were described as dark brown or almost black, and knotted together so thickly in a four-square-block area that they formed a dense mat resembling a "mess of thread or yarn."

The next day the *Memphis Public Ledger* ran an article calling it a "Shower of Snakes" though the official Army report pointed out that there were no snakes found on rooftops, rain gutters, or in rainwater cisterns, as there should have been if the wriggling reptiles had fallen from the sky. The newspaper added that the snakes averaged a foot to a foot and a half in length, had small black heads, and small black spots.

The newspaper also reported that "the sight is not pleasant," and that they may have been ". . . harmless, but they are unwelcome visitors."

Saucers over Secret City

Oak Ridge, along with its "spooky science installations" like K-25, S-50, Y-12, and X-10 (see Fabled People and Places chapter), has been a major draw for Little Green Men ever since its hush-hush founding back in the early 1940s. There have been hundreds of sightings and many witnesses to corroborate multiple encounters with strange objects in the Oak Ridge skies. But before Oak Ridge was built there was almost no discussion of anything unusual.

According to international UFO authority George D. Fawcett, such sightings in association with nuclear facilities are not unusual. UFOs, he says, seem to be drawn toward major electrical energy sources such as dams and reactors—a correlation that hasn't gone unnoticed. When the Manhattan Project got underway at Oak Ridge to develop the first atom bombs, an enormous amount of electricity was channeled to the site in secret. Millions of kilowatts of electricity were consumed—more than 13 percent of all the electric power in the nation at the time—and UFOs were drawn to Oak Ridge like moths to a candle. But why?

It's a question that has never been answered satisfactorily. Some defense experts have worried openly that alien spacecraft may be sizing up points of weakness in our

energy grid in order to plan a future attack. But others, like Fawcett, have speculated that there may be less-threatening reasons behind it. Perhaps they are just using such areas as a kind of "interplanetary service station" and picking up our electrical leakage. (If your radio has ever buzzed as you drove under a power line, you know there is electrical leakage.) Dams and reactors offer easy access to both electric power and water. Our own atomic submarines stay submerged for months at a time by manufacturing their own air by converting electricity and water into hydrogen and oxygen.

Oak Ridge might have been an attractant to UFOs because of its concentration of mercury. At one time, 99 percent of all the mercury in the country (some 2.4 million pounds) was stashed at Oak Ridge. Now nearly all of it is gone, and no one can account for where it went. Could UFOs have siphoned it off? In the cold of deep space, liquid mercury from Earth would become a hard metal. Who knows? Maybe it was used for intergalactic construction projects.

Here are a few Oak Ridge area sightings over the years:

September 18, 1944—A metallic-looking tubelike object is spotted hovering over the road near the K-25 (shown on previous page) plant. The object moves away when a crowd starts to gather and its sighting is later reported to the FBI.

October 16, 1950—Shortly after 3 P.M. the Atomic Energy Commission Patrol reports a "silver disc" hovering over the K-25 plant. An F-82 fighter plane is sent to intercept. The fighter-plane radar picks up only a light aircraft, but ground observers report that the F-82 passed under the "silver disc" while in pursuit of the light plane. (See below for a telegram from FBI director J. Edgar Hoover, dated December 5, 1950.)

June 21, 1952—At 10:58 P.M. a Ground Observer Corps spotter reports a slow-moving object nearing the Oak Ridge Laboratory. F-47 aircraft on combat air patrol in the area close in on it. Several times the object makes what appear to be attacks of blinking white light, six to eight inches in diameter.

June 23, 1952—At 3:30 A.M. Martha Milligan sees a bullet-shaped object with burnt-orange exhaust fly straight and level.

```
                          TELETYPE

FBI WASHINGTON DC              12-5-50      4-47 PM      GAR
SAC, KNOXVILLE                 URGENT
DETECTION OF UNIDENTIFIED OBJCXXX OBJECTS OVER OAK RIDGE AREA, PROTECTIO
OF VITAL INSTALLATIONS.  REURTEL DECEMBER FOUR LAST REGARDING POSSIBLE
RADAR JAMMING AT OAK RIDGE.  ARRANGEMENTS SHOULD BE MADE TO OBTAIN
ALL FACTS CONCERNING POSSIBLE RADAR JAMMING BY IONIZATION OF PARTICLES
IN ATOXXX ATMOSRHERE.  CONDUCT APPROPRIATE INVESTIGATION TO DETERMINE
WHETHER INCIDENT OCCURRING NORTHEAST OF OLIVER SPRINGS, TENNESSEE,
COULD HAVE HAD ANY CONNECTION WITH ALLEGED RADAR JAMMING.  SUTEL
IMPORTANT DEVELOPMENTS.
                          HOOVER
END
                                                        1950-DEC-20
```

Coincidental Combustion

Fire has long been associated with the more choleric of human emotions. Common expressions such as "That really burns me up," or "He was like a house on fire," or "She was really steamed about that" usually invoke images of excitability. All the more peculiar, then, that a mild-mannered college professor suddenly burst into flame one day for no apparent reason at all.

That is exactly what happened to Dr. James Hamilton, an instructor at the University of Nashville, on January 5, 1835. Born in Princeton, New Jersey, in 1796, he had graduated from that town's eponymous college before moving to Nashville to accept his position in 1829. The gentle scholar was known about town as a loner, regarded with a bemused tolerance reserved for harmless eccentrics.

When he wasn't tutoring or teaching classes, Hamilton went on solitary strolls with his eyes skyward, meanwhile keeping copious notes on daily temperature readings, air pressure changes, humidity levels, rainfall, dense fogs, or powerful tornadoes. He made diary entries for sightings of comets, auroras, planetary movements, and meteor showers. He wrote a regular column for the Nashville newspapers that attracted little attention except on those rare occasions when he was able to forewarn locals of an imminent eclipse.

Due to his carefully maintained observations, we know that the Nashville weather on January 5, 1835, was a bright, brisk 8°F. Professor Hamilton had just finished his morning lectures and had strolled home at midday for lunch when he decided first to check the meteorological instruments in his backyard to compare their readings with those he had already recorded at the university.

As he was examining the wind speed gauge on his anemometer he suddenly felt a terrible pain on the surface of his leg. Thinking it might be a hornet (even though it was winter), he slapped at it, only increasing the pain.

Hamilton then ran inside and lifted his trousers to see what was happening. To his intense amazement, as well as intense pain, he saw a small bright flame shooting out of the side of his leg. Slapping at it hadn't worked, so he immediately cupped a hand over the spreading fire to deprive it of oxygen and snuff it out. After a moment the flame died, leaving only a burned place on his skin about the size of a dime. His private physician, Dr. John Overton, had read about other such bizarre occurrences and diagnosed Hamilton's malady as an extremely rare example of spontaneous human combustion (SHC). Even more unusual was that Hamilton had survived the experience, since most known cases of SHC resulted in flames consuming the hapless victim in a matter of minutes. After literally "going up in smoke," typically all that is left of a victim is a pile of ash or perhaps only a pair of feet, since damp socks and shoes tend to prevent them from burning. To this day, no one knows what causes these weird events. Lucky for the rest of us, they are among the rarest of anomalous phenomena.

But if they're so rare, then just how astronomical are the odds against it happening again in the same vicinity? In October 1989 a Brentwood yard worker was admitted to the Vanderbilt University Medical Center with second-degree burns over 7 percent of his body. He'd struck a match and briefly turned into a human fireball.

His name was also James Hamilton.

UFO Flap!

One of the nagging mysteries of UFO studies has to do with the cyclical nature of UFO sightings. Like sunspots, locust plagues, tree ring records of droughts, cheese consumption, hemlines, and the stock market, there seems to be some kind of regular rhythmic pattern to the appearances of anomalous aerial phenomena, though no one knows why. UFOlogists call such outbreaks "flaps." They are mostly detected in hindsight and tend to occur in cycles lasting from six and a quarter days to more than five years.

For a prime example, consider a major flap that took place in Tennessee in the autumn of 1973. On Sunday, September 23, 1973, several Shelby County sheriff's deputies and Memphis policemen reported seeing a UFO. That same night there was a "spate of sightings" in the southeastern United States, according to the *Nashville Tennessean*. Deputy P.M. Pilalas was quoted in the *Nashville Banner* as saying, "We let our blue light shine twice and then stopped. The vehicle then flashed its white beams twice and then both the white and red lights went out. . . . It made a whirring-type noise for about thirty seconds to a minute, then it was gone."

A few minutes later, and some eighty miles away in Jackson, Tommy Robbins of the Illinois Central-Gulf Railroad also reported seeing a hovering object with red and white lights that "was very bright and seemed to give off a light like a strong fluorescent light." It headed west and then disappeared.

More reports phoned in by ordinary citizens came in the following night, but law officers discounted them, thinking they were mostly crank or "copycat" calls from people who had become nervous after reading about the deputies' encounter. About 8:45 P.M. on September 25, Maury County sheriff's deputies and numerous others saw two brightly lit orange objects that were "crisscrossing back and forth from north-northeast," over Highway 431 near Spring Hill. The FAA reported no local air traffic in the area. Danny White of the *Banner* also saw them and wrote: "The sighting at Spring Hill was no prank. The two objects were there, whether they be stars, planets, space junk, atmospheric gasses, airplanes or UFOs. They are as real as the residents of that community ever want them to be."

On Saturday, September 29, Obion County sheriff Nathan Cunningham saw three UFOs, one of which passed low enough over Union City that at least twenty people reported hearing its humming sound as it swished by. "It stopped over the north for four or five minutes, then came back over south and finally disappeared," Cunningham said. According to the *Banner*, witnesses saw "a bright red light" that very nearly caused a seven-car pileup when it passed over Highway 78 near Reelfoot Lake.

On Monday afternoon, October 1, a robotlike creature with a large round head emerged from an egg-shaped UFO and approached three witnesses in Anthony Hill. That same day at about 6 P.M. near Brighton, a woman and her son saw a "large domed disc" cross the sky and two people in Giles Town saw an egg-shaped object emitting bright light as it vanished behind the tree line.

On her way to work at a Wilson County restaurant on the morning of Sunday, October 14, Lebanon resident Mrs. Fred Singleton saw a silent, cigar-shaped UFO hover near her car. When a beam of light from the object hit her car, the tape player stopped dead and the car "quit running like it was out of gas." The UFO remained stationary in the air for about five minutes. As soon as it was gone, everything began working normally again. "I'd never seen anything like it in my life," she told the *Banner*. "It scared me out of my wits."

Cecil Whitson, a dairy farmer in Putnam County, called the *Tennessean* after he was "buzzed by a UFO" on October 15. As described in the paper, "He said he mistook it first for a tractor with headlights lumbering toward him until it took off over his head about fifteen feet [overhead], then climbed straight up and cleared a seventy-foot silo."

The Clarksville Police Department was overwhelmed with a barrage of more than a hundred frantic calls on the evenings of October 16 and 17. Cone- or saucer-shaped objects with red and blue lights were seen over the northern areas of the city. Meanwhile, just south of Clarksville in New Providence, three objects approximately fifteen feet in diameter were reported "jumping across the sky" before they departed "like a streak of lightning."

October 17 was especially busy with circular multicolored objects flying across and hovering over Tennessee.

At 7:30 A.M. on Friday, October 19, Lebanon schoolbus driver Dennis Sircy saw a "shiny, silver-looking, round" UFO on Leeville Pike and Tucker's Gap Road. The kids in the bus saw it, too. Jerald Phillips, chief of rescue for Wilson County Civil Defense, investigated the area and said it had left "three large circles in the broom sage, with four large places where something "had blown the grass off the ground, exposing the dirt." Radiation was detected at the spot. That evening, several witnesses called police after seeing a light hovering over radio station WCOR's tower.

Finally, about 8:30 P.M. on October 20, three witnesses in the Powell Valley, Claiborne County, watched in fascination as an orange sphere shot out a brilliant beam that lit up the entire side of a mountain. Once the object disappeared, the skies were unusually quiet. Across the state, few if any law enforcement centers received any more calls that evening. After that, the sightings quickly dwindled, as if the saucers had headed back to their mother ship or home planet to regroup. But what had happened? Why so many UFOs all at once?

Several years later, Nashville psychiatrist Otto Billig attributed such clusters of UFO sightings to social, economic, or psychological stresses. "UFOs do exist," he explained to *Tennessean* reporter Adell Crowe, "but only in the minds of men." When people are under stress, he insisted, they start "seeing things." He pointed out that during the Tennessee flap in the autumn of 1973, the nation was rocked by Vietnam, Watergate, a gasoline crisis, legalized abortion, American Indian activists in a standoff with the FBI at Wounded Knee, and more.

Confronted with Billig's theory as another flap was apparently getting underway, with nine different UFO sightings in central Tennessee in January 1979, law officers weren't buying it. Veteran Nashville police Lieutenant Robert Ezell was one of seven Metro policemen, several Tennessee Highway Patrol officers, and numerous others who spent an hour observing two objects that were discovered hovering above the vicinity of 10th Avenue North and Charlotte Avenue.

"I don't think *that* many people could be wrong in what they saw," Ezell told the *Nashville Banner*. "Does [Billig] consider that all twenty-two people that saw this thing have an emotional stress problem?"

Nowhere to Land

On May 10, 1989, Nashville city councilman George Darden introduced a bill at a meeting of the city council to have a Metro UFO landing pad erected in Nashville. He was dead serious. "Many people have come to me expressing the fact that they are seeing these unidentified flying objects," he told the Rules Committee. According to *Nashville Tennessean* reporter Gail McKnight, Darden said he was worried that with all the WELCOME TO MUSIC CITY USA billboards around the city, country & western loving aliens might be attracted to the city from outer space, find nowhere to set down their saucer-shaped rigs, and get mad about it. "They'll go back and say we lied."

Zoning denied permission to erect signs to welcome spaceships.

The Rules Committee nixed the idea in a twenty-seven-to-one rout. The Metro Board of Zoning appeals also unanimously denied Darden's application for permission to erect large signs in his own back yard to welcome the spaceships. Councilmen recalled that a similar point-spread had resulted from Darden's previous introduction of bills to install quieter sirens on emergency vehicles and to ban sex in the Metro Courthouse. However, that last defeat, as wags later pointed out, could have been interpreted in a number of different ways.

Mystery Message in the Field

On May 14, 2006, Capt. Bryan Graves of the Monroe County Sheriff's Office was flying his small plane a few miles south of Madisonville when he made a startling discovery. In a field below he saw a strange image. Five large circles interspersed with smaller circles made a clearly defined geometric pattern on the crops. No visible entry trail led to the image, and no recent tiremarks were visible on the edges of the field. A nearby road showed no sign that anyone had even pulled off the road to look at a map.

Graves noted the spot on his map and came back later on the ground to investigate. The owners of the Rocky Springs Road property—the family of former Tennessee senator Estes Kefauver—said they had not noticed any unusual activity nor had any idea, in fact, that anything had happened to their crops until the officer told them. They could think of no motive for anyone to want to create something like this in their field, if indeed it had been done by humans.

Up close, no footprints were found, nor were there any clues to indicate how the patterns had been made. The pattern was almost 160 feet in diameter, and each of the larger component circles was a little more than forty feet across. Perfectly straight lines linked the individual circles in a radial pattern.

Within hours, word got out and hundreds of curiosity seekers began flocking to the farm to see the circles for themselves. The landowners were forced to put up NO TRESPASSING signs to save the rest of their crops. A week or two later, trained investigators from the Cincinnati-based Independent Crop Circle Research Association (ICCRA) arrived on the scene and conducted a field study, collecting 1,500 samples of the soil and crops, and taking radiation and atmospheric measurements. The crop samples later showed abnormal elongation of the wheat nodes and small pits in the stems of the crops called "expulsion cavities," which can be duplicated in a lab by bombarding plants with microwaves, but doesn't happen under normal natural conditions. The centers of the circles also revealed elevated levels of radiation, which is consistent with many other "authenticated" crop circle sites (i.e., crop circles that aren't later revealed to be hoaxes).

Researchers pointed to the large numbers of springs, caverns, and archaeological sites in the vicinity. The area has been occupied by humans for at least ten thousand years, and the more recent Cherokee centers of Chota and Tanasi (namesake of the state) are not far—though now submerged under Tellico Lake. It may only be coincidence that Chota, the mound where the famous Bat Creek Stone was found, the Lost Sea, and the Madisonville Crop Circle form a near-perfect rectangle, but some investigators read significance into that arrangement, comparing it to the ley lines of Europe and England.

A year later, another crop circle turned up in Monroe County, in Johnnie Helms's fifty-acre wheat field. This one, however, turned out to be a copycat hoax. Researchers from ICCRA determined that a board or garden roller was used to flatten the crops, and that a walking path with footprints leading to the image proved that several people had participated in what was later termed an act of vandalism rather than an anomaly. Furthermore, in more than seven hundred samples taken, no microwave-like effects were observed on the plants nor detectable elevations in radiation. "I don't like it," landowner Helms said, upset at the damage to the crops, "and if I find out who did it I am going to prosecute them."

If anything, the hoax only heightens the mystery of the authenticated circles on Rocky Springs Road, for as to who—or what—created them, or how they could have been formed, no one yet knows.

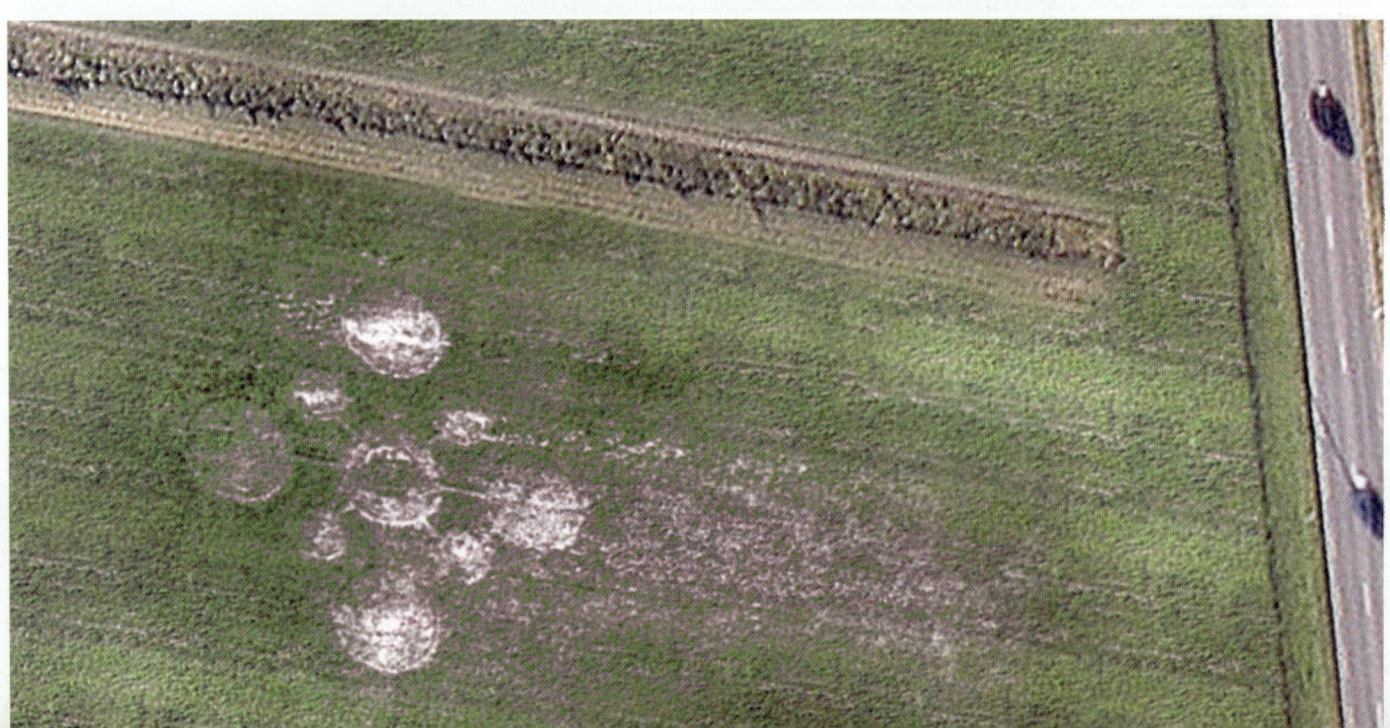

The Unfleeting Shadow

"Life's but a walking shadow," Shakespeare's Macbeth complains as he's contemplating the brief and seemingly meaningless life he's stuck in. Problem is: Some shadows stick around longer than others. When they tore down the old St. Thomas Sanitarium at the corner of Hayes and Twentieth Streets in Nashville, a number of witnesses reported seeing a shadow of the Virgin Mary.

The building seems to have been named after Nashville Bishop Thomas S. Byrne, who was never actually canonized. However, the Bishop was an aggressive builder with a number of churches, schools, and hospitals erected to his name across Tennessee, so he may have invoked the name of the particular St. Thomas who is the patron saint of architects. Bishop Byrne purchased a mansion on Church Street in Nashville's West End in 1898 and had it converted into a sanitarium. The hospital operated for the next seventy years, expanding across the block to Hayes Street. It was to be demolished in the mid-1970s to make way for a parking lot for Baptist Hospital just across the street. Although a new St. Thomas Hospital had already been opened in 1974 on Harding Road, the Holy Mother departed the old building only reluctantly. For a brief time the shadow caused a sensation and drew crowds to see it. When the Baptists indicated no intention of maintaining a pilgrimage shrine, the phenomenon faded away.

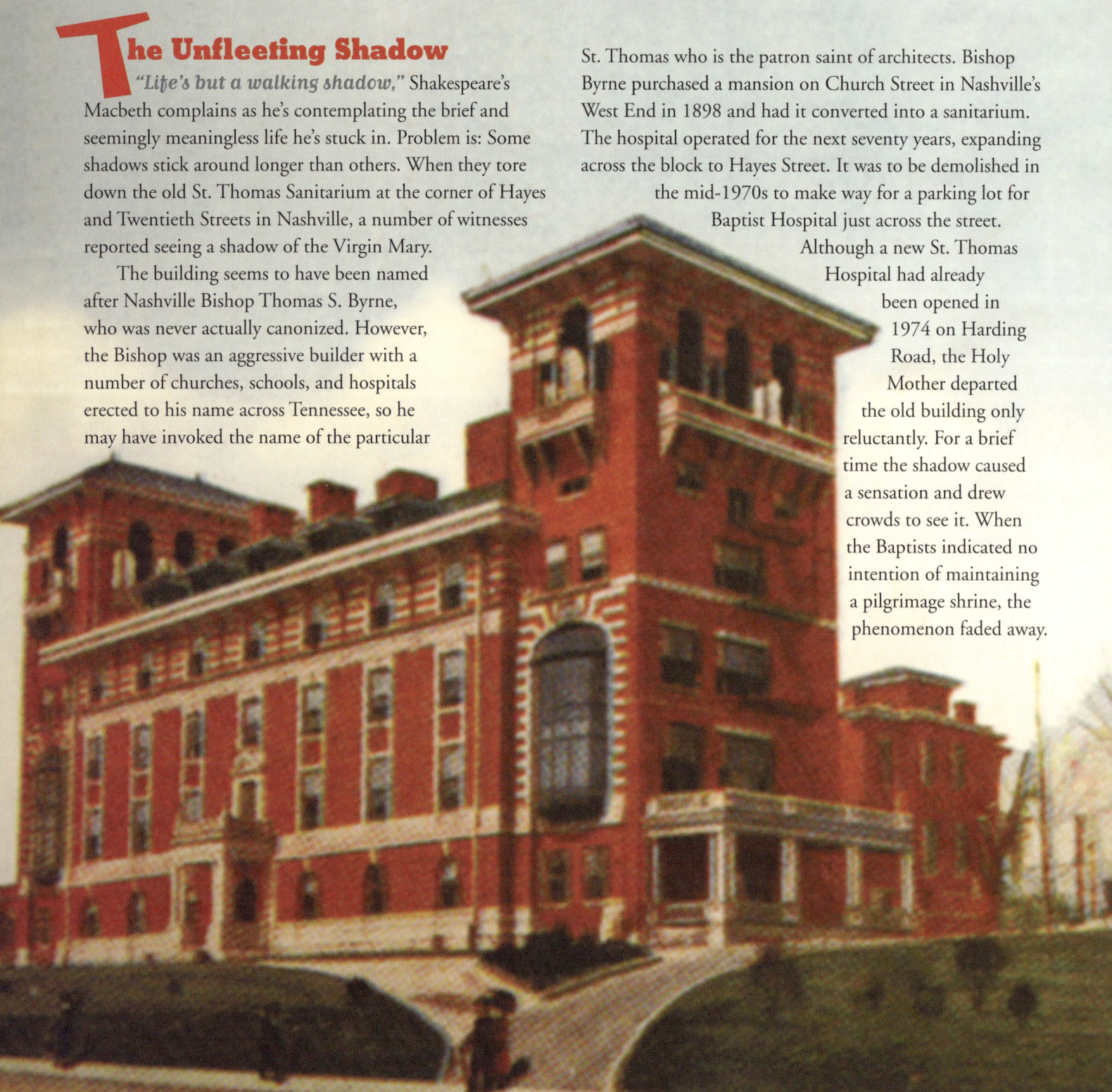

Great Balls of Fire

A steep, twelve-mile ridge named Doe Mountain nearly divides Johnson County down the middle. For a number of years, it has been the site of a marvel known both eponymously and descriptively as the Doe Mountain Fireball. No one has figured out if it is an anomalous natural phenomenon such as ball lightning or St. Elmo's Fire, or a paranormal apparition of some sort. In support of the first theory, it has been described as a blindingly brilliant spherical object (if a flame can be considered an "object") estimated at somewhere between the size of a basketball and a weather balloon. It seems to roll rapidly, bounce, or hover the way certain kinds of static electrical phenomena do.

On the other hand, it seems to be completely harmless, coming in contact with trees or dry grass without leaving so much as a scorch mark, and there seems to be no correlation between sightings of the weird ball and the weather. On rare occasions it has even appeared during the day, under perfectly ordinary weather conditions.

Doe Mountain is surrounded by gentle valleys on all sides, from which it juts up almost like an island in a sea. Some scientists have hypothesized that its relative isolation (and insulation) from other nearby ridges and mountains may have something to do with the burning orb, but they are at a loss to point to any single causal force or feature. Manganese, used in the production of hardened steel and batteries, has been extracted from mines on and around the ridge, but whether this has anything to do with it, no one knows.

Proponents of the paranormal theory say that the fireball could have something to do with Native American burial caves in the region. Just a few miles away on the north side of Watauga Lake, a cave called the Lake Hole Mortuary Cave was found in 1990. It contained thousands of beads and pottery fragments as well as human remains more than a thousand years old. Perhaps the burial caves on Doe Mountain are threatened by mining, leading to the possibility that perhaps the mysterious fireball is some kind of warning. But a warning for what?

Pleasant Sightings

"I don't know what it is, but it sure is pretty" is how Mt. Pleasant police officer James Johnston described a UFO he saw to Nashville Banner reporter David Lyons.

Everyone in the police department could see it from the porch of the station—an object with blue, red, green, and orange lights that had appeared over southwestern Maury County for three days in a row in September 1976. Police departments in nearby Columbia and other communities poked fun at the reports. "Mt. Pleasant must have found a still," the Columbia dispatcher said. "They're seeing UFOs again."

But five law officers had kept an eye on it ever since it first appeared. "We saw it a week ago Monday," Johnston said. "It looked egg-shaped then." On September 6, 1976, as many as fifty people gathered at 3 A.M. in Mt. Pleasant's downtown square to watch it, including drivers of eighteen-wheelers who had spotted it from the highway. "I know people think we are crazy down here, but the whole town can't all go crazy at once," the police officer said.

The same week, exactly three years earlier, a similar series of sightings had enthralled the town. The September 1973 phenomena were never explained either.

Miracles on Copper Ridge

Back in the mid-1990s a minor miracle began to unfold on Majors Road in northern Knox County, in what used to be called the Copper Ridge Baptist Church. Starting November 8, 1995, congregation members realized that, out each window of the main sanctuary, they could see a cross floating in the air nearly a hundred feet away. The crosses were about six feet tall and hovered thirty or forty feet above the ground, clearly visible enough to be photographed. They could be seen both night and day. During the day the weird images were brilliantly white, and at night they were a burnished gold or copper red color.

Rev. Joe Bullard described his first encounter with the strange light phenomenon. "One evening . . . my wife, Mildred, and I drove by. . . . We stopped the car in amazement when a radiant white light seemed to surround the entire building for a short time. We went home wondering what that meant. . . . We didn't have to wait long for an answer. . . . The next time I spoke to the congregation, a bright light hit the side of the church and, as we looked out of the window, we saw our first cross of light. We could hardly believe it, but as they continue to appear, we know they are real."

One night a tall turbaned man appeared in the church and slowly walked forward toward the front of the church. Two other less visible people accompanied him. "Every couple of steps the last person in line turned slightly toward us and waved in a friendly manner," Bullard reported. "When they reached the front of the church, they turned around. . . . When they had made the walk three times, they disappeared. [They] certainly caught the attention of some of our members!"

Before these strange happenings, the congregation had dwindled to just fourteen individuals, though the building could seat sixty. After this, more than a thousand people lined up to see the crosses and seek a blessing. As word spread, the crosses got brighter and brighter, to the point that worshippers had to wear sunglasses to avoid being blinded by the light.

One afternoon a blind man was guided into the sanctuary flanked by two attendants who guided him toward one of the windows. As Reverend Bullard told it, "Suddenly, he jumped up screaming that he could see, throwing down his cane and dark glasses, and rushed out of the church and down the road. His attendants frantically tried to get their car out of the parking lot to follow him, and we haven't seen any of them since." Many more claims of healing, ranging from cures for deafness, cancer, and drug abuse to failed marriages and bad breath soon followed. Within a few months, some sixty miracles were reported—roughly the same number of authenticated miracles that have occurred at the famous shrine of Lourdes in France since 1858, and nearly twice as many biblical miracles as Jesus performed in his earthly lifetime.

Miracles don't last forever, and in this case, the tolerance of some members eventually began to wear thin as thousands of visitors continued visiting the church. By 1998, Reverend Bullard was asked to resign, "but I refused, so they cut off my $250-a-month salary and went to court to remove me. . . . [M]y wife and I were physically attacked and sprayed in the eyes with pepper spray and we were taken by our children to the hospital to recuperate. To protect my family, I turned the church over to the congregation. . . . [Now] the church is closed to all outsiders, [and] the windows are being removed to keep the crosses out." The reverend and his wife attained some closure when, during a clandestine visit to the church, they witnessed the turbaned gentleman at roadside with "a marvelous smile on his face. As we passed, he raised his hand up as if to say: 'Do you feel better now?' . . . I slammed on the brake and tried to back up quickly to take a closer look, but he had disappeared."

The congregation, meanwhile, has tried to put the whole strange episode behind them, even going so far as to rename the church. Nowadays the church is called New Beginnings Baptist Church.

Susan Caroline Godsey's Big Sleep

Most people who become famous get that way either by accumulating a long list of achievements, or else due to some accident of life, such as by winning the lottery, getting struck by a meteorite, or being born into a royal family. But Susan Caroline Godsey of Trenton, Gibson County, achieved fame starting in the 1850s by doing almost nothing at all. In fact, she snoozed her way to national recognition by spending nearly twenty-three hours of every day fast asleep.

In 1849, at age eight, Godsey had a recurring fever and was treated by an itinerant doctor. Local historians insist that the healer was only a quack from a traveling medicine show hoping to prove the efficacy of his snake oil, but a short while later Godsey began having intense spasmodic seizures, immediately followed by deep sleep. Over time, the violence of the spasms tapered off. But they were so frequent that she awoke only several times a day, just long enough to eat a bit of food, relieve herself, and share a few words with her family before another paroxysm would send her off to sleep again.

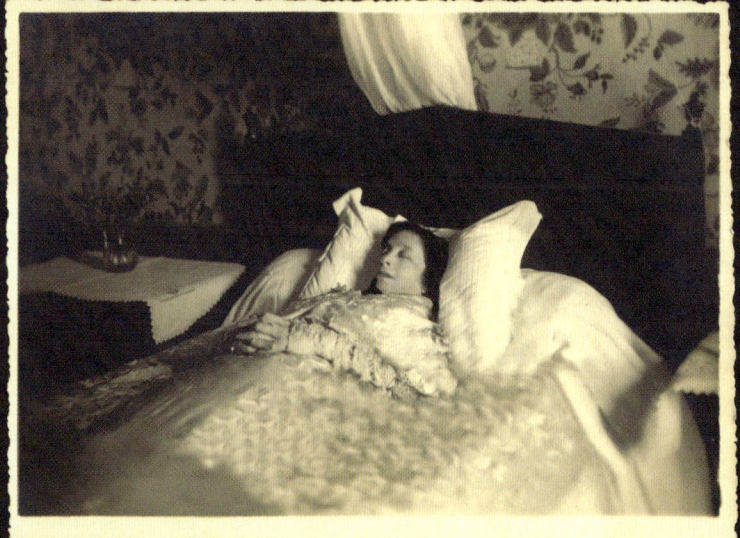

Months became years, and years decades as the "Sleeping Beauty of Tennessee" spent more than 93 percent of her life sleeping. Her fame spread, with articles about her strange malady appearing not only in local county newspapers but in the *New York Times*, the *London Daily Mail* and international medical journals. In the late 1850s consummate showman P. T. Barnum took a brief interest in the possibility of including Sleeping Susie in his great American Museum in New York, alongside such well-known oddities as the midget General Tom Thumb (Charles Stratton), bearded lady Josephine Clofullia, and the famed FeJee Mermaid.

The deal was never struck, but after that the Godseys began taking Susan on trips to medical schools. In 1867 she made an appearance in Nashville. After months spent dissecting smelly old cadavers, male students in Dr. Robert Eve's classes welcomed the chance to study a pretty twenty-six-year-old in her sleep. In 1870, a team of physicians in St. Louis enjoyed their examination as well, noting in their report that she had "attained the normal development of her sex" and that the "general development of her body . . . [which was] . . . more full than could be expected under the unfavorable circumstances of her apparently-disturbed health."

Twenty-five years after she slipped into her famous hypersomnic situation, she finally began emerging from it. In 1873, presumably with her whole life ahead of her (she was in her thirties), she died of an uncertain cause.

Telltale Tail Tale

Here's a thought to lull yourself back to sleep the next time you've eaten too much spaghetti and wake up with your guts churning. Back in the 1870s a young woman who lived out in the country east of Christiana in Rutherford County named Thankfull Taylor (sometimes spelled Thankful) endured years of excruciating stomach convulsions and abdominal pains after every hot meal, while only cool water seemed to calm her intestinal jitters. As her condition gradually worsened, her parents sought the advice of local doctors, but none of them seemed able to come up with a diagnosis that fit the description of the malady, nor any cure that proved even mildly effective. In fact, the medicines they prescribed only seemed to make the convulsions worse. Any wine or medicine that contained alcohol would result in peculiar spasms and rippling tremors in the girl's stomach that could be seen from clear across a room.

In June 1874, after suffering for more than four years with the inexplicable disorder, Thankfull awoke with one of her frequent, but always horrible stomach spasms and cried out for her mother. Thankfull's mom, Didama Carroll, ran into the room with a lantern and saw a dark object protruding from Thankfull's throat and managed to grab it. Called to the scene, Dr. J. M. Burger grasped the wriggling protrusion with his surgical forceps, extracting a twenty-three-inch water snake. Like a biblical miracle, the girl's pains and convulsions immediately vanished. The snake died within minutes after the extraction. Thankfull later recalled having swallowed something like "a string" when she'd taken a big gulp of spring water on a particularly hot day years before.

Dr. Burger kept the snake in his office in a jar of formadehyde for the rest of his life in case anyone doubted the incident. Its present whereabouts are unknown.

Apparently the girl went on to lead a normal and relatively uneventful life.

David Lang, the Vanishing Farmer

An otherwise perfectly ordinary field alongside Long Hollow Pike (State Road 174) a few miles west of Gallatin, Sumner County, is said to be the scene of one of Tennessee's most enduring mysteries. Around 3:30 P.M. on the afternoon of Thursday, September 23, 1880, farmer David Lang was strolling across this field in full view of two neighbors and three members of his own family when all five of them witnessed his sudden disappearance before their very eyes. Lang was only about forty yards away when he melted into thin air in midstep.

When neighbors rushed to the scene and thoroughly examined the area, they found no holes or cracks in the ground—nor have any ever been found in all the years since then. Test pits dug here quickly reached solid bedrock. Though many regions of Tennessee are subject to sinkholes and underground cavities, the old Lang farm site is apparently not one of them.

Emma Lang remained hysterical and distraught for many weeks after the event, while the farm fell into disarray. Servants and field hands left to seek employment elsewhere when further unnatural affairs were soon observed. For instance, all the grass within roughly a ten-foot radius of the spot where Lang had disappeared began to grow rank and yellowish. The Lang children then noticed that the area where the odd grass grew was eerily free of insects, mice, or other critters that should normally occupy open fields in Tennessee.

One day Lang's daughter Sarah cried out for her father and beat on the ground with a stick in the spot where he had last been seen. Upon doing this, both she and her younger brother could hear him faintly crying for help for a brief period of time, followed by silence. The cook, too, later admitted that she had sometimes heard Mr. Lang's disembodied voice at the site, but hadn't wanted to mention it for fear of upsetting the family or endangering her employment.

Years went by. Emma Lang never held a funeral service for her husband, and eventually others took over the farm after she passed away. The two children moved to Virginia, where Sarah Lang began to practice Spiritualism, holding séances in an effort to contact her lost father as well as her deceased mom. Using a technique intended to allow "automatic writing," she was finally able to channel her dead mother, who in due course informed her that she and long-lost husband David were together again in the hereafter.

Many locals claim that even today a nearly perfect circular patch of ground still turns sallow, despite all attempts at plowing, planting, or fertilizing it. However, no newspapers ever covered the event. No records of any David Lang farm can be found in the local county courthouse, nor have any census listings, cemetery stones, or other genealogical sources ever confirmed the earthly existence of either the Langs or the two witnesses (a Judge Peck and his brother-in-law) who were said to have been present on the day the vanishing took place.

But as any physicist will tell you, there are still many mysteries in the universe. After all, entire star systems can disappear into a black hole, and time itself can come to a standstill in their vicinity. Could it be that vanishings of farmers, their families, and all record of their existence could take place not only in space, but time as well?

Perpetual Motion of Jackson's Wheel

Before the Civil War, Confederate inventor Asa Jackson had hit upon the solution to a problem that even the Renaissance master Leonardo da Vinci himself had failed to solve. Using simple carpenter's tools, and perhaps inspired by the biblical description of a vision in Ezekiel 1:16, the Tennesseean from Lebanon built a machine that could generate its own impetus. In other words, he had found the secret to "perpetual motion." Once it began to turn, the wheel-within-a-wheel would turn itself by itself until its parts physically wore out. That was the concept, anyway.

Jackson, born in 1792, was already sixty-nine when the Civil War began. During the hostilities he feared his invention would fall into enemy hands, so he took it apart and hid it in a cave. Even without Jackson's epoch-making device, the Union won anyway. Jackson retrieved his contraption, put it back together, and set it in motion long enough for witnesses to vouch that it worked. It ran, they said, for many days, perhaps weeks, before Jackson stopped it. Satisfied that he'd made his point well enough, he removed some of the key pieces and left it that way. Four years later he was dead.

Since then, no one has been able to figure out how the detached parts fit back together or how to make it run again. The weird mechanism sits in a case by itself in John Rice Irwin's oddball Hall of Fame in Norris, tantalizingly daring some other brilliant soul to come along and solve its puzzle. This could be your ticket to the Nobel Prize in Physics.

Crowning Angel of Death

Among its gathering of rare and amazing artifacts from the rural hinterlands and mountains, the Museum of Appalachia in Norris includes a small collection of peculiar swirling feather balls or wreaths that were once known as Death Crowns or Angel Crowns. Found inside the feather pillows of children or the elderly who had died in bed, people believed that it was a sign that the deceased had gone directly to heaven and that his or her soul was now safe in the arms of the Lord. So strong was this belief in the old days that if someone had died and a careful search of their pillow did not reveal a Death Crown, their mortal soul was considered to be at risk. On the other hand, if a crown was found by accident in the pillow of someone who was still alive, it wasn't such a good omen—it meant that they had already been marked for death, and wouldn't be around much longer. Folklorists theorize that the belief in their significance may go back to Wales (home of the Druids), brought to Tennessee by Welsh miners many years ago.

The feathers are hard and compacted, but no apparent bonding material holds them together. They mysteriously form inside pillows on their own.

Remember: Just because something is a legend doesn't necessarily mean that it is untrue.

Bizarre Beasts

In 1926 folklorist *Frederick Thomas Nettleinghame* published a prayer of petition that he had heard chanted in a small rural church in the West Country of England. At first, it may seem comical—

From Ghoulies and Ghosties
And Long-Leggetty Beasties
And things that go bump in the night
Good Lord, deliver us

—until you realize it was deadly serious. It was already a very old prayer when he copied it down, and the West Country was (and still is) a largely rural place, with lonely farmsteads where people knew full well that at night certain Dreadful Things were likely to be waiting for them, out there in the dark. Although the open moors of places like Devon and Cornwall are different from the swamps, hills, and mountains of the mid-South, the things those folks understood about their surroundings were not all that different from the things that Tennesseans knew about their backwoods until not so long ago. If anything, all those Tennessee trees offered even more places to hide.

Sure, we've got our TVs, smartphones, and little Bluetooth devices sticking in our ears to drown out the sounds of nature, and our GPS gizmos rarely let us get lost anymore, and scarcely a minute goes by when we're not texting or talking to someone, somewhere, but has that *really* affected the critters who are lurking in the backwoods?

We doubt it. Just because we don't always see them says more about us than them, and certainly doesn't mean they aren't out there. And every now and then—just often enough, in fact—someone actually *does* have an encounter with a tall, hairy, apelike thing, or find a set of strange, long-clawed footprints, or see something with glowing red eyes quietly observing them from the edge of the forest, to reassure us that the Wild Things haven't gone away, but have only gotten better at hiding.

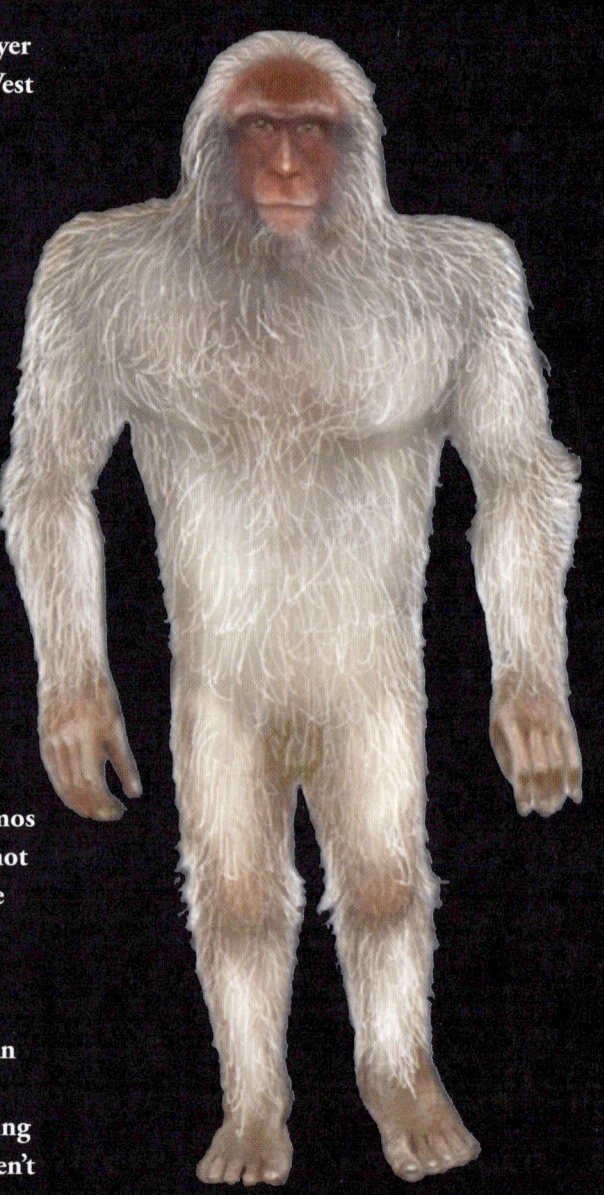

The Wampas Cat

Other states may have their Devils and Woolyboogers, their Sasquatches and Mothmen, but Tennessee's favorite native cryptid is the Wampas Cat (sometimes spelled Wampus or Wumpus). For centuries—long before the arrival of Europeans—there have been reports of a large, catlike creature in the forests and mountains of eastern Tennessee. It was reputed to be able to kill deer or even bears, and when Europeans arrived, it wreaked havoc with their livestock.

Although sightings by humans have been relatively rare, the descriptions of Wampas Cats have been remarkably consistent. The figure is always about four feet tall with dark, sometimes striped or mottled fur, and has large yellow eyes that glow like hot coals. It is catlike in all its movements and facial features, with erect ears projecting above its head just like other felines, but unlike any other cat it typically walks upright, standing only on its hind legs.

In past centuries, Wampas Cats were sometimes accused of stealing infants left in cribs out on the porch and making meals of them, although zoologists believe that only a wounded or very sick Wampas would stoop to such a thing. This is because, frankly, to most other animals, we human beings tend to smell gosh-awful. Scientists point out that humans invented deodorants, mouthwashes, and perfumes because we even smell bad to ourselves and each other, despite the lucky fact that we have some of the least sensitive noses of any mammals.

Now that unattended babies are mostly parked indoors in front of TVs, incidents of baby snatchings by Wampas Cats have significantly tapered off. Even so, stories of brief and terrifying encounters with the fierce creatures still crop up from time to time, not only in remote areas but also in more populated places like Cleveland, Rogersville, Erwin, Bristol, and Chattanooga. Sightings have occurred in downtown Knoxville so often

that one urban legend maintains that the cats inhabit a series of caves or dens beneath the city itself.

Even more frequent are reports of Wampas cries, which have been compared to the screams of freshly jilted girlfriends. Small surprise, then, that one of the old Cherokee legends had it that the cat had once been a jealous woman who so mistrusted her husband that she disguised herself in the skin of a mountain lion and spied on him during hunting trips. When her ruse was finally discovered, a curse permanently covered her with cat's fur. She became a kind of half woman, half cat, forced to live like a beast and hide from the eyes of humans.

To the early settlers the Wampas was also female, but they believed she was a witch who spent her days disguised as an old widow hermit but transformed into a cat at night to work her evil deeds. One evening during a full moon she was in the midst of her transformation ritual when some townspeople happened upon her and startled her before she could complete the incantations that effected the makeover. Unable to complete the spell, she was stuck halfway between her catlike and more womanly states. The townsfolk were as terrified as she was, and in their panic she managed to escape into the night—but ever since then she's never been able to return to human form.

Author Charles Edwin Price reported a sighting in the 1950s that suggests the Wampas may still be desperately seeking some way to change back into a person. A friend he refers to as "H.W." told Price that his father had been walking down Spring Street in Johnson City late one night when he saw a four-foot-tall cat standing up with its paws on the windowsill of the Jones-Vance Pharmacy, peering inside the drugstore. "After the cat had seen all it wanted to see inside Jones-Vance," H.W. said, "it turned and, still standing on its hind legs, continued walking down the street and disappeared around the corner. Daddy said that his blood ran cold."

We dare say that ours would too, if we were to see such a thing. Write and let us know if you have.

Wampus Cat Sightings in Knoxville

During the school year, my girlfriend lives in Strong Hall on the UT campus. One night she told me that during the first week of school she looked out her ground-floor window toward the corner of Sixteenth and Cumberland, and saw what appeared to be a human-sized cat walking on its hind legs, with glowing eyes. I don't remember the details she gave me, as far as how long it was there or how long she saw it. She's asleep right now or else I'd ask her for more details, but I wanted to let you know about that before I went to sleep and forgot all about it. It should be noted that my girlfriend came down from Minnesota for school, and I have no reason to believe she would try to trick me by reading about the Wampus cat and then trying to pretend she saw it. We're very close and I have no reason to believe she would lie to me. —*Jimmy, posted on johnnorrisbrown.com*

I was up on "The Hill" at UT walking along at night when it was cold and the moon was out full and suddenly I saw something sitting in the grass like it was looking at the river. I could just barely make it out, the black shape I mean. At first I thought it was a person then I thought it was a big dog, but when it stood up I could see it was some kind of big cat, but almost big as me. I yelled and it made some kind of wild noise and then ran away on two legs! I don't know which one of us screamed more, but it scared the heck out of me for sure. —*Carla*

Jacksboro's Killer Primate

The next time you look at a large-scale topographic map of Tennessee, or happen to be gazing at satellite imagery, take a moment to check out the area around Jacksboro, Campbell County. You'll notice something odd: The mountains and valleys make a strange right-angle junction here where a row of long, undulating ridges lead down from Kentucky and Virginia only to suddenly come to a screeching halt at Jacksboro, as if they were suddenly boxed in. Geologists say that, indeed, the mountains *were* boxed in here, by three big fault lines—the Pine Mountain Fault parallels the Hunter Valley Fault, and across them both cuts the Jacksboro Fault. In the middle of this geological dead-end sits Norris Lake, created when a dam was built across the only place where the waters of the Clinch and Powell rivers could leak out of the corner of the "box."

For some reason there seems to be a concentration around this part of Tennessee of what most folks would probably call Sasquatches or Bigfoots (not "Bigfeet"). From LaFollette to Briceville, this little corner of the state (and in this case we mean "corner" literally, since the mountains meet at right angles) has had more than its share of run-ins with mysterious, big, hairy apelike critters. If our theory is right, Ice Age glaciers herded them down there, and they decided to stick around for, like, the next twenty thousand years, laying as low as can be, but from time to time having run-ins with the locals.

For example, Larry Thacker has pointed out how there was a string of sightings in Jacksboro beginning in October 2003, when citizens began describing encounters with a four-hundred-pound apelike creature that seemed to coincide with the disappearance of about a hundred pets in the vicinity. A segment released by Channel 6 WATE's Vince Lennon around the middle of the month reported the story:

> "I didn't really get a good look at his face because he didn't hang around all that long," Donna Keathley said about when she saw an ape-like creature last week in LaFollette. "But he's big and he's got a really bad stinkful odor to him."

A few days later, a report by Chloe Morroni on Channel 8 WVLT reported that the county's 911 call center received emergency calls for weeks. Residents reported that their cats were being killed.

> "They're saying it's a chimpanzee, a large chimpanzee," said 911 dispatcher Kamille Barnes. "It's killing their cats." Barnes lives in the College Hill community, which is where the creature has been sighted. She believes it came into her house. "My basement door was left open, and something came in and scattered all the clothes and stuff stored in the basement," she said.

UT Veterinary School primate expert Dr. Edward Ramsey pointed out that chimps rarely make good pets. He seemed unconvinced of a killer primate since they're virtually all herbivorous.

Cliff Hightower of the Knoxville *News Sentinel* picked it up on October 21, 2003. "'It could be a cinnamon black bear,'" [LaFollette animal control officer George Moses] said. "'But that's just speculation.'"

Over the ensuing weeks more than fifteen more news reports followed what was variously called the Jacksboro Skunk Ape, the Campbell Beast, the Killer Primate, and the Mad Monkey. Eventually the sightings dwindled until the creature—Skunk Ape, Bigfoot, Woolybooger, or what-have-you—dropped out of everyday conversation. But that doesn't mean that it—or they—went away. Other sightings not far away led to stories of the Norris Lake Critter, and further reports by the *LaFollette Press* mentioning killer monkeys suggest that there are still undiscovered, unexplained, and uncaptured creatures in this part of the state, awaiting discovery.

The "Thing" the Preacher Saw

My brother-in-law and some other local people have experienced something large and hairy on the ridges here in Briceville, Anderson County, always late at night and off the beaten path. I have heard these stories for years about the "thing" on the ridge, and my family has had experiences with it. I know my brother-in-law wouldn't dare make this up because he is a preacher.

There is a lady here that anything I say she says the opposite. She says that the hairy thing was just made up by the drunks so that they could leave home and look for the black panther, this would get them out of the house so their wives wouldn't know what they were really up to. One man would go out and scream like the panther and this would start the "search" for the animal. But believe me, this is not a black panther that we're talking about. —*Daphne, Briceville Public Library*

It Ripped My Dog in Half

It was about 1:30 A.M. and I had gone outside to bring my dog in, but heard a growling sound in the woods. So I ran back in the house, grabbed my flashlight and my gun, and went into the woods to see what was there. My dog ran to where the sound was coming from and eight seconds later, I heard a yelp and a sound like blood splattering on the forest floor. I turned my flashlight on and saw a wolfish-looking creature that walked toward me. I ran back to my house, locked every door, and stayed there.

When I got up the next morning, I went back into the woods and found my dog ripped in half. The top of his head was bit off and his legs were chewed down to the bone. I called the cops and they did not believe my story, but a month later someone else saw something similar. In that case, the person said the victim was a young woman in her early twenties, all ripped to pieces. That was the last I heard about it. —*Donovan*

The White Screamer

Nicky McNeil at Tennessee Attachment Company (makers of sewing machine parts) maintains a Web site there called Blufwatch (http://blufwatch.tripod.com), which pokes gentle fun at the rural community of White Bluff. "You are SO White Bluff," the site comments, "if you refer to the stoplight; if you don't bother to use turn signals because everyone already knows where you're going; if you miss church just once and receive get-well cards; if loitering at Bibb's Garage isn't a bad thing—it's the only thing; if you hear that a McDonalds might finally be coming to town, but there are rumors they are only bringing one arch. . . ." There are more than fifty Bluffisms in all.

"You are SO White Bluff," the list continues, "if you have ever hunted for the 'White Screamer' on Trace Creek." The White Screamer may, in fact, be the one serious difference between White Bluff and any other Tennessee town of a similar size, because it is probably the one thing about their town that the locals take dead seriously. For many years they've had to endure something no one can quite explain, and no one quite knows what they ever did to deserve it, either.

People disagree as to whether the Screamer is a ghost, a wild beast, a man, a woman, some kind of semihuman monster, a peculiar natural phenomenon like a mirage or will-o'-the-wisp, or a hallucination shared by all. All they know for sure is that it is terrifying.

Most of those tales trace the first appearance of the White Screamer to events that befell a family that lived along Trace Creek (although some folks insist it really took place off Nosegay Road near Claylick). The basic story is the same: Not long after the Civil War ended this family was finally getting back to farming as a complete family, after years of making do without the dad. One night the old veteran heard strange and horrifying screams coming from the woods nearby. He bolted the doors and shutters and shivered in fear at the awful noise.

The next evening the screams returned, and he spent the whole night roaming the house, making sure that every possible point of entry was secured. When the sun finally rose again, he was bleary-eyed after two sleepless days.

When the incessant screaming returned the following night, he couldn't stand it anymore. Darkness or no, he was determined to confront whatever it was that was keeping him awake. He seized his rifle, collared his dogs, and told his wife to keep the doors locked after he left.

With a lantern in one hand and a gun in the other, he headed out into the woods in the direction of the awful sounds echoing through the trees. The screaming receded in front of him, however; and as he slowly crept ever farther into the forest with the gun pointed cautiously ahead, it seemed as if the beast, or whatever it was, was keeping its distance, remaining just out of sight beyond the farthest trees illuminated in the flickering light he was carrying. It was still screaming now, but in a softer and softer voice, until he could scarcely hear it at all.

Then he suddenly heard other screams coming from far behind him, in voices he immediately recognized. The shrill cries of his wife and children came from the direction of the farm, as if they were being attacked. Realizing he'd been tricked, he turned and ran stumbling through the pitch-dark underbrush toward home.

Halfway back, the screams of his family abruptly ceased. When he got there and clambered up onto the porch with his chest heaving for air, his worst fears were realized. The door hung at an angle on its hinges as if it had been ripped open. Inside, the front room was a wreck, the chairs all in a broken heap and the fireplace tools tossed aside as if a terrible struggle had taken place there. But the worst sight awaited him in the bedroom, where his wife and both their children lay dead in pools of gore, their clothing soaked red with blood and pieces of their hair and fingers torn away. Tears of grief and helpless rage soon mercifully blinded him to the awful sight of the shredded bodies of his loved ones.

Then, in the distance, he began to hear screaming again. He knew it was waiting for him alone. With nothing left to lose, he decided to go after it again, no matter how tired he was. But in case any of his neighbors might come along and wonder at the awful scene, he tore a page off the wall calendar and wrote a description of what had happened and where he was headed. And it's a good thing he did, for he was never seen again.

It took many years for the community to get over the atrocity of an entire family massacred, and the mystery of what could have happened lingered on. There were some among the neighbors who blamed the husband himself. Even though post-traumatic stress disorder wouldn't become a known condition for well over a century, people already recognized that veterans sometimes returned home damaged from wartime experiences. It was likely, they believed, that the farmer killed his own family and then made up the story in the note and ran away to escape justice.

Their theory didn't explain the Screamer, though. Something scary really was out there and roaming the area, and soon people began to catch glimpses of it. As far as anyone can tell for sure, it hasn't murdered again—but it could. According to folks in White Bluff, it is still out there.

Contemporary eyewitness accounts differ in the details, but here is one witness's tip for finding the White Screamer.

> *If you want the experience of being around this creature, I can tell you where you can camp.... If you're on Hwy 70, turn by William James Middle School onto Trace Creek Road. Keep going till you go down the big hill. Right as you get to the bottom of the hill, there will be a house on your left and a driveway on your right. Go to the driveway on your right. You will have to go through the creek and up a small hill. There is an old gate but just go over it. This is where I used to hunt during the day, but I wouldn't be caught dead there at night. —Ashlee*

Critter from Sugar Flat

Some "things" just love harassing lovers, for apparently all you have to do to bring the escaped convicts, criminally insane, space aliens, and swamp creatures—not to mention local cops—out of the woodwork is to park your car somewhere on a dark night with your sweetheart and begin to make some lip-smacky.

That's what they say happened a little more than twenty years ago at what was then Lebanon's local trysting spot, old Sugar Flat Road. On January 5, 1989, one young fellow and his illicit lover left their spouses at home and went for a joyride that wound up with them parking along Sugar Flat in a particularly poorly lit stretch of the road. The windows of the pickup fogged over with the heat of their "conversation" and for a time the outside world ceased to exist. Eventually things came to their usual conclusion, at which point they suddenly realized it was well past the appropriate time to head home. They sped away.

The rest of the story is perhaps best told by the late legendary local Lebanon cutlerer Frank "Cuz" Buster:

> As the couple rounded a curve on the bumpy old road, two figures burst directly into the path of the truck from the line of small scrub trees and bushes that lined their route.
>
> The brakes of the battered old truck did little to slow the vehicle; and in the midst of crunching metal, breaking glass, and skidding tires the couple heard a horrible groan. Thinking he had hit a deer or a small bear, the driver swung his door wide and leaped out of the truck.
>
> The thing (that's what we'll call it for the time being) lay toward the rear of the truck. The driver could barely make it out despite the full moon and

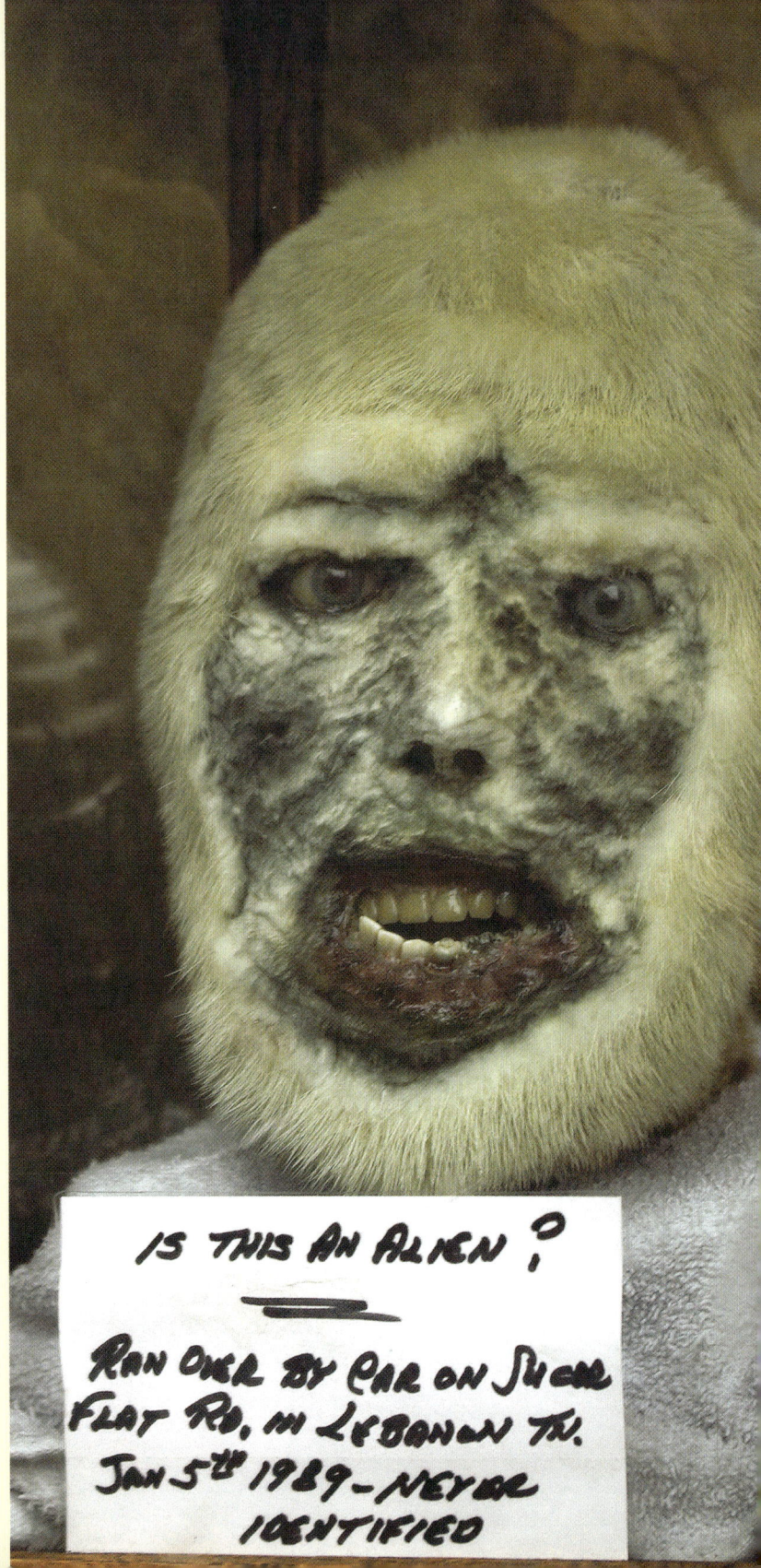

IS THIS AN ALIEN?

RAN OVER BY CAR ON SUGAR FLAT RD. IN LEBANON TN. JAN 5TH 1989 – NEVER IDENTIFIED *the glare of his taillight. He took a flashlight from his lady friend inside the truck and went back to get another look at the lifeless form lying in the road. As he approached the thing, he heard an animal-type cry from the other figure standing just outside his field of vision. Frightened by this cry, he was also fascinated at the thing in the road. As the beam of his flashlight settled on the thing, he forgot all about its partner in the bushes.*

Whatever he had run over looked for all practical purposes like a medium-sized man with one exception. It was covered with what looked to be hair or fur. It was also definitely dead. As he stood over the creature, his lover's voice trickled in from the darkness and he realized that the most important thing he could do right now was get her home before they both had too much explaining to do.

He pulled the creature to the side of the road, disguised it as well as he could and got back into the truck. Despite her questions, he did little talking during the trip. After dropping her off he went home and drank the better part of a bottle of whiskey hoping it would calm him and put him to sleep quickly after the harrowing experience. But try as he might, sleep evaded him. The solution to his restlessness seemed to be to return to Sugar Flat Road and find out exactly what it was he hit. . . .

[I]n the quiet of the dawn he inspected the creature again. It wasn't a man. Of that he was sure. But what was it? With a shudder he took a shovel from the back of his truck intent on burying the thing deep in the ground and forgetting this night had ever happened. But as he dug into the soft earth, he began to reason that since the creature wasn't a man it was obviously an animal. And he should have a trophy. When the hole had been dug he deftly severed the creature's head with the point of the shovel, scooped it up and tossed it into the bed of the pickup. He kicked the thing's body into the hole, covered it with dirt and drove into town to a taxidermist's shop. The taxidermist shook his head in disbelief when he saw the creature's head, but despite never having seen anything like it before he agreed to preserve it.

How the stuffed and mounted head later wound up at "Cuz's" junk shop in the center of Lebanon is a story that followed Buster to the grave when he passed away in 2007. It's hard to tell if the expression captured on the face is one of consternation, threat, puzzled surprise, or most likely, some combination of the three.

Lost Bigfoot Sighting

For several years there were a number of Bigfoot sightings reported on South Second Street in downtown Memphis. But the big guy is no longer putting in many appearances these days because Kooky Canuck, a Canada-themed restaurant, now occupies the site. The food there seems designed to entice *something* big anyway—for instance, one of the items on the menu is a seven-pound hamburger estimated to provide 12,387 calories, and 266.8 grams of fat. Can't say we recommend it—in fact, the knowledge that at least five hefty Memphians have managed to eat one is what may have scared off Mr. Big. He's known to be frightened by the fizzy sounds of antacids in water.

Fishy Story

One of the most famous Tennessee hoaxes of the early twentieth century was a photo of what appeared to be a five-hundred-pound catfish. Warren McConnell of Hardin County reputedly reeled the thing out of the Tennessee River near Cerro Gordo in 1914. While catfish in the Mekong River in Cambodia may sometimes reach this size or larger, the next-nearest claim for a giant North American catfish is a 315-pound monster supposedly caught in the Missouri River shortly after the Civil War. But even that contender is considered awfully unlikely, given how fishermen have been known on rare occasions to exaggerate the size of their quarry. In modern times (that is, since scales, photos, and measuring tapes have been invoked to establish something more closely approximating the truth), the largest North American catfish have been blues and flatheads with the current officially confirmed records for either species hovering around 124 pounds.

So what about that five-hundred-pounder? Tennesseean Joe Bradlow Pitts of Savannah claims it was a joke played by his dad that quickly took on a life of its own. According to Pitts, his dad took the fish, which actually weighed a little more than eighty pounds, and then draped it across a toy wagon. His uncle, who was an amateur photographer, propped up a small cardboard cut-out figure of a man borrowed from a clothing store display and took the picture. So his dad could then claim in all honesty that the picture was a "real picture of a giant fish—not a fake picture at all" by his never pointing out that the man and the wagon were faked. After all, the best and most believable lies are the ones people tell themselves.

The Triune Terror

On July 5, 1868, the *Nashville Banner* reported the discovery of one of the largest snakes ever found in North America. The paper described it as black in color, more than thirty-five feet long and eight or ten inches in diameter, or "about as thick as a large man's thigh," according to an article written by J. L. Scales, *Banner* reporter. Since it had been sighted near Triune, in eastern Williamson County, the paper dubbed it the "Triune Terror," though locals said they'd occasionally encountered it for almost twenty-five years without ever reporting it. They hadn't considered it all that newsworthy, and they referred to it simply as the Big Snake.

One of the article's sources, a Mr. Allen, came upon the snake, which raised its head about eight feet in the air and stared at him. Worried it might be preparing to strike, Allen beat a hasty retreat and ran to tell his neighbors about it. When they went in after it with sharpened farm implements as weapons, however, all they found were a cluster of broken bushes where it had evidently been resting.

Then almost ten years later, with local consensus being that the snake had died, two Nashville men spotted it crossing the pike near Burke Knobs. They thought it was a large pole lying across the road, until it lifted its head above the top of the fence next to the pike and began wriggling over it. From two hundred yards away they watched it

rear up and suddenly strike at something in the underbrush, then saw it swallow a whole rabbit. Then they tracked it to the property of Thomas Burke, where it disappeared into a hole.

With Burke's help, the Nashville men attempted to capture the snake using a box trap about fifty feet long and eighteen inches square, baited with a leg of mutton.

According to a follow-up article in the July 8 issue of the *Banner*, the trapping attempt failed. The snake managed to break through the iron bars (some of which were found fifty feet from the rest of the trap) and had last been seen knocking over "fences and other obstacles in his pathway."

Rhode Island Red Rover

Larry Guy of Polk County knew of a rare and amazing creature: a rooster named Hank that could bark like a dog. The little peeper, owned by his aunt Hattie, was raised by a motherly coonhound after its biological mother—a Rhode Island Red hen—died. The chicken barked and for several years it was a major attraction among the people who knew to ask about it.

One day the barking chicken disappeared, never to return. Some people believed that Hank had been stolen by a passing circus that needed an attraction to replace the Half-Man who quit after she was revealed merely to be an extremely ugly woman with a permanent five o'clock shadow.

Crossover Connections

Hank, the barking rooster, was hardly the only result of interspecies motherly love to have garnered notoriety in the annals of Tennessee. In the Whitehead Cemetery near Tiger Creek, Carter County, is the grave of Sallie Garland, whose epitaph reads,

> She was not only a mother to the human race, but to all mankind as she gave nurse to one fawn and two cubs. She is now resting from her labor.

Her husband, James "Tiger" Whitehead, is buried next to her, and his epitaph mentions that he was a "noted hunter" who had killed ninety-nine bears. On more than one occasion he discovered too late that he'd killed a female animal with a cub or fawn in tow, and had brought the babies home. If Sallie was breast-feeding one of her own offspring already, they said, she simply made room for the forest baby as well. Tiger Whitehead died at the age of ninety-two in 1905, and Sallie outlived him by five years.

Home of the Freeloading Furry Friends

Signs along the approach roads leading into the community of Kenton, Obion County, warn drivers to keep their eyes peeled for squirrels, for the local variety is one of its proudest features. Kenton is home to a population of about two hundred white squirrels that, according to local lore, arrived in 1869 with a Gypsy caravan and then stayed when the Gypsies headed on to their next destination. Some sources claim that the original mating pair was a gift to a local man for letting them set up camp on his land. Others point out that exhibiting exotic animals was a major source of income for traveling people—would they have endangered their livelihood by giving away the show? An alternate explanation has the critters escaping the Gypsies.

Could they have evolved right there? Maybe, but how do we to account for the ample numbers of white squirrels in a brown and green world—which would make them easy pickings for predators? Well, they live in town, where they tend to attract benign human attention (i.e., feeding), which reverses the odds.

This would certainly explain the presence of other white squirrel colonies on a number of college campuses, where students often have nothing better to do than toss the remains of their cafeteria lunches at cute little tree rodents. Communities in Ohio, North Carolina, Illinois, and elsewhere have documented white-squirrel populations. Marionville, Missouri, claims the oldest colony (first reported in 1854); Olney, Illinois, advertises the largest colony (roughly two thousand); and Brevard, North Carolina, boasts the prettiest (theirs have dark eyes).

None of this is to knock the bright little fellers of Kenton, of course. Perhaps Kenton can claim that their colony is the most welcome since, as the town billboard proudly asserts, it's "The Home of the White Squirrel."

Murderous Mary, the Executed Elephant

In 1916 the Sparks Circus stopped in the railroading town of Erwin with its thirty-year-old elephant named Mary. Citizens there are still talking about it.

Mary was reputedly the largest land animal on earth (three inches taller than even P. T. Barnum's famous Jumbo), and she could play baseball (.400 batting average) and musical horns. However, she had a temper and had already killed two of her handlers. (The circus had changed her name after each previous killing to conceal this fact.) Inexplicably, Mary was put under the charge of a completely inexperienced handler for a parade through Erwin.

When Mary broke from the parade to pick up an errant piece of watermelon, her handler hooked Mary in the ear instead of guiding her by the chin. This proved a fatal mistake. Mary wrapped her trunk around the rookie trainer's waist and flung him so hard that he slammed into the side of a nearby lemonade stand. W. H. Coleman, who was nineteen at the time, reported that Mary then "just walked over and set [her] foot on his head . . . and blood and brains and stuff just squirted all over the street."

Destroying her seemed the only option and the Clinchfield Railroad offered use of a rolling derrick as a gallows. Twenty-five hundred people showed up for the public hanging. Unfortunately, when Mary struggled against the tightening noose the chain broke and she fell to the ground, breaking a hip. She screamed pitifully.

The second attempt was more successful, and the elephant hung suspended for half an hour so everyone could get a good look. Photos were taken, and a few people clipped elephant hairs as souvenirs.

A steam shovel carried the body to a huge pit that had been dug near the tracks. The exact burial location was neither marked nor recorded, and after weeds obscured the site, it was eventually forgotten. Though various museums and historical associations have requested permission to dig for Mary's remains, their applications have been denied. So it'll probably be up to archaeologists of the future to find her. And we can't help but wonder what conclusions they'll come to when they do.

BIZARRE BEASTS 123

Where Beasts Still Walk the Earth

There's a safe haven for elephants in the Volunteer State. Northwest of Hohenwald, Lewis County, is the Elephant Sanctuary, a 2700-acre retirement home for old, sick, or needy elephants, most of whom have had careers in zoos or circuses. Elephants, frequently living to seventy years or more, eat so much—a hundred and fifty pounds of food a day—that they were often euthanized or allowed to starve to death before the Sanctuary was founded in 1995.

With affordable land and a climate and terrain similar to northern India, Hohenwald was a natural choice for an elephant sanctuary. Each of them arrives from a different background, with a different personality and past. Tarra had a career as a roller-skating performer. Shirley survived a shipwreck. Sissy had been in a Texas flood. Delhi had chemical burns on her feet. Barbara had worked in Asian logging camps as a living timber skidder. Minnie, Lottie, Debbie, Ronnie, Tange, Zula, Billie, Frieda, Liz—they each arrive like the new kid in school and have to make new friends and try to fit in. Both Asian and African elephants live here: The two species must be kept in separate parts of the reserve, though, since their habits, traditions, and ways of interacting are different.

Not all of the elephants make an easy adjustment to their new life in Tennessee, and some arrive with severe psychological damage. Winkie II was born in Burma in 1966 and was kept at a small zoo in Wisconsin, where she was chained in a small, cold concrete pen most of her life. After she arrived in Hohenwald, she took weeks to emerge from the barn and venture into the open, and was slow to make friends, although Sissy extended a friendly trunk and tried to incorporate her into the daily activities of the rest of the group. Winkie was extremely uneasy around humans. In 2006, the 7,600 pound elephant killed one of the most experienced Sanctuary employees and injured one of its founders, who tried to intervene when she attacked. Following its policy of letting the animals live as freely in a state of nature as possible, no "disciplinary action" was taken against Winkie. She and another elephant were later diagnosed with post-traumatic stress disorder and a new set of rules for interacting with them was enacted.

Both because of the dangers and because the elephants need to be away from the gaze of humans, the Sanctuary is not open to the public. But if you park your car along Darbytown Road about four miles out of Hohenwald and listen carefully, you may hear a sound that hasn't been heard echoing across the landscape of Tennessee for more than 11,000 years, when the last mastodons and mammoths disappeared: the trumpeting calls of excited pachyderms.

Mammoths of Williamson County

In 1821, giant bones were discovered in "stone graves" in Williamson County. Stories of an oversize race of monstrous humanoids soon swept across the region, although most scholars now believe that the bones probably belonged to mammoths or mastodons that had been buried by Ice Age hunters, either as a ritual or to prevent the meat from being scavenged.

Soapy End

In the summer of 1948 a large elephant was killed when a circus driver failed to slow down for "Dead Man's Curve" on Highway 70N/24, three miles southeast of Monterey. As the truck headed toward Monterey rounded the famously deadly curve, the elephant shifted its footing and caused the vehicle to swerve, sending the hapless animal crashing through the sideboards and down an embankment. The giant carcass was later sold for commercial soapmaking.

Duck Strut, a Web-Footed Wonderment

In a state with a Duck River, several Duck Creeks, national headquarters for Ducks Unlimited, at least two Ducktowns, and plenty of aging Rockabilly legends waddling around still sporting ducklike hairdos, it's no surprise that ducks have carved out a place of honor in Tennessee. Since 1932 Memphis's Peabody Hotel has provided luxury accommodations. During that inaugural year, hotel manager Frank Schutt thought it would be a hoot to toss ducks in the main lobby fountain. Guests were delighted to have something unusual to look at, while the ducks enjoyed being fed, so it was not only a win-win situation; it was just ducky.

To this day, ducks emerge from an elevator at 11 A.M. to stroll happily down a red carpet and hop into the fountain while the "King Cotton March" plays in the background. Then at precisely 4:55 P.M. the Duck Master, fitted out in his proper red uniform, announces the ducks' return to the Duck Palace on the hotel roof. The red carpet is rolled out once more, the ducks line up in formation, and at a signal given at the stroke of 5 P.M. they head back to the elevator for their ride to the top. Ducks are true creatures of habit, and once a new duck gets the hang of the routine, he or she seems only too willing to enact this transfer twice a day exactly like the day before.

We suppose it beats winged migration.

Local Heroes and Villains

Just as one person's trash may be another person's treasure, the same holds true for heroes and villains. An individual can be a hero to some and a villain to the rest—or vice versa. Whether, for example, Tennesseans consider Civil War general Nathan Bedford Forrest to have been a true native hero, or else only a white supremacist war criminal, often depends on whether their ancestors fought on the same side as he, or were enslaved by those who did. With others, the divide is not always so clear-cut—or so controversial. There are those whom nearly everyone would agree were villains, and those whom most people would find heroic. The best thing we can say in either case is that these characters were always fascinating.

What follows is only a sampling. Whether you admire these folks or despise them is, of course, entirely up to you.

Buford Pusser Walked Tall

When Teddy Roosevelt was governor of New York (before he became president), he waged a political battle against the Republican Party. He eventually triumphed. After his win, one of his friends asked how he had achieved it. "I have always been fond of the West African proverb," he said. "Speak softly and carry a big stick."

Apparently McNairy County sheriff Buford Pusser took TR literally when it came to this advice, for he became a law enforcement icon with his collection of big "beating sticks" with which he loved nothing better than to whup bad guys. The sticks, most of them quite a bit heftier and scarier-looking than a Major League–grade Louisville Slugger, are part of the display at Pusser's last residence, now open to the public as a one-man museum and shrine at 342 Pusser Street in Adamsville.

Frozen in time, the house is just as it was when Pusser lived there until his death in 1974. The place is gloomy, not merely because it is a temple of death, but also because it was specially built with thicker-than-normal brick walls and smaller-than-average windows, above floor level to prevent drive-by shooters from killing the sheriff or his family. Pusser's own bedroom was in the basement, with his bed up against a wall shielded by a dirt embankment. His garage was arranged so he could enter and leave the house without being exposed.

Pusser was a man with lots of enemies, and he knew it.

Pusser came to law enforcement naturally, since his father had been chief of police of Adamsville. After stints in the marines (he was discharged early because of asthma), as a professional wrestler (he had been a six-foot-six football star in high school), and a few courses in mortuary sciences, he returned to Adamsville to serve as chief of police. Two years later, he ran for election as sheriff. In 1964, at age twenty-six, Pusser became the youngest sheriff in Tennessee history.

He immediately stepped into the crime-fighting fast lane, since just across the state line, north of Corinth, Mississippi, was the stronghold of the State Line Mob, a crime syndicate that had taken advantage of McNairy County's sparse population and central location between Nashville and Memphis to thrive as a center for bootlegging, smuggling, prostitution, robbing tourists, and other organized crime ventures. Determined to put an end to their activities in his county, the young sheriff destroyed eighty-seven stills in just his first year on the job.

During the "war" that Sheriff Pusser waged against both the State Line Mob and the Biloxi, Mississippi–based Dixie Mafia, he was shot eight times and stabbed seven times. His face was a mass of scars from the various assassination attempts, of which his wife Pauline was the most tragic victim. Before dawn on the morning of August 12, 1967, Pusser was called to the scene of a disturbance near the state line. Pauline, worried about his going out without a deputy to back him up, got in the car with him. Heading down Highway 22, they passed New Hope Church when a black car pulled out, drove up alongside the sheriff's vehicle, and began firing. Pauline was hit in the head and most of Pusser's jaw was blown away. The sheriff survived, more determined than ever to take on the criminal elements in his community.

By 1970 Pusser had been reelected three times and could not run again. That year, a film about his one-man anticrime war, *Walking Tall,* was released, soon followed by *Walking Tall II* (1975) and *Final Chapter: Walking Tall* (1977), feeding the public's hunger to see something done about the nation's ever-increasing crime rate. Unfortunately, the former sheriff did not live long enough to enjoy his new status as a celebrity for more than a brief time. Driving home from a Memphis press conference on August 20, 1974, during which it was announced that he would play himself in a movie titled *Buford,* his Corvette spun off Highway 64 between Selmer and Adamsville, wrecked, and burst into flames. His neck was broken in the crash. Only thirty-six years old, Pusser was pronounced dead on arrival at Selmer Hospital.

Analysis of the scene later suggested that he had been approaching 130 miles per hour when the car hit the embankment. A swirl of conspiracy theories followed his death, ranging from the possibility that the vehicle had been tampered with to the notion that he'd been poisoned with nerve toxins made from Amazon rainforest plants secretly slipped into his Coke. The most likely explanation, however, was that he had been ignoring the speed limit to an excessive degree. This was his fourth serious wreck, his third single-car accident, and the second time he'd been in a fiery crash. Pusser had often admitted to feeling like he lived "on borrowed time" but probably didn't do as much as he might have to extend the loan.

Request to watch a short videotape at his house museum to reach your own conclusions. Other items on display include his toothbrush, TV, credit cards, report cards (mostly Fs), revolving blue light, toilet bowl brush, and of course, those big sticks.

Nathan Bedford Forrest

Even people who honor the memory of Confederate general and KKK founder Nathan Bedford Forrest find the sculpture south of Nashville on the east side of Interstate 65 between Exits 74 and 80 a challenge to warm up to. Looking like a lunatic, with an oversized head and demonic eyes, the fiberglass figure has attracted more than a few bullets since its unveiling in 1998. But situated where it is, on an island of private land donated by William Dorris to the Sons of Confederate Veterans, and sandwiched between the relentless flow of traffic on the interstate and a busy railroad switchyard, it is almost completely inaccessible.

Before the Civil War, Forrest was a wealthy plantation owner and slave trader. By war's end he was nearly broke but quickly rebuilt his fortune while also helping to found the original Ku Klux Klan. He was the organization's first "grand wizard." Three years later he tried to dissolve it, after becoming concerned about its increasing tendencies toward mob behavior. By then, however, the evil genie was already out of the bottle. The Klan reorganized in 1915 near Stone Mountain, Georgia, and remained a plague for the next seventy years.

Monuments and historical markers celebrate Forrest's wide-ranging escapades in nearly every county in the state. Yet ever since the Confederacy first formed, Tennesseans have always been divided. More than 100,000 Tennessee men joined the Confederate Army, more than any other state. At the same time, some 50,000 Tennesseans joined the Union Army to fight against the Confederacy. That's more enlistments than about half the states that supported the Union.

Reverend Reanimator

Knoxville came close to having its own Dr. Frankenstein, in the person of one Rev. Stephen Foster (no relation to the songwriter), who had vivid dreams of resurrection. Reverend Foster, who is buried in the old First Presbyterian graveyard downtown, was born in Massachusetts in 1798 and went to Dartmouth and Andover seminary, where he was ordained as a priest. He was still in his twenties when he became a professor of Latin and Greek at Greenville College (now Tusculum College), and then professor of classics at East Tennessee College in Knoxville.

Foster's tombstone describes him as an "able Instructor of Youth," a "devoted Minister of the Gospel," and a "Kind and affectionate Friend." There is no mention, however, of his fascination with galvanism, which may have been inspired indirectly by the 1818 science-fiction bestseller by Mary Shelley, *Frankenstein, or, the Modern Prometheus*. Galvanism involves sending jolts of electricity into muscle tissues to cause them to move or contract. Although the same principle would eventually lead to inventions like today's cardiac defibrillators, pacemakers, and artificial limbs, early practitioners thought it might be capable of bringing the dead back to life.

Foster may also have been moved by the story of three-year-old Catherine Sophie Greenhill, considered the first person to have been resuscitated by electric current. In 1774, little Catherine was pronounced dead after she fell out of a high window onto the flagstone pavement of London's Pudding Lane. Using a portable electric generator, an apothecary named Squires was able to get her heart and breathing restarted within twenty minutes, and eventually she regained consciousness. Ben Franklin heard about this case and later promoted the use of electricity in "revivifying" other apparently dead victims.

Rather than comforting the population, however, incidents like this contributed to the wave of panic about premature burial that obsessed vast numbers of people in the nineteenth century. If an apparently dead person could be brought back to life with a few electric shocks, how could anyone be sure that someone was truly dead?

As a minister, Foster would have been aware of biblical accounts of resuscitation, like when Elisha reanimated dead children in I Kings 17:22 and II Kings 4:35, or the resurrection of Lazarus in John 11:44. Experimentation, then, was not necessarily unethical, especially if it might prevent someone from being buried alive. But rather than wait around on the chance that someone might die conveniently nearby, Foster went where he was sure to find a recently dead person: the Knoxville gallows on a hanging day.

The good reverend took a corpse from a criminal execution and hooked it up to a generator or Leyden Jar (an early form of battery), administering a series of electric shocks. To his great satisfaction, the executed criminal began breathing again. But at that point Foster stopped, satisfied that the technique worked. "I don't mean to cheat justice," he reportedly said.

Why was Reverend Foster so intrigued by the process of resuscitation to go so far as to see if he could actually make it work? Perhaps it was because he somehow sensed that his own death was already impatiently awaiting him. The final words on his tombstone sum up what happened next:

Amid the most eminent usefulness,
Respected, esteemed, beloved, [he] Departed
this life Jan. 11, 1835, aged 37 years.
"Mysterious are Thy ways, O Lord!"

Casey Jones—Hot Dog or Hero?

If a tardy airline pilot were to land his craft the way "Casey" Jones drove his train, we at *Weird Tennessee* wonder if he would be considered a hero or a villain . . . or if he'd have earned a catchy song that got the public singing about him.

John Luther Jones got his famous nickname because he grew up near Cayce, Kentucky. In 1888, he moved to Jackson, Tennessee, to begin work as a railroad fireman, the guy who shovels the coal to fire up the boiler on a steam locomotive. In time, he became a conductor and engineer, with a reputation for doing whatever it took to arrive on time, including exceeding the speed limit if need be. He was known up and down the line between Jackson and Water Valley, Mississippi, for running fast and for blowing the steam whistle to yield a long-drawn-out mournful moan, so that everyone would know that Casey Jones was roaring through.

Jones's reputation for speed earned him a transfer from the Jackson–Water Valley run to the Memphis–Canton (Mississippi) run, where in early 1900 he became the driver on

the famed Cannonball Express. But when he pulled into Memphis from Canton at 10 P.M. on the night of April 29, 1900, Jones was told he'd have to pull a double shift, driving an unfamiliar engine back down into Mississippi. An hour later, Jones and his fireman, Sim Webb, had Illinois Central No. 638 fully stoked and steamed. Not long after 11 P.M. they cleared South Memphis and rolled across the state line.

Just before dawn on Monday, April 30, Casey and Sim were approaching Vaughn, Mississippi, when they saw a freight train ahead. They didn't slow down, though, since it was on a side track. But what they didn't know was that the freight was unusually long, and that at the other end of the side track, it overlapped the rails they were on. Instead of slowing down, Jones ran the 638 past the standing freight at fifty miles an hour, even though the standard speed was thirty. As they reached the other end of the siding, he suddenly realized that the tracks ahead weren't clear, and that with all the momentum of his speeding train, a wreck was inevitable. Jones screamed at fireman Webb to jump from the engine, while he pulled on the whistle and airbrakes as hard as he could. The train began to slow, but it was too late.

The 638 exploded in a cauldron of steam, fire, and boiling water as it crashed through the last few boxcars, through the caboose, and rolled a few hundred feet farther down the tracks before flipping on its side. According to the legend, when Jones's remains were pulled from the wreckage, one hand was still on the brakes and the other still on the whistle cord, but that sounds a little fanciful, since the explosion would have been like a bomb going off.

The lawyers stepped in to sort out who was owed what and how much or how little the company and the victims were going to walk away with. When dealing with Jones's widow, the railroad company maintained that her husband had ignored a flagman and had failed to slow down for all the warning lights. But when they faced off with the passengers, they insisted that all possible safety precautions had been taken.

In the end, the version of what happened that morning was decided not in the courts but in music halls and on phonograph recordings. In 1902 the first of a number of ballads about the wreck rose to the top of the music charts, making Casey Jones a familiar household name from then on. The earliest release mentions some of the reckless risks that Jones took:

> *They rated him down to a thirty mile gait,*
> *Threw the south-bound mail about eight*
>   *hours late.*
> *Fireman says, "Casey, you're runnin' too fast,*
> *You run the block signal the last station*
>   *you passed."*
> *Jones says, "Yes, I think we can make it though,*
> *For she steam much better than ever I know."*
> *Jones says, "Fireman, don't you fret,*
> *Keep knockin' at the firedoor, don't give up yet;*
> *I'm goin' to run her till she leaves the rail*
> *Or make it on time with the south-bound*
>   *mail."*

Casey Jones's small frame house is in Jackson. Check it out and decide for yourself: was he a foolhardy hot dog or a real American hero? Or—as is often the case—both?

George Maledon, Prince of Hangmen

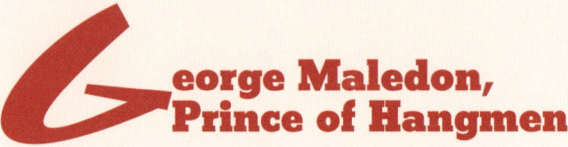

All by himself in Section E, Row 5 at the Mountain Home National Cemetery in Johnson City, George Maledon, aka the Prince of Hangmen, was the most accomplished executioner in American history. There's nothing on his stone to record this achievement.

Maledon was born in Germany in 1830, then moved to Detroit with his parents. As an adult he headed to Arkansas, where he found work as a policeman. During the Civil War he joined the Arkansas Light Artillery, but as soon as the fighting was over he went back to police work as a deputy marshal in Fort Smith, mostly as a prison guard at the federal jail there. Described as a scrawny "little wisp of a man" who dressed in black and rarely laughed or smiled, Deputy Maledon was no Barney Fife. When the prison needed someone to execute a prisoner, he quickly volunteered for the job—and found his true calling.

It seems almost like one of those historic convergences that not long after Maledon got his first taste of jerking the trap catch and watching a felon fall, President Ulysses S. Grant appointed Isaac Parker as federal judge of the Western District of Arkansas. It was 1875, and the Western District was one of the rowdiest, most corrupt, and habitually violent places on the continent, since it included the Oklahoma Indian Territory. Like a Third World country embedded in the side of the nation, the territory had become a magnet for desperadoes, cattle rustlers, and fugitives, but previous federal judges had been only too willing to ignore those activities in exchange for bribes.

Parker immediately initiated a massive anticrime effort that aimed at bringing swift justice to the region. Within months his new team of federal marshals brought nearly a hundred defendants to trial, and he quickly sentenced eight to hang. Maledon was in the right place at the right time, for he earned $100 each time he tied the fatal knot.

Over the next twenty-two years Maledon terminated sixty men on the gallows and shot two more dead when they tried to escape the prison. The *Fort Smith Elevator* published the gruesome details of each hanging for the "entertainment and education" of its readership, and was the first to call little George the "Prince of Hangmen." Judge Parker, meanwhile, earned the moniker of "The Hanging Judge" and his bailiwick came to be called "The Court of the Damned." Each man was dependent on the other for the success of his endeavors.

Maledon used an unusual gallows that had a beam (for attaching the ropes) and trap (for allowing the floor to fall away) that were sixteen feet wide, so that if necessary, as many as eight to twelve prisoners could be hanged at the same time (depending on whether they were shoulder to shoulder or lined up back to front). The gallows never ran at full capacity, however, and there were only a few occasions when half a dozen men were dropped at once, although twofers and triple features weren't uncommon. The larger events naturally drew the biggest crowds.

On September 3, 1875, Judge Parker and Deputy Maledon sought to make their first big impression on the local outlawry with a well-publicized six-at-once demo that brought reporters from as far away as Kansas City and St. Louis and attracted a standing audience of five thousand. It was also a show of Parker's firm belief in "blind justice" for the distribution of sentencing was markedly race-blind. Standing before the excited crowd that morning were a full-blood Cherokee murderer named Smoker Mankiller, a mixed-race Indian named Sam Fooy who had killed a school teacher in the course of a robbery, a black farmer named Edmund Campbell who had killed a Native American, a white horse-thief named James Moore, a white man named Daniel Evans who had killed a man in order to steal his boots, and a white man named John Wittington who had gotten into a drunken brawl and clubbed a man to death. Maledon rigged the ropes around each man's neck and when the signal came, all six dropped at once.

Maledon kept at his painstaking task until he was sixty-four. In 1894 he retired from his grim business to became a greengrocer, but business was slow since people hesitated to buy their tomatoes from one who had handled so many dead bodies. The following year, his eighteen-year-old daughter ran away with a man. Shot and wounded by the man, who turned out to be married, she managed to get back to Fort Smith to tell her dad what had happened before she died of infection. When his daughter's killer escaped the death penalty—the Supreme Court commuted the sentence to life in prison—Maledon left Arkansas, intending to take a show on the road of the relics he'd collected over his years as a hangman. He had sample ropes that had been stretched by the weight of human corpses, before-and-after photos of the hangings, pieces of the gallows beam, straps, leg irons, blindfolds, and other gruesome souvenirs of his peculiar trade. But although his traveling show was successful, it didn't last long.

In 1905 he checked himself in at the old soldiers' home in Johnson City, where he reached the end of his own rope six years later. According to the medical records, his last years were spent in a state of dementia during which he relived and retold the stories of all the men he'd relieved of life. Someone asked him if he'd experienced a guilty conscience or worried that the ghosts of all those dead men would come back to bother him. He answered, "No, I have never hanged a man who came back to have the job done over."

Bush Breazeale's (Next to) Last Hurrah

It's probably too late to find out if Lester Flatt and Earl Scruggs were inspired by "Uncle Bush" Breazeale to write their classic song "Give Me My Flowers While I'm Living" but it seems entirely possible. In late June 1938 seventy-four-year-old Felix "Bush" Breazeale achieved nationwide fame for deciding to go ahead and have his funeral while he was still alive to enjoy it. The gathering it generated turned out to be the largest event ever held in Roane County.

The *Roane County Banner* alerted the national media and word quickly spread. On the day of the funeral reporters from both major press syndicates and photographers from *Life* magazine showed up, along with a crowd that swelled, according to some estimates, to twelve thousand people. Cars leading to the Cave Creek Baptist Church southeast of Kingston were backed up Howard Road for miles, all the way to Highway 70. Hot dog and soft-drink vendors cashed in on the festivities.

The traffic was so thick that the hearse and funeral procession had trouble getting to the cemetery. Breazeale rode in the front of the hearse next to the driver, while the empty walnut coffin that he himself had built filled the rear of the vehicle. Breazeale proudly took his position in front of the bier and beamed broadly at all his friends and well-wishers. Afterward Breazeale autographed (with his "X") hundreds of the printed programs and shook the hands of thousands of the people who had come. He told everyone that the sermon, delivered by Rev. Charles Jackson, was "the finest I ever heard."

With all the media attention, Bush Breazeale became a celebrity and went to New York to appear on Robert Ripley's *Believe It or Not!* radio show. On his return to Roane County, someone asked him how he liked the trip. "Them folks up in New York City were nice and everything, and they treated me like a king, but their vittles weren't worth a dern!"

Felix Breazeale lived for five years after his funeral. A second, smaller service was held the day his lifeless remains were lowered into the ground.

Maybe there's something to this. Perhaps we should rethink the standard way funerals are timed. Certainly Lester Flatt and Earl Scruggs gave this notion some careful consideration when they wrote their song:

> *Won't you give me my flowers while I'm living,*
> *and let me enjoy them while I can.*
> *Please don't wait till I'm ready to be buried,*
> *and then slip some lilies in my hand.*

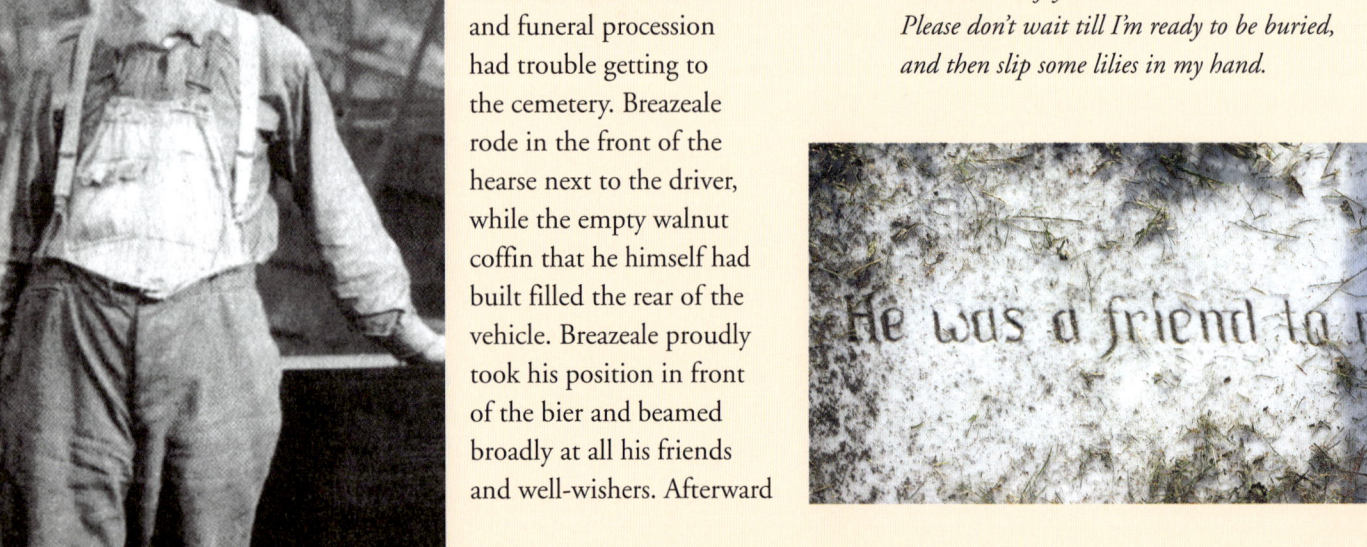

Marvin "Popcorn" Sutton

Once in a great while a pursuant of illegal activities does so with such panache and derring-do that folks helplessly find themselves rooting for the scofflaw, hoping that somehow he'll succeed. The "Gentleman Bandit" Melvin Dellinger, for example, captured the public imagination for a while when he politely robbed dozens of banks without hurting anyone and refusing to take the bank customers' money. From Robin Hood to the Sundance Kid and beyond, we admire criminals who break the law with style.

The legendary Marvin "Popcorn" Sutton earned his nickname after a dome-topped popcorn dispensing machine ended up on the wrong side of a barroom dispute with him. He earned his living as a moonshiner and prided himself on the quality of his product. Popcorn never made a secret of what he did, and he was well known and well liked around his native town of Parrottsville, Cocke County.

He often appeared on PBS television documentaries showing exactly how to set up a quality still and operate it, wrote an autobiography called *Me and My Likker*, and helped a North Carolina bed-and-breakfast decorate a themed "Moonshiner Suite," complete with copper worms, barrels, and other paraphernalia that he'd actually used. Sutton insisted on using clean copper, pure mash, and fine white sugar in his distilled beverages. Visitors to the Misty Mountain Ranch in Maggie Valley applauded his performances when he played the banjo and sang about the way he made a living.

His status as a beloved folk hero and mountain character grew in proportion to his difficulties with the law. Sutton was first convicted of selling untaxed liquor in the early 1970s, and had regular run-ins with agents from the Bureau of Alcohol, Tobacco, and Firearms. After years of raids and other crimes (including felony assault with a deadly weapon), a 2007 raid netted 850 gallons of grade-A moonshine, three thousand-gallon stills, hundreds of gallons of mash, and several guns. In 2008 the sixty-one-year-old Popcorn was denied the chance to remain under house arrest and was ordered to report to federal prison for his eighteen-month sentence.

He continued to evade the law until at last, on March 16, 2009, he went missing. His wife, Pam, found him slumped in a seat in his "three-jug" Ford Fairlane, which he'd bought for three jugs of liquor. Sutton had died from carbon monoxide poisoning.

Asked by news reporters why her father had apparently killed himself, Sky Sutton said, "He did what he said he would always do; death before dishonor."

Machine Gun Kelly— Bad Guy Wannabe

To most folks, little Georgie Barnes seemed to have it made. He had a lot of siblings and a loving mom, and they lived in a reasonably posh part of Memphis. His dad was rich, a self-made man with his own insurance agency downtown. But like a lot of self-made men, he had a sink-or-swim approach to parenting. "Give a child too much and they'll grow up spoiled" was pretty much the way he saw things. For the most part, it worked.

Georgie's siblings did okay—one brother even followed his dad into the insurance business—but George wasn't a good student, often getting into fights and preferring to cut classes to hang out at a billiard hall most afternoons, instead of doing his homework. He barely managed to get his diploma from Memphis Central High, and when he applied for college, none of the Tennessee schools would take him. The best he could do was Mississippi A&M's agriculture program, but even there he failed to make the grade, earning a C+ for "personal hygiene" in phys ed. That was his best grade. Threatening professors only made things worse, and after a short time he was kicked out.

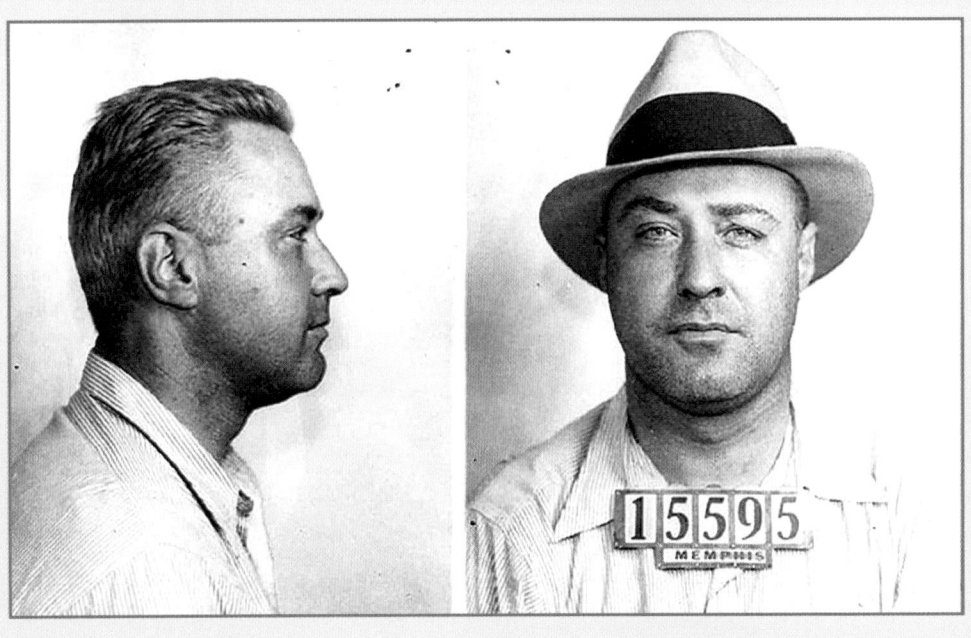

Back in Memphis, his deeply disappointed dad refused to come to the rescue. So Barnes got his own place to live and tried to make a living selling used cars and raising goats. Then he took a job as a cabbie, keeping his hat pulled low every time he had to drive through the nicer parts of town where the rest of his family lived. He got married and had two kids, but the marriage fell apart before long.

Barnes was in his early twenties when Prohibition passed. This led to some new opportunities, first as a runner for some liquor smugglers and then as a full-fledged bootlegger with his own still, in business for himself.

After a few arrests, Barnes left town. In the days before computerized records made one's past accessible to nearly everyone, changing identities and shedding one's rap sheet was almost as easy as changing addresses. By the time Barnes got to Oklahoma he was no longer George Kelly Barnes, but George R. Kelly.

Without a new line of work to accompany the new name, however, it was only a matter of time before "George Kelly" began accumulating another criminal record to match that of George Barnes. Caught bootlegging again, he served another stint behind bars, this time in New Mexico. Then in 1928 he was arrested for driving a loaded "flagon wagon" onto an Indian reservation. Selling alcohol on federal property landed him in Leavenworth Federal Penitentiary in Kansas, facing a three-year sentence. The former rich kid from Memphis stayed on his best behavior to gain a quick release.

When he got out again he met and married his second wife, Kathryn Thorne. He was her fourth husband. If anything, the former prostitute and convicted thief, said to be able to "drink liquor like water" and who knew "more bums than the police department," was a more natural-born criminal than he was. Kathryn bought George his first machine gun and insisted that he practice using it. With the tommy gun, George felt invincible, once showing off his prowess by spelling his name in bullet holes in a billboard.

Kathryn told her drinking buddies that her new hubby was "Machine Gun" Kelly, and she began managing his criminal career like a stage mom, capitalizing on his puffed-up reputation to gain the admiration of her underworld cronies. The two of them pulled off a series of small-town bank robberies in Texas and Mississippi, suddenly making Kelly the FBI's "Public Enemy Number One."

George and Kathryn bit off more than they could chew with their last major crime, however, when they kidnapped Oklahoma City oil tycoon Charles Urschel in July 1933. They held him for what was then the largest ransom ever: $200,000. Urschel was released unhurt nine days after they had captured him, but, though blindfolded the whole time, he had memorized the sounds of oil pumps and airplanes, animal smells, and weather conditions and driving times, all of which helped the FBI narrow down their investigation to an area outside Paradise, Texas. By the time they raided the farmhouse hideout and arrested some of the accomplices—including Kathryn's parents, who owned the place—the Kellys had left. But since the law officers had catalogued all the serial numbers of the ransom money, it was only a matter of time till they were able to trace Machine Gun Kelly and his moll back to a friend's house in Memphis.

On Tuesday, September 26, 1933, federal agents raided the bungalow-style home of John Tichenor and Seymour Travis at 1408 Rayner Street. Kelly, hungover, was caught in his underwear. According to J. Edgar Hoover, when the agents surrounded him, he cowered and begged, "G-men, please don't shoot me, G-men!" but Kelly later denied ever having made such entreaties. By then he'd been arrested so many times that he even recognized some of the agents, and said, "I've been waiting all night for you."

The Urschel kidnapping case led to the first convictions under the new "Lindbergh Baby Law," which made interstate kidnapping a federal offense (and which had put the FBI on their trail). Even though Kathryn tried to pin it all on her husband, she and her parents also received life sentences in federal prisons.

Kelly was among the first group of Leavenworth convicts shipped to the newly renovated Alcatraz Island prison, along with Al Capone, Doc Barker, Robert "Birdman" Stroud, and Floyd Hamilton (Bonnie and Clyde's getaway driver).

At Alcatraz, Kelly acted like he'd finally found the place where he fit in. He was a model prisoner who happily participated in the prison laundry, served as an altar boy in the prison chapel, and spent most of his free time writing letters. After seventeen years on "The Rock," he was sent back to Leavenworth, where he died behind bars in 1954.

At least half of the $200,000 ransom, which was buried inside thermos bottles somewhere near the farm that belonged to Kathryn Kelly's parents, was never recovered.

Despite his frightening moniker, "Machine Gun" Kelly never hurt anyone or even fired his gun during the commission of a crime.

Richard Halliburton: The Modern Icarus

A Gothic-style bell tower on the Rhodes College campus in Memphis, just across from the Memphis Zoo, commemorates the strange life of one of the city's weirdest sons, the adventurer and travel writer Richard Halliburton. Born in Brownsville in 1900, Halliburton grew up in Memphis, then went to Princeton University. But halfway through his college years, he dropped out to join a freighter crew bound from New Orleans to Europe. He eventually returned and graduated, but by then the travel bug had already bitten him good and hard.

In the 1920s and 1930s, when travel was still a rugged and challenging affair, Halliburton managed to see more of the world up close than almost anyone has before or since. And he did so in the most adventurous ways he could dream up: crossing the Alps on an elephant like Hannibal the Carthaginian did in 218 B.C.; swimming the Panama Canal from end to end (and paying the lowest toll—which is based on gross tonnage—for any "vessel" ever to pass through the canal: just thirty-six cents); visiting the emperor of Ethiopia and the last emperor of China; diving into a Mayan sacrificial well; following Odysseus's route around the Mediterranean; mapping Cortés's explorations of Mexico; flying around the world in an open cockpit biplane (taking the first aerial photos of Mount Everest and landing among the headhunters of Borneo); living as a castaway on the Caribbean island of Tobago; briefly joining the French Foreign Legion; climbing the Matterhorn, Mount Olympus, Mount Fujiyama, and Mount Popocatépetl; seeing the seven wonders of the world; and sneaking into the sacred grounds of the Taj Mahal so he could spend the night (illegally) swimming in its reflecting pool under the moonlight. After each of these adventures, the stories and books he wrote about his experiences funded his next forays into the wide world that all throughout his youth was waiting just beyond the Mississippi River.

Adventure may have been his life, but it was also his death. Halliburton had barely turned thirty-nine when he set out from Hong Kong in a gaudily outfitted Chinese junk named the *Sea Dragon*, attempting to sail it to San Francisco. Almost a thousand miles from Japan and some three thousand miles west of Hawaii, the *Sea Dragon* ran into a raging typhoon. The hapless vessel was last seen by crew of the SS *President Coolidge* on March 23, 1939, and shortly thereafter Halliburton and his mostly inexperienced crew of young Ivy League grads vanished. Despite massive search efforts following their disappearance, no trace of their ship's wreckage was found. Six years later, a piece of wood found washed up a California beach was tentatively identified as a part of the lost craft, but otherwise, like so many other real explorers, Halliburton disappeared.

The bell tower at Rhodes College was erected by his grieving parents in 1962. A plaque at its base quotes his *The Royal Road to Romance*: "I wanted freedom, freedom to indulge in whatever caprice struck my fancy, freedom to search in the farthermost corners of the earth for the beautiful, the joyous and the romantic."

Wonder, like weirdness (and beauty), is always in the eye of the beholder.

Peach Pit Prodigy

At first, Roger Smith may come across as one of those guys who don't seem to care what other people think about him. Call him a seedy character and he'll hardly blink. Accuse him of being fruity, and he'll only laugh. Tell him his art is the pits and he'll probably just smile and agree with you. But there's a good reason for all his seeming equanimity. For more than forty years he's whittled away most of his spare time carving peach pits, challenging himself to see how many different things he can make from the same gnarly rock-hard pits.

Born in 1943, Smith was a part of the generation that fought in Vietnam. He served time in the marines there and in the Dominican Republic before getting out of the service in 1968. Since then, he's held a variety of jobs: as a teacher of civics and general business at a high school, as a welder and iron worker, as an essential materials operator for DuPont, and, for twenty-three years, as a meter reader for the Duck River Electric Company before finally retiring from public work to run his small farm near Culleoka in Maury County. At some point along the way he had a little extra time before his lunch hour was up, so he took out a pocketknife and began carving the pit left over from the peach he'd just eaten for dessert.

Ever since then, peach pits have been a perpetual passion. Working in his spare time, he's carved everything from elephants to Edsels, spending up to eight hours to turn a pit into a pint-sized art piece. On request, he'll make baskets, butterflies, gorillas, sows with piglets, penguins, praying hands, rocking chairs, Santas, or an entire village. Though nearly everything is carved from a single seed, there are exceptions: to create a pipsqueak pachyderm, he uses the pointy ends of rattlesnake ribs to make the tusks. Snake ribs serve as horns for itty-bitty buffaloes as well.

Smith already has more than a lifetime supply of raw materials to work with, since, as word of his pastime spread along his meter-reading route, his customers began saving their own pits and leaving sacks of them hanging by their electric meters. "I must have a hundred thousand seeds," he says, pointing at a row of barrels filled with them. "But just like people, every pit has its own personality. I've never seen any two that were a perfect pair."

One of his most extensive achievements to date is the creation of an entire baseball game from peach pits. All the spectators, players, media personnel, popcorn vendors, mascots, and even the cars and trucks waiting in the parking lot are made from peach stones. At the middle of the ballpark, standing atop his lonely little mound, is what can perhaps probably only be referred to as the "peacher." He's no belly "eecher."

Creeping Bear

The last killing in Tennessee known to have been committed with a tomahawk by a Native American took place on Main Street in Memphis on New Year's Eve, 1902.

Creeping Bear was a full-blooded Indian who had come to Memphis on a train with one of Buffalo Bill's Wild West shows. (Most reports say he was Sioux from the Dakotas, but a Memphis police researcher says he was a Cheyenne from an Oklahoma reservation.)

On New Year's Eve, he walked past the No. 4 Engine House of the Memphis Fire Department on North Main Street. The firemen were all off at a fire, and the only person still there was an ex-cop named George Millard, who taunted Creeping Bear as he walked by, then tried to assault him (or tried to snatch his blanket, depending on what story you read). The Indian dealt Millard a single swift tomahawk blow to the noggin. So much blood gushed out of the two-inch wound that a bucket was supposedly used to catch the flow. Millard died on January 16.

Creeping Bear was tried three times for the crime. First he was found guilty of first-degree murder, but the Supreme Court rejected the verdict as inappropriate for an unpremeditated act and ordered a second trial. The second conviction of manslaughter was also rejected on appeal, because it hadn't been disclosed that key witnesses for the prosecution were friends of the deceased. Halfway through the third trial, the proceedings were abandoned and Creeping Bear went free. The lasting lesson of his trials was what became known as the Creeping Bear Doctrine—the need to establish the friendliness or hostility of witnesses.

Most historians assume Creeping Bear returned to his reservation, but a tiny 1905 obituary notice for a Miss Kittie Johnson in Memphis stated she'd been murdered by her boyfriend, One George "Creeping Bear" Webb.

Riding the Range and Acting Strange

On June 6, 1927, twenty-one-year-old Memphian Evelyn Estes put on her khaki riding britches, strapped a gun around her waist, climbed onto her horse Billy, and galloped across the Harahan Bridge. She wore a man's wristwatch and felt hat, while in her knapsack were three bandanas, a pencil, a toothbrush, a change of pants, and some socks, and BVDs. A canteen, canvas bucket, knife, and compact, and lipstick rounded out her kit. She had $25 in her pocket.

Determined to have an adventure, Estes said she was heading to California the old-fashioned way, just like the pioneers. Most people who heard about her quest thought she'd only last a few days, a week at most. Some even said she'd be back before sunset the same day. She proved them all wrong.

Over the next two years, Estes rode her horse across the country, staying on ranches in Oklahoma and Kansas and camping out with Indian tribes in the Southwest. She met Lou Gehrig and Babe Ruth in Wyoming and visited President Calvin Coolidge at his summer home in the Black Hills of South Dakota. With her short haircut and felt hat she was often mistaken for a boy, but when most people realized their mistake they usually invited her in. She earned her keep whenever possible by pitching in to help with farm work, doing laundry, and milking cows. At one point she helped deliver a baby.

She arrived in Los Angeles in February 1928 and, after her 3,800-mile adventure, she got lost. As the Memphis *Commercial Appeal* later told it, "Somehow, after dark, she took a wrong turn off Mulholland Drive, and wound up in the woods just below the famous Hollywood sign. A park ranger rescued her, and sent her to a stable, where she met her friends." By then she was already a legend, referred to in the newsreels as "Calamity Jane's Little Sister." Over the course of the following year she rode back to Wyoming and finally made her way back to Memphis, twenty-three months after she began.

> She was a legend . . . "Calamity Jane's Little Sister."

Asked why she did it, she said, "There is an old English saying, that every life is entitled to one great folly. I had a great need to be free. . . . [I]t was as hard to obtain as it was to explain."

Estes married in 1940, but the marriage didn't survive long. She died in 1999 at the age of ninety-three.

Semper Fido

One of the world's few monuments to enlisted dogs is in front of the Tickle Small Animal Hospital on River Drive in Knoxville. The War Dog Memorial honors Pepper, Tam, Missy, Bunkie, Hobo, Tubby, and nineteen other canines who served in the marines during World War II and lost their lives during the liberation of Guam in 1944. The dogs were employed to detect land mines, look for booby traps, carry messages, and act as sentries.

Military dogs earned rank. They entered the service at the rank of private and could be promoted. Occasionally they outranked their own handlers. Doberman pinschers, German shepherds, Labrador retrievers, and the occasional collie served during the war.

The Knoxville memorial is a replica of a monument at the U.S. Marine Corps War Dog Cemetery at the U.S. Naval Base on Guam.

"Captain Jack" Hinson's Revenge

An uninhabited and unpaved dirt road west of Stewart in Houston County ends at a promontory with an impressive view of Kentucky Lake, the impoundment created in 1944 when the TVA dammed the Tennessee River to control flooding. Before that, this same spot afforded an unobstructed view of the river itself, winding far below the steep bluff where the road ends. This was something that John W. "Captain Jack" Hinson turned to his advantage when he decided that the only manly response he could offer after what had happened to his family was bloody-minded revenge.

Born in North Carolina in 1807, Hinson had settled in this part of the country because it was the kind of place where an independent-minded guy could do what he wanted and be left alone. There were few large plantations, no big towns to speak of, and few industries, so a small-time planter like he was could enjoy a life of hunting, fishing, raising a family, and tending a farm—at that time, the American Dream.

Hinson wasn't completely isolated from the rest of the world, though, and when the states began to quarrel over the issue of slavery, he voted for Lincoln. Within months of the start of the Civil War, this part of Tennessee became a hotbed of guerrilla activity, contested by rival warlords. Both sides included criminals and opportunists all too eager to prey on local folks caught in the middle. Hiding behind their respective "noble causes," thugs from both North and South would kidnap and torture local farmers for money and supplies, then commandeer their property and livestock for their own use.

Perhaps the most hated Union officer in the region, was Col. W. W. Lowe of the Fifth Iowa Cavalry. Tales of his ruthless approach spread as his men slaughtered livestock, burned houses, wrecked mills, and carried out summary executions. His soldiers dragged two men out of

Sunday School at a church just north of Erin, told them to kneel and say their last prayers, and then shot them before they could say "amen." Seven more men were killed in short order, without trial or tribunal.

In the winter of 1862, Jack Hinson's own boys ran afoul of the cruel colonel. They were hunting in the "coaling grounds" between the Tennessee and Cumberland rivers, accused of guerrilla activities because they weren't wearing a uniform (for either side). On Lowe's orders, the two boys were shot by firing squad, their heads mounted on their father's gateposts to serve as gruesome examples of his command.

Despite his leanings toward the Union, Hinson swore vengeance on the spilled blood of his sons. Taking a specially made seventeen-and-a-half-pound .50-caliber long-range hunting rifle, he left his family, walking into the woods to kill as many Yankees as he could.

Knowing that he could trust no one, Captain Jack entered a self-imposed exile, shunning contact with his home and former neighbors. For years he had hunted through every ridge and hollow of the country between the rivers, and he could silently steal through its forests on even the darkest nights. He knew how to live off the land and kill his own game, carefully retrieving the lead from each deer carcass so he could remold the flattened balls and fire them again. Meanwhile, soldiers began mysteriously disappearing from Forts Henry and Donelson whenever they'd go out on solitary sentry duty, or—if they were on patrol with their platoon—suddenly dropping dead in midsentence, a split-second before the distant crack of that rifle would reach the ears of their comrades.

Hinson's favorite targets, however, were the gunboats that patrolled the Tennessee River. He lay in wait on a high promontory, hidden behind an outcropping of rock. Anything in blue was fair game, but officers in particular learned to hide below decks or risk sudden death delivered by the invisible sniper on the ridge above. After each confirmed kill, Hinson carved a small circular mark on the stock of his gun. By war's end there were thirty-six circles, but historians think he was being conservative, only marking the gun when he was sure he had taken down his prey. Many claim his true toll was more like eighty or a hundred Union soldiers.

Later in the conflict Hinson sometimes served as a scout, guide, or intelligence source for the Confederates. Meanwhile, the Union forces had assigned cavalry and infantry soldiers from nine regiments, along with a specially outfitted team of marines, to hunt down the "one-man battalion" who was now nearly sixty years old. At one point, speaking with Confederate Maj. Charles Anderson, he admitted to finding some satisfaction in his lone quest. "They murdered my boys and may yet kill me," he said, "but the marks on the barrel of my gun will show that I am a long ways ahead in the game now, and am not done yet."

When the war ended, he hung up his rifle (eventually giving it away) and moved to Magnolia, Houston County, to run Magnolia Mill on White Oak Creek with his wife, Elizabeth, until his death in 1874.

There's no plaque or monument to indicate where Hinson carried out most of his self-imposed mission. But not far beyond the end of the road overlooking the water, there's a sudden drop-off, and hidden in the face of the bluff below it is a nearly forgotten outcrop of yellowish strata that old-timers in the area call Name Rock. It's hard to find if you don't know exactly where to look, but if you do, it's easy to see how it got its moniker. Though covered with a skein of names, dates, and initials, it is still possible to discern the oldest marks among them: "Hinson," dated 1863. The "C.S." scrawled before it seems to be a claim of allegiance.
—*Thanks to Chris and Bettie Card*

Loco Gringo

Let it never be said that William Walker lacked the ambition or the gumption to pursue his dreams. Toward the end of his short life, he wrote, "Unless a man believes that there is something great for him to do, he can do nothing great." Despite his fierce intellect and determination, he is unfortunately not well remembered in the annals of history.

William Walker was born in 1824 on Nashville's fashionable High Street, where the Tennessee Performing Arts Center is now. He was a prodigy with a near-boundless ability to absorb and digest information. After studying astronomy, math, navigation, French and English literature, philosophy, theology, Latin, and Greek, he graduated summa cum laude from the University of Nashville when he was only fourteen. He graduated from the University of Pennsylvania medical school with highest honors before age twenty. His immense intellect, however, was accompanied by a tendency to get bored easily.

Abandoning his successful medical practice, he first attended the University of Edinburgh in Scotland, in his father's homeland. But after two months, he moved on to Paris and Heidelberg, where he studied sword fighting. By age twenty-three, he was married to a deaf-mute woman and was a practicing attorney in New Orleans. A year later, already bored with the legal profession, he began his third career as a journalist. When his wife died of yellow fever, he edited a California newspaper that had sprung up from the Gold Rush.

Soon Walker wanted an even bigger challenge. He mastered the Spanish language in preparation for his next inexplicable career move: invasion. Backed by an "army" of forty-five men, mostly Kentuckians and Tennesseans who had failed to get rich in the gold fields, Walker staged an invasion of Sonora, Mexico. In October 1853, they sailed into La Paz at the tip of Baja California, took over the town square, and lowered the Mexican flag. In its place they raised a red-starred flag to declare it the new capital of the Republic of Lower California. Walker declared himself president of this new country.

But Mexican and Indian forces retaliated, forcing Walker and his men to walk overland back to the United States, where he was arrested for his stunt. Though his first foray was a failure, he apparently found the rush of conquest addictive. At age thirty-one he gathered fifty-six would-be soldiers of fortune (called the American Phalanx) and led them off to Nicaragua. At the time, Nicaragua was in a politically fragile state and unable to organize an effective resistance against even such a small number of invaders. After several bloody skirmishes, Walker gained control of the Nicaraguan government and managed to stage an "election" in 1856 that made him president of the country.

In conquering Nicaragua, he had interrupted the plans of the shipping and railroading magnate Cornelius Vanderbilt, who had invested over a million dollars in a company that intended to build a canal across the country. When Nicaragua plunged into political turmoil, Vanderbilt's scheme fell apart. Vanderbilt pressured the United States, Costa Rica, and the United Kingdom to undermine Nicaragua's new government.

Without the support of wealthy Americans, Walker couldn't fund his new government, but the only wealth he could tap quickly was from Southern plantation owners. To get their support, he revoked Nicaragua's previous laws against slavery, making him enormously unpopular with Nicaraguans. Walker was forced out of Nicaragua in 1857, yet greeted by cheering throngs in the United States and welcomed by President James Buchanan. After two attempts to reclaim his presidency were thwarted by the U.S. Navy, Walker slipped out of Mobile Bay with 150 men, took the

Nicaraguan town of Castillo Viejo, and seized several of Vanderbilt's steamships. An American Navy attack promoted by Vanderbilt forced Walker to surrender yet again.

His last adventure in Central America took him to Honduras, where in 1860 he arrived with a hundred followers to take over the town of Trujillo. Attacked by Hondurans on one side and the British Navy on the other, Walker surrendered to the British, believing they would escort him safely back to the United States. But because Walker insisted on surrendering as the president of Nicaragua (not as an American citizen), the British turned him over to the Hondurans. On September 12, 1860, William Walker was executed by firing squad on the Honduran beach.

In a few months the American Civil War began, and in the chaos that followed, the Nashville know-it-all who was so determined to rule was forgotten.

In Honduras, a legend called the "Fantasma del Gringo Presidente" still persists. One night a year, they say, a ghost emerges from his sandy grave and attacks anyone it encounters.

Bad Brassell Boys of Baxter

Just a few yards from Cornerstone Middle School in Baxter are the remains of two brothers who were hanged by the neck until dead.

The Brassells weren't exactly the kind of kids that teachers delight to find staring back at them on the first day of school. All four brothers and their sister were known throughout Putnam County for being rowdy, but the two youngest boys were the ones who as grown men ended up paying the ultimate price for their misdeeds. One evening in November 1875 the family gathered at older brother Jim Brassell's house along with two men from DeKalb County to cook up a plan to rob the old Allison Stand Inn a few miles away.

The inn was thought to be holding $4,000 in its strongbox as well as $600 in "operating funds" hidden in an old clock, since it was owned by the mother-in-law of the Putnam County tax collector. The tax collector made regular stops at the inn between each of his rounds, and the Brassells were sure he was leaving the money there instead of taking it to a bank or back to the treasury. His next scheduled stopover was to be on November 29, so they thought they'd maximize the take from a robbery if they waited and attacked the inn that night.

For some reason the two older brothers, Jim and Buck, backed out, but Joseph Lewis "Joe" Brassell and George Andrew "Teek" (sometimes spelled "Teke") Brassell were determined to go through with it, with the help of the two men from DeKalb. So they smeared soot on their faces as a disguise and approached the inn with their pistols drawn.

Robbery turned into murder (of Russell Allison), and the four men dashed away. Among the posse of men who tracked and captured the fugitives the next day: Buck Brassell (Joe and Teek's older brother) and John Allison (deceased Russell's older brother). John Allison died in that skirmish.

JOE BRASSELL — TEEK BRASSELL

The trial in Nashville dragged on for next three years. In the end one DeKalb man received a long prison sentence, the other was released for testifying against his partners in crime. Joe and Teek Brassell were hanged on March 27, 1878; then their bodies were displayed to send a message to other would-be criminals.

A weird thing happened a few days after the hanging—lightning struck the building where the Brassell coffins had been assembled—but the burials seem to have occurred without a hitch.

Some years later, Baxter Theological Seminary bought the land behind the farm where the Brassells were buried. Over the years it changed names until finally it became Cornerstone Middle School, which it remains today.

Belle of Riverview
In Clarksville's Riverview

Cemetery an 1892 stone reads, "Sacred to the Memory of Belle." According to local legend, Belle was a "lady of the evening," known to one and all only by her first name. Her funeral was reportedly a major event, made even more unusual by the fact that none of the scores of attendees actually saw one another there. They'd all borrowed or rented closed carriages and paid their last respects by slowly cruising by the fresh grave with the curtains closed, barely parting the drapes wide enough to toss bouquets of flowers onto the mound of dirt that covered Belle's coffin. No one knows who paid for the tombstone, and the only visible male present was a minister, though all the horse-drawn vehicles were assumed to have held only men.

In late-nineteenth-century Clarksville prostitution parlors operated openly. In fact, in the 1890 federal census fifty women openly identified themselves as "ladies of the evening." Despite local tales claiming that Belle was one of these women, researchers for *Cumberland Lore* found mention only of a three-year-old Belle in the 1880 census, living in a brothel with her prostitute mother.

If this is the same Belle marked by the stone in Riverview—which seems likely—then one of those curtained carriages might have contained her unknown father.

Personalized Properties

"**E**very man's home is his castle" goes the old saying, but a lot of Tennesseans seem to have taken those words to heart. From Memphis to Mountain City, scattered across the state are places to live that are all about uniqueness, and quite a few of them are literal bastions of individuality. Not all of them are as elaborately detailed as the thirteenth-century-style fortress that juts above a hill near Triune, or as paranoid as the Armageddon-proof house in Alcoa, or as out-of-place-looking as the Warren Street Mart in south Memphis. Nor are any of them quite as scary and inaccessible as the ultra-secret HEUMF (Highly Enriched Uranium Materials Facility) castle located inside the Y-12 National Security Complex at Oak Ridge. That's where the nation's stockpile of bomb grade Plutonium and U-235 is watched over from the vantage point of high-tech but surprisingly medieval-looking turrets outfitted with super-powerful Gatling mini-guns instead of crossbows and Greek fire. Talk about a fabled place!

But even when—as is the case most of the time—self-made environments have been built more for personal delight than personal defense, quite a few folks in the Volunteer State have let their energies and imaginations go full throttle to create something that reflects their desire to live as they darn well choose in a setting that suits them best. The lyrics from "I Gotta Be Me" by Sammy Davis Jr. probably best sum up the attitude we're talking about: "I want to live, not merely survive / And I won't give up this dream / Of life that keeps me alive . . . I gotta be me!"

Castle Gwynn

Once in a great while it happens that suddenly everything snaps into place at the most unexpected moment: a vision, seemingly coming out of nowhere, clarifies what needs to be done. For high school senior Michael Freeman, it happened in 1970, in the middle of an architectural drafting class. Instead of sketching a brick ranchette or split-level condo like the other kids, he found himself absorbed in making a meticulously detailed rendition of a medieval castle. Four turrets, a great hall, a fireplace large enough to roast a side of ox—he could see himself living in such a place. But this was Tennessee, and as far as he knew, no such places were available.

The castle idea took hold of Freeman and wouldn't let him go. After graduation he opened a school and family photo portrait business that soon began earning him enough wherewithal to purchase a piece of property where he could begin to realize his vision. Near Triune, on the eastern edge of Williamson County, he found a forty-acre hilltop site that commanded a view of the surrounding countryside.

Knowing that a medieval lord would have approved, he bought the place in 1976.

Four years later, the first tower was under way. Its ground-floor kitchen took two years to complete, involving hand-molding fourteen thousand bricks to build sixty arches. A second tower was begun in 1985, which has a second-floor dining hall with a twenty-eight-foot vaulted ceiling for banquets and celebrations. In time, a third-floor suite will be added so that further additions to the castle can be funded in part by renting out the space to romantic visitors. Two more towers are planned, and construction is still under way.

Castle Gwynn, as Freeman named his fortress, is modeled to some degree after Castell Coch, a Victorian folly built in the late nineteenth century on the foundations of an older castle near the village of Tongwynlais, Wales. Both Gwynn and Coch are romantic reinterpretations of life in the thirteenth century, but with better lighting and easy access to modern dentistry. Castell Coch wasn't finished until a decade after its owner's death, but we can hope that Mike Freeman will still get to see his dream finally take shape as he envisioned it.

The castle is a private residence and not normally open to visitors except during each full weekend in May and on Memorial Day. But you can get a good glimpse of it from New Castle Road off Highway 96, about two miles east of Triune.

Millennium Manor, a House for the Ages

In 1937, sixty-year-old carpenter and mason William Nicholson left the marble-quarrying country of north Georgia and moved to Blount County to start a job at the Alcoa aluminum plant. Within a year, he began work on what would eventually be known as Millennium Manor, a barrel-vaulted bunkerlike structure that he fully intended to occupy until the End of Days. Inspired by Roman architectural techniques, he built curved wooden forms to create six long tunnels, three for each floor, divided into fourteen rooms. After making the forms, he covered them with rubber tarps, then carefully laid blocks of marble over them to create barrel arches. Pouring more than four thousand bags of cement over the marble solidified the ceilings into rigid structures capable of supporting enormous weight.

The residence has about three thousand square feet of living space, as well as an underground two-car garage. It took eight years to make it livable, but Nicholson was a man on a mission. He was a follower of Seventh Day Adventist leader Victor Houteff, whose wife, Florence, prophesied that the world would end on April 22, 1959. According to her prophecy, on that day 144,000 righteous people would be saved and get to live for another thousand years. Bill Nicholson intended that he and his wife, Fair, would be among them.

To survive the end-time, Nicholson planted an extensive fruit orchard and vegetable garden on the property

(including bitter oranges to prevent scurvy), and dug a well five feet in diameter and six stories deep to provide an independent source of water. There are seven chimney flues to heat the upstairs rooms, so that after society collapsed and the electrical grid ceased to function, the Nicholsons would be able to heat with wood scavenged from the no-longer-occupied homes and yards of their neighbors.

Time and biology's relentless processes proved the undoing of these best-laid plans. Born in 1878, Fair Nicholson died of cancer in 1950. After more than fifty years of marriage, her husband was clearly disappointed that now she wouldn't be among the 144,000 to survive Armageddon. "My wife believed in me, but her faith in eternal life was weak," Nicholson said. "She tried to believe but she had her doubts. There came times when she talked of dying."

When 1959 rolled on by and nothing more cataclysmic had happened than the first TV broadcasts of the *Twilight Zone* and the deaths of Buddy Holly, Ritchie Valens, and the Big Bopper, Nicholson suspected that the end had been miscalculated by a decade. In 1965, nearly deaf and blind and unable to maintain his home alone, he told a neighbor, "If God doesn't intervene soon, I will die." A few weeks later he passed away.

None of the Nicholsons' ten children wanted to live in his odd house, so it sat abandoned, victimized by vandals while it became a hangout for teen drinking parties. Six years after Nicholson's death, the house that had been appraised during his own lifetime for $150,000 was so trashed that it sold at auction for less than $4,000. It saw use as an Odd Fellows club, and a Halloween haunted house after that, but it continued to fall into disrepair. Then in 1995, Knoxville fire captain Dean Fontaine and Rural Metro senior paramedic Karen Wells bought it to save it from being condemned by the city of Alcoa and torn down.

Fontaine and Wells have devoted much of their spare time and energy to restoring Millennium Manor to its former condition. As much as possible, the new decor matches the defensive setting. A suit of armor stands in a niche, while medieval axes, spears, shields, and heraldic flags adorn the walls. Fontaine points out that, after seeing so many other buildings burn, he enjoys living in a house that is absolutely fireproof. "It's also extremely dark and quiet in the underground parts," he says. "Since I often have to work nights and sleep days, that suits me fine."

If he's awake, Fontaine is happy to show random visitors through, and the couple has an open house each Memorial Day. The rest of the time you are welcome to take a respectful look. It is located at 500 North Wright Road in Alcoa.

Floyd Banks's House of the Almighty

Floyd Banks Jr. was going about the perfectly ordinary activity of building a full-scale medieval castle when a bit of concrete stucco he had just applied to one of its ramparts began to look like the face of Jesus Christ. As soon as he saw that, he changed the name of his massive fortress from the Castle of Truth to the House of the Almighty.

Banks had been a farmer most of his life, but in 1993 he had been inspired to begin building a ten-thousand-square-foot castle on one corner of his property, which is located on a dirt lane off Lee Shirley Road, south of Greenback. Once he saw the Jesus face, he kept his eyes open for other signs and wonders. Sure enough, they were everywhere: Old Testament prophets, animals, birds, historical figures like George Washington and Sam Houston, and dozens of "Satan heads."

After he realized that other people weren't seeing the same images he was, he began "framing" them or silhouetting them with rectangles of red or black paint. "They come up just about anywhere," he says. "I can be laying down some mortar and when I put a cinderblock on it, out'll come a little Satan head when the mortar squeezes out. There's got to be some kind of message to it, don't you think? I'm sure of it." He believes that the message is spelled out in what he calls "picture-graphs" instead of words, because "to be fair to the world, the 'Big Guy' would have to leave each message in at least five hundred different languages. He's not going to do that."

Ten years into the castle-building project, the Jesus face appeared, so Banks quit farming and began giving away parts of his property and his possessions to folks who seemed needy or deserving. The grounds of the castle are planted with row crops like corn and beans, but anything he doesn't eat gets given away as well.

"It's like the loaves and fishes," he says, referring to the biblical miracle described in Luke 9:16. "The more I give away, the more there is." Made from found and recycled materials, the thirty-three-room, two-story structure has cost him less than $8,000 so far.

According to Aaron Littleton, Banks sees miracles here, from full-blown prophetic visions concerning North Korean atomic threats to the 1998 National (football) Championship by UT Knoxville. Banks achieved the big win for the university by embedding a metal "U" and "T" in

a propitious place in the castle. Just as planned, they won one for the Gipper that year.

Still very much a work in progress, the citadel is only about half completed so far, with most of the dozens of rooms and passageways still unroofed and open to the sky. One crenellated turret provides several floors of finished living space, heated with fireplaces and outfitted with strange altars. One room has a Native American decorative theme going on. Another has homemade Egyptian hieroglyphics. The overgrown central courtyard of the castle includes an extensive pet cemetery, sometimes augmented by additional dead animals provided by his neighbors. In yet another part of the castle is a throne room within earshot of the torture chamber, which is complete with whips, chains, and iron rings embedded in the walls for attaching the victims. We couldn't tell if it was intended for serious use or not, though. "It's just a place to have a little fun," was the only explanation he offered.

Throughout the labyrinth of passages and rooms are homemade wall plaques that lay out Banks's philosophical ideas concerning moral behavior, scientific theories about things like gravity and buoyancy, and even his culinary beliefs. The latter provide recipes for various "happy foods" that are easy to cook and provide a balanced diet.

Banks certainly seems happy enough. Now in his mid-sixties, he's got a lot more to do to finish the place, but appears to be undaunted by the task even though nature seems to be as eager to engulf the walls with vegetation about as quickly as he can lay more masonry.

No matter. This place is already well on its way to becoming a wonderfully magnificent ruin.

High and Mighty Tree House

Like a kid's dream playhouse on steroids, what may very well be the world's largest tree house stands at the end of Beehive Lane, northeast of Crossville in Cumberland County. This isn't some rickety platform wedged in the crotch of a branchy old beech tree, but a ten-story ark of a building reached by a spiral staircase, mounted on seven stalwart oaks. Three floors up and in the heart of the structure is a sanctuary the size of a basketball court (in fact, basketball has been played in it), with rows of pews, balconies, and a rustic altar. Seven levels above this is a bell tower with chimes made from ten empty oxy-acetylene tanks dangling from copper cables. From here the view to the horizon is unobstructed, since it's several stories taller than any trees around it.

The tower, which weighs nearly three tons, was the only part of the building that Horace Burgess wasn't able to build by himself. He had to use a construction crane to set it in place. But other than that, the only powered tool he has used is his chain saw. Over the course of fifteen years he's hammered more than 258,000 nails into an estimated sixty thousand pieces of recycled scrap lumber to build his ten-thousand-square-foot wooden edifice.

The idea came to him in a 1993 vision that lasted only four seconds and happened while he was fully awake. In a flash, he not only could see the building, but also understood that he was being called upon to achieve it. He could even see the sanctuary with a basketball court included, as well as the form of its altar, with four rustic crosses ("one for Jesus, one for each of the thieves that were crucified with him, and one for [mankind] to bear").

A professional landscaper, Burgess had the physical strength, know-how, and sheer perseverance to make it happen. But he was also an ordained minister, and believed that when God plants a mission in your head, you'd better follow through. However, as he told Morgan Simmons, reporter for the Knoxville *News Sentinel*, he isn't the first religious visionary to experience a momentary crisis of faith. "God didn't do me like Noah," Burgess said. "I never got the dimensions. If I had known it was going to end up this big, I never would have started it."

A maze of passageways and staircases leads through the vast building, often emerging in surprising places after bypassing some floors altogether. Near the top is Burgess's "penthouse suite," with carpeted floors, shelves, a woodstove, and a ladder leading still farther up and away to reach a sleeping loft. From the parapets at this level, it's possible to see how the nearby garden is laid out in the shape of a radiant cross atop an American flag (with crop furrows for stripes), and the name JESUS spelled out in irises and lilies below.

Although it has often been used by worship groups and asylum seekers, the building remains unfinished. The first seven years of construction went quickly, when the determined minister was mostly ignored and left alone. But now it is hard, Burgess admits, to make as much forward progress since vandals destroy things almost as quickly as he builds them. Whenever he can, he arranges for trusted friends and helpers to stay in the house at night to protect it. Still, he feels that God will stand by him until it is completed. Eventually Reverend Burgess hopes to install a Swiss Family Robinson–style elevator, operated with ropes and pulleys, along with a fully functioning kitchen and bathroom, and lots more hidden panels and secret passageways. Water will be supplied by rainwater collected from the roof and stored in a cistern.

"This tree house belongs to God," he said. "Sometimes people ask me if it is haunted, and I tell them yes, it is. It's possessed. But it is haunted by God, and possessed by the spirit of the Holy Ghost."

Wickham's Pantheon of Heroes

Ever wonder why so many of those Greek and Roman statues in art museums are headless and armless? It's because meanness and stupidity are age-old strains that have run in human bloodlines in tandem with inspiration and ingenuity, and for every talented artist who can make something from nothing, there's an equal and opposite dim-witted vandal who can tear things apart.

Despite nearly forty years of vandalism at Enoch "Tanner" Wickham's Stone Park near Palmyra, Montgomery County, this place is still impressive enough to hint at how truly amazing the site must have been in its heyday.

E. T. Wickham was born across the Cumberland River from Clarksville in Montgomery County in 1883, and grew up in a farming family. He was nine when his father died, and twelve when he quit school to help run the family farm. For most of the next sixty years, Wickham lived in a house down in a hollow near Palmyra, where he tended his farm, got married, raised nine children, and went to Catholic Mass as regularly as he could.

In 1952, at the age of sixty-nine, he built a small log cabin using recycled logs that he'd cut and hewn himself when he was just fifteen. After he and his wife, Annie, moved into the cabin, he built a statue of the Blessed Virgin Mary from concrete and erected it in the garden, then surrounded it with a low wall marked with the hours of the day. He later claimed that the shadow cast by the statue on the garden wall made it the world's largest sundial, accurate to within two minutes. Statues of Joseph, Fatima, Jesus, and the Crucifixion soon joined Mary in the garden, while a large archway topped by a cross and guarded by two concrete foxhounds marked its entrance. In a 1964 newspaper clipping, Wickham said he wasn't sure why he

had started making sculpture, but it was just something that he'd wanted to do for a long time.

After the Virgin, he built statues of Tecumseh, the Shawnee Indian hero, Revolutionary hero Patrick Henry and other war and folk heroes, his parish priest, and some fondly missed relatives. Equestrian statues of Andrew Jackson and of his own brother, a circuit-riding physician astride an Appaloosa mare, were among his largest works. Many of the columns that support the sculptures were made by pouring concrete into metal stovepipes. A pair of concrete oxen memorialized his own ox team, and a Liberty Bell symbolized his patriotism and sense of justice. Over the course of eighteen years, Wickham made more than thirty life-size statues, often celebrating their unveilings with elaborate dedication ceremonies involving state and local dignitaries.

After Wickham's death in 1970, vandals began regularly abusing the site, possibly because his surprisingly liberal political stance and religious beliefs were somewhat out of step with the rest of his community. His pair of statues of Bill Marsh and Sam Davis, for example, identifies Marsh (his maternal grandfather) as the "First Man That Voted a Union Ticket" in the county. Wickham's self-portrait stands in a thin pine woods a little apart from all the others.

Thick vines and undergrowth hide much of the original site now, and some of the statues have been moved for safekeeping to a farm farther down the road.

To find Wickham Stone Park, head south on Hollow Road from Highway 149 near Palmyra, then turn left (east) on Shiloh-Canaan Road, then left on Buck Smith Road. The statues are at two locations along this road about a mile and a half apart. More information can be found at www.wickhamstonepark.com.

Voodoo Village

The correct and proper name for this place is the St. Paul Spiritual Temple. Using any other name in the presence of the people who live here or in its immediate vicinity is likely to earn you a quick hustle off the premises, or worse. So many Memphians refer to it as Voodoo Village that we want to be sure everyone knows the real name. It's the most mysterious thing in the whole city.

Mystery is, of course, the offshoot of the unknown. The temple belongs to a religious cult, centered first around founder Washington "Wash" Harris, and now focusing on his son, James Harris. The elder Harris, a long-term member of a radical branch of Freemasonry influenced by both Roman Catholic dogma and Nation of Islam (Black Muslim) ideas, founded the cult around 1955, when he was in his late forties.

The two-acre religious compound erected at 4596 Mary Angela Road, a dead-end lane in extreme southwestern Shelby County, contains strange symbolic structures adorned with unusual groupings of objects—red-painted cow horns, turtle shells, crosses, a silver-painted building covered with spikes, Egyptian-style masks, Native American thunderbird symbols, totem poles, hearts, stars and crescent moons, rockets, dolls, and Masonic compass-and-try-square signs—intermingled with clusters of altars, pathways, and gardens representing ancient Egypt, Heaven, and the Garden of Eden to create a highly charged religious environment.

In the center is the temple itself. Visitors who saw the compound in its early days said that it generally looked more playful than sinister, comparing it to a "cross between Alice's Wonderland and the Wizard's Oz."

The site probably began like many other outsider art environments, as one man's visionary and mostly artistic (and probably harmless) creative self-expression. In the late 1950s and early 1960s, white Memphis teenagers taunted Harris's religious group (including blacks and Native Americans) with racist epithets. Then the group withdrew from the rest of the city when Harris was accused of impropriety with a fourteen-year-old congregant (he was about sixty) and for practicing medicine without a license.

In time, the temple members—always a hundred or fewer—started throwing stones and bottles at unfamiliar vehicles. They erected a barbed-wire-topped fence around the complex.

When Memphis newspapers dubbed the place Voodoo Village, temple dwellers completely separated from society at large. Vigorously denying any association with voodoo, magic, Satan worship, or any other dark activities, temple members insisted that all they did was worship the Lord, and that their temple was erected as a holy site. Still, tensions continued to grow, with each side's actions only reinforcing the hostile responses of the other. The rift never healed. Even now, curiosity seekers are liable to be warned off with the same phrases used twenty or thirty years ago: "Don't come too close, don't stop too long, and don't take any pictures!"

So complete is the wall of silence that it is not known whether Wash is still alive or not. If still alive, he would be at least a hundred years old (according to various records, he was born around 1905 or 1911), but in a handful of encounters between outsiders and members, he is still referred to in the present tense, as if he is still alive and among them.

The St. Paul Spiritual Temple soul purification bath, according to a recipe collected in the mid-1970s, requires three baths at exactly twenty-four-hour intervals. (This recipe is provided for informational purposes only and under no circumstances do the authors or publishers accept any responsibility for any results or damages to either health or household plumbing.) Add the following to a half-filled bathtub: one cup of salt; a box of baking soda; a half gallon of red vinegar; and one cup of graveyard dirt, dug from the middle of a grave about six inches deep (according to the recipe, the hole must be refilled with fresh soil after collecting the dirt). After the bath, dry with a clean white towel and say the Lord's Prayer.

Chopper Heaven

There are certain places that, if the Smithsonian were *really* trying to keep its curatorial fingers on the pulse of down-home America, they should consider trying to buy, preserve, and save for the edification of the greater American public. S & G Custom Cycles in Columbia, Maury County, is one such place. Happily for the national debt, though, this is one potential government expenditure that doesn't need to be made, for this place is self-curating. As its owner, third-generation motorcycle man Sam Goodman, likes to say, "We are much more than a bike shop; we are a destination!" So the next time you get bored watching candle dippers and basket makers at the typical "living history" museum, you can come here and see master craftsmen of a more recent era still plying their trade, in a setting that is as much a museum of the weird as it is a historical treasure.

Earl Jacobs, Sam Goodman's grandfather, was a pioneer in the twentieth-century sense. In 1919 he opened one of the first Harley-Davidson salesrooms in middle Tennessee as an addition to his Mount Pleasant wagon and buggy repair shop. During World War II it passed down from him to Sam's uncle Dempsey Goodman. In 1973 Sam opened his own shop and soon joined with two buddies, Tom "Bird" Cardinal and Mr. Gordon Willis "G.W." Turpin (who once drove for Bonnie and Clyde), and moved to nearby Columbia in 1979.

A lifelong phobia about being buried underground led to an agreement with Goodman that would allow Turpin to continue to participate in the life of the shop. After Mr. Turpin was cremated, his urn full of ashes was brought back to Chopper Heaven. "He" remains on a shelf in the showroom when he isn't off on the road somewhere with his living buddies. As Sam Goodman points out, "Mr. Turpin has been to more bike rallies dead than most folks get to go to when they're alive." He admits, however, that while Turpin still "loves to travel, he is not much of a conversationalist." Turpin is not the only biker whose remains remain in the S & G Collection, along with jackalopes, scaredy cats, antique gag jokes, memorabilia, hundreds of vintage bikes, and at least one 1936 Maytag washing machine with a kick-start motor.

The general aura of good fun is a big reason to visit the shop, even if you don't see yourself as a "chromosexual" (people who will do anything to roll on the fanciest ride they can probably not afford). Disparaging certain California-based TV bike customizers as mere novices, the S & G gang is proud of their masterful skills and low rates ("We cheat the other guy, and pass the savings along to you" is their motto). They're more than happy to show their collection to anyone for free. Trust us, it's weird and it's worth a visit.

PERSONALIZED PROPERTIES 165

Big Buddha

On the corner of Mendenhall Road and Dargen Avenue in southeast Memphis there's a multi-ton chunk of yard art guaranteed to give pause to any unsuspecting passersby. Lolling atop a small platform that faces inward from the corner toward the house is a giant stone Buddha—or more properly, a Budhai, since it doesn't represent Siddhartha Gautama (the Indian prince who lived around 500 B.C., founded Buddhism, and is generally referred to as "the" Buddha). Budhai was a monk who lived about the same time period. Many traditional Buddhists believe Budhai will become a Buddha in the future, but for now he occupies a place in Buddhism roughly similar to that of Santa Claus in Christianity.

The revered Buddha is typically depicted as a serene and meditative figure with normal body weight (or sometimes even gaunt to the point of being skeletal) whereas the jolly monk Budhai is always shown as a roly-poly guy with a potbelly and a happy-go-lucky grin, often holding a never-emptying bag crammed with candy, gifts, money, and other treasures. In Buddhist folklore, Budhai has become the deity of good luck, riches, and success, which is why he's often represented as a fat golden statue in many Asian restaurants. With such a large statue of Budhai out in front of this house we can assume that the folks who live there must already be very lucky, or are desperately hoping to overcome some terrible streak of bad luck.

In any case, we wish them every success!

Arda Lee's Hidden Hollow

Theme parks have been around since at least the 1780s, when Marie Antoinette had a fake peasant village built on the grounds of the French royal palace at Versailles (which already had the first merry-go-round, first pirate boat swing, and first roller coaster, all built for Louis XIV). They became popular in America in the 1950s in destinations offering good, clean family fun. During the 1950s Disneyland, Children's Fairyland, Enchanted Forest, Tweetsie Railroad, and dozens of other family-oriented theme parks like them sprang up all over the country.

In 1952 Arda E. Lee bought an eighty-six-acre farm near Cookeville, Putnam County, that had belonged to his dad and uncle. But his work as a tool design engineer for Lockheed Martin left him with little time to do much with his property. After he retired in 1972, he finally seized his opportunity. By then he'd had plenty of time to think and besides, God had given him a vision for creating a theme park that not only offered lots of fun things to do, but a religious message to boot. Building most of it himself with materials scrounged from all over the county in his 1964 Dodge pickup (now on display), Hidden Hollow offered a nostalgic smorgasbord of old-fashioned fun. It combined picnic areas, swimming holes, fishing ponds, horseshoe pits and a petting zoo with a gristmill, a gingerbread house, an Indian teepee, and a covered bridge. At night, fountains and buildings were lit up with colored lights, while an illuminated fifty-foot cross, chapel, tomb of Jesus, and other shrinelike religious sights completed the effect.

After Lee died in 2004, the park went downhill for a while, closing when his offspring could no longer afford to maintain it. But in 2008 Hidden Hollow reopened under new management, with a new mini-golf course. It remains one of the few true down-home family theme parks in the nation. It's also one of the cheapest.

If you like your fun really fun-ky, then we recommend it!

Time Collectors of Memory Lane

There are collectors for nearly everything you can name, from stamps, ashtrays, and coins to dentures, string, and mule dung that looks like famous celebrities (we're not making this up). Otis and Kathy Eldridge collect the past. The forties and fifties were the years of their childhood and youth—and that era is preserved in a sprawling gathering of buildings behind their house on Caney Creek Road north of Rogersville, Hawkins County. The site is called, appropriately enough, Memory Lane.

Memory Lane began when Otis Eldridge decided to buy an old coffee grinder from a country store that was going out of business. From that beginning, the collection began to snowball. Now a working diner, a 1950s Texaco service station, a movie theater, an airplane hangar, an ice cream parlor, a collection of mobile homes and carnival rides, and a rare 1940s enameled-metal Lustron Home have been rescued and erected on the Eldridge farm, along with an auto body shop, a bowling alley, a TV and radio repair shop, a bank, and a city hall, complete with police station and jail. Near the original country store is a blacksmith's shop and train station, while down below is a covered bridge, a church, a school, a creek-fed swimming hole, and a reconstruction of the house where Otis was born, including the original house's doors, windows, and furnishings. More than a hundred vintage cars and trucks round out the collection.

Memory Lane is a private collection and on private land, but if you are polite and call in advance the Eldridges may be able to accommodate a visit. Otherwise, it is normally open to the public on the Saturday of Memorial Day weekend. It is located behind Eldridge Auto Sales on Caney Creek Road, just west of the intersection with Old Mill Road, north of Rogersville.

Stone Clinic and the Wizard of Oliver Springs

At the northern tip of Roane County is the picturesque little town of Oliver Springs, which enjoyed brief attention from Hollywood when it was chosen as the setting to film *October Sky*, the story of a (West Virginia) coal miner's son who became a NASA rocket scientist. But an equally true and intriguing local story could be told about a hulking tower that many folks call "the castle," which juts up strangely in the middle of town. Many residents trace their lives back to that castle, since "old Doc Stone" delivered some five thousand babies there over the course of his long and colorful career.

Fred Stone's childhood ended at fourteen when his parents divorced and his father died. A few years later—yes, while he was still a teenager—he traveled west to homestead a ranch in the scrubby mesa of eastern New Mexico. Then he moved to Oregon to farm wheat and pick hops. A few years later he returned to Tennessee to earn a medical degree, then volunteered as a medic for the British forces in France during World War I. He was awarded a Military Cross for bravely tending the wounded during a particularly intense artillery attack. Military life suited him, and he served as a U.S. Army physician all over the world for a full twenty years.

Back in Tennessee he set up camp as a country doctor in Claiborne County, while he began building a huge and, by all reports, strange house on the banks of Bear Creek. Twenty-ton boulders went into the creation of a four-story castlelike structure that jutted from the side of a cliff. Several streams flowed directly through the house, one of them used to generate electricity. Passageways and staircases meandered from room to room, which were filled with the treasures he had acquired on his overseas travels.

Stone was still building the Bear Creek house when he bought an abandoned medical clinic and applied the same eclectic approach he had used to building his home. A large maple tree stood in front of the building, and rather than cut it down he configured the new additions to accommodate it. (The tree is gone now, leaving an odd indentation in the streetside facade.)

Eventually the clinic stood five stories high, taller than any other building in town, and was topped by a turretlike observation post that commands a fine view of the surrounding countryside. Like the house, wandering hallways connected the examination suites and recovery rooms, while hidden chambers allowed the doctor to live in relative privacy. Visitors to the private parts of the complex told their friends how easy it was to get lost in the confusing warren of stairwells and passages, sometimes comparing Doc Stone to the Wizard of Oz in how he could hide and disappear when he needed a few moments' rest. Since he was always on call and rarely slept more than three or four hours a night, it was understandable.

In his eighties, Stone finally moved back to the Bear Creek house. Shortly after moving in, the house burned to the ground. The fire was so hot that the boulders he'd used to build it cracked and powdered. A year later Stone, the builder of Tennessee's weirdest private hospital, was dead.

Klaatu's Ride

Not long ago Tennessee's most bizarre residential property—at 1408 Palisades Road in Chattanooga—was put up for auction. The two-thousand-square-foot, three-bedroom home—a large, flattened ovoid resting on six splayed concrete legs—sold for $135,000. The only way in or out is via a flight of stairs that can be raised or lowered just like an alien ride from a fifties sci-fi flick. We have to admit that that holds a certain kind of appeal, for once you are snugly ensconced in your flightworthy home you can press a button to raise the drawbridge and no one can get in.

Of course that could work against you, too. There have been some apocryphal stories circulating about the couple who built it having an argument one day that culminated with the wife running out of the house, raising the stairs (there is a switch at ground level, too), and then parking the family truck under the stairs and trapping her husband until he finally apologized.

We don't know if the trapped-husband story is true or not, but we kind of like it. —*Adam Ferguson*

Elvis a Go-Go

Michelangelo Buonarroti had his Sistine Chapel, Gutzon Borglum had his Mount Rushmore, and Ansel Adams had his Yosemite Valley. Each creation was a tribute, a transformation, and a mark on history. Each artist took something great and made it greater. Just as, you could say, Churchill Winston Hill had his 1962 Chevrolet Corvair 95 van.

Hill, a native of Norway, Maine, ended up in Tennessee in 1967 after a stint in the Army. He was an employee of Tennessee Eastman in Kingsport for ten years while his wife, Roxie, worked in the Trim and Inspect Department of the Levi's jeans plant. In 1978 Churchill quit his job to settle near Elizabethton. Here, following a lifelong dream, he built a custom auto body workshop and art studio.

When he found a Corvair Van for sale for $300 a year later, it was a classic convergence of man, opportunity, talent, and material. His experience with airbrush-painting church murals and baptisteries paid off when he had a chance to pay homage to the second-most-worshipped king in Tennessee.

The "Elvis Van" took two years to complete. Sixty-five paintings on the outside of the vehicle

tell the life story of the King of Rock and Roll, accompanied by scaled-down reproductions of posters from all thirty-three of Presley's movies. Replicas of the gates of Graceland allow visitors a chance to look inside whenever it is parked with the doors opened, while 120 buttons arrayed around the outside activate a vintage 1954 Rock-Ola jukebox mounted in the blue and gold velvet-lined interior, making the van a rolling museum of all things Elvis.

"I wanted to do something that nobody had ever done before," says Hill. We think he succeeded.

172 PERSONALIZED PROPERTIES

Bucketman

To amuse some kids, on July 4, 1987 Danny Hoskinson torched some plastic picnic utensils with a Bic lighter to make a stick figure. Somehow the ad-libbed art project ignited a passion in him. Years later, he said, he "graduated to the plastic bucket" and the blow torch to create fantastic sculptures: totem poles to whimsical animals, and flying angels to demons.

Some were larger than life, like the Centaur, a half man, half horse that stood guard at the entrance to a three-acre art environment he built near Benton, Polk County, called the Polk Art Park. Some of his creations took as many as fifty melted buckets to make. He said, "I am teaching the plastic to be art and the plastic is teaching me to be an artist." Because he rarely wore shoes, locals referred to him as "the barefoot bucketman," a nickname he happily accepted. People still fondly recall the Bucketman's roadside stand six miles south in Ocoee, where he sold his weird plastic figures to tourists heading up Highway 64 for their mountain holidays.

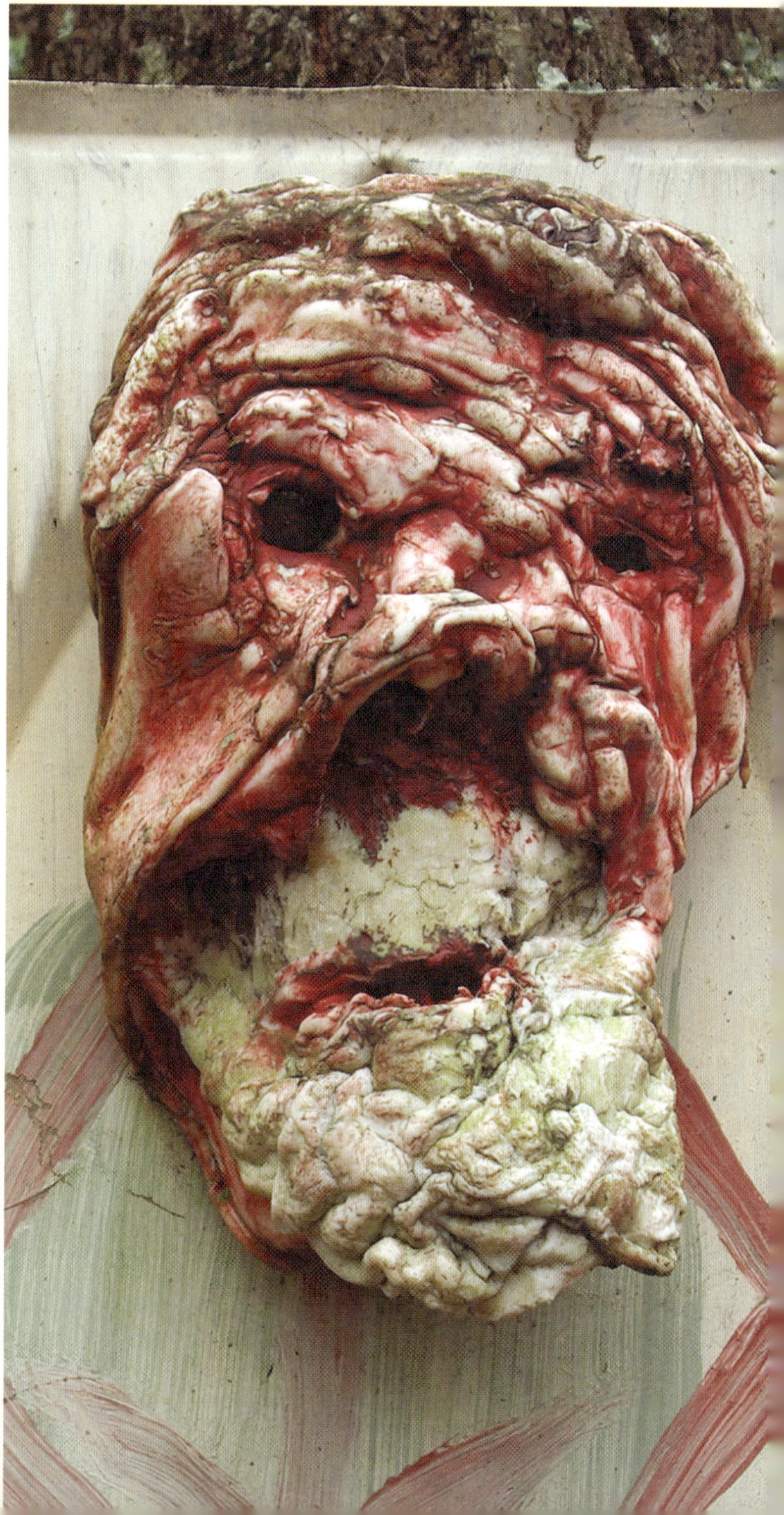

When death came for the Bucketman, it came quickly. In mid-June 2008 he went to the doctor, complaining of abdominal pain. On July 2, he sent an e-mail to a close friend:

> *I tell you this with a dry eye for life has been too good to me to be whining about anything. It's not over till it's over, but I have cancer and cirrhosis of the liver. It's too much for the doctors to deal with so there's nothing to do but take care of the pain at this point. . . . They haven't said how long I have but if you can believe what you read it won't be long. That's why I'm not wasting any time telling you this. . . . It's a time to celebrate. I've waited all my life for this.*

A few hours later he was gone.

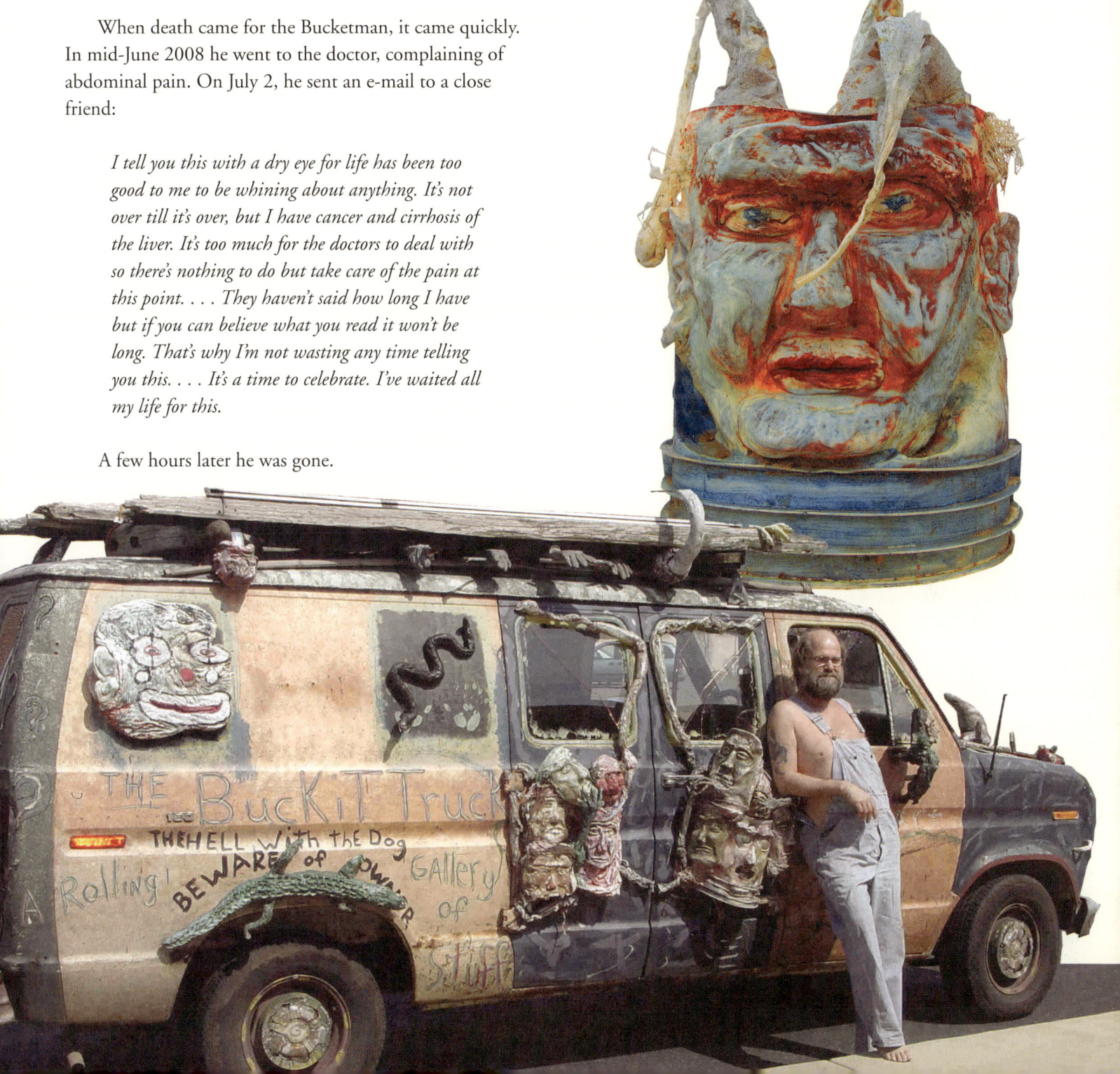

Roadside Oddities

Variety is the spice of life, or so the old saying goes. We humans seem to be attracted to the un-usual, the ab-normal, and the out-of-the-ordinary, and we tend to hate the same-old same old. More than anything else, it's monotonous routine that turns prison into punishment, that makes commuting along the same route to work every day such a drag, and that makes assembly-line work so hard. Despite all the manicured landscaping and the easy-to-read signage in the journey of life, most of us find ourselves craving to come upon a little something "different" now and then that will make our eyes bug a bit and give us an excuse to turn to whoever's with us and say, "Wow, take a look at that! Now that's weird."

Most of these things, of course, aren't found along the four-lane speedways; they're on the smaller back roads. And that's a good thing because we want to encourage you to get off at the next exit and see the real Tennessee once in a while. With all the recent emphasis on eating locally (sightings of locavores are becoming increasingly common) and shopping locally to support hometown merchants, we think there should also be an emphasis on driving locally. Call it "localmotion" and turn it into a moving movement!

We'd like to help you encourage your friends try it out. On the pages that follow are a number of reasons to get away from the fast lanes and onto the side roads, with your eyes peeled for something . . . well . . . a little different.

Powell Airplane

Time was, when a journey involved meeting and interacting with everyone along the way. Creeping along on foot, or by horse or horse-drawn wagon, you looked every bystander and oncoming traveler in the eye, either to wave or at least to assess whether or not they meant you any harm. Nowadays you can spend hours on an interstate and never really notice anything but the trunks of the vehicles just ahead of you.

The late 1920s inaugurated the golden age of the roadside attraction, when buildings shaped like animals, teepees, or food were in vogue and fun to see and visit.

In 1930 Elmer and Henry Nickle cashed in on the roadside attraction craze by building their Airplane Filling Station on the newly widened and resurfaced US-25 in a gap near Powell, west of Knoxville. Elmer Nickle was fascinated by airplanes and reasoned that even if not all passers-by shared his fascination to the same degree, they'd at least find the sight of a plane parked so close to the road unusual enough to take a second glance. The high-wing lifting surfaces sheltered the pumps while a set of rotors on the roof helped make the craft seem even more futuristic, by turning it into a combo airplane and helicopter.

Ever the eager entrepreneurs, the Nickle Brothers built a tea room on the same property with lattice-trained rosebushes, making the junction of the Clinton Highway and Pleasant Ridge Road a must-see for anyone heading in that direction out of the city.

Harland Sanders advertised on the backside of the Nickles' reversible business cards and began his own roadside attraction, Kentucky Fried Chicken.

Despite its curious shape, the Airplane Filling Station began to look more out-of-date as its hand-operated pumps and relatively small underground storage tanks rendered it obsolete as a gasoline outlet. After that, it saw other uses as a produce stand, bait shop, used car lot, and package liquor store, before finally slipping into empty abandonment. Happily, the Airplane Filling Station Preservation Association (www.powellairplane.org) is now actively involved in restoring this classic of American enterprise and saving it for future generations to enjoy.

Beware of Pink Elephants Bearing Fire Water

It's probably just an accident of weather caused by high winds torquing under-reinforced fiberglass, but the oversized Fellini-esque tableau that greets visitors at a desolate parking lot east of Interstate 65 exit 112 in Robertson County looks like a surreal scenario begging for a script. A huge pink elephant quaffs a massive martini, complete with an olive the size of a basketball. Meanwhile a dazed-looking giant of an Indian decked out in beige chinos and wingtips seems to stumble toward the highway, leaning with one arm outstretched toward a flagpole as if to steady himself or wave at passing cars.

Grand Guitar

It's bigger than big but not quite colossal, more mellifluous than huge and way classier-sounding than mega or humongous. Hence the name Joe Morrell cooked up for his now-defunct music shop and homemade museum at exit 74 off Interstate 81 near Bristol: the Grand Guitar. The guitar part of the name is more than obvious. At three stories tall and more than seventy feet long, it may be the world's largest stringed instrument, but you'd need a flat pick the size of the hood of a 1975 Cadillac Fleetwood to play it.

Joe Morrell was born in Bristol in 1934 and as a young man often performed on the country-and-western circuit under the stage name of Herbie Hootenauger or as backup in Curly King's band on the *Farm and Fun Time* radio show. By 1960 he was ready to settle down and become more respectable, so he founded Joe Morrell Music Distributing Company. In the early 1980s the company moved into the guitar-shaped eye-catcher he designed and built out near the interstate. A few years later, he bought radio station WOPI and moved its broadcast studios into the capacious ax as well.

After Morrell died in 2006, the museum and music shop closed. There have been some intermittent efforts at reopening, but when we visited, the place was in serious need of new strings and a tune-up. Closed or open, it's worth a visit if you're in the area.

Glass Eye and Museum Madness

In 1910, when Gol Cooper was six years of age, he was tying his shoe with an opened pocketknife in his hand. He was stooped over, pulling tight the string, when it suddenly broke, thrusting the knife blade through his eye. He lived between Clarksville and Paris, in a place his grandfather had named Needmore because, he said, everybody there "needed more" than they had.

Gol's father had an eye made for him and he wore one until he died (in 1979 in Norris, where he had been employed by the Bureau of Mines for many years). The eye and the knife were presented to the Museum of Appalachia in Norris by Gol's daughter.

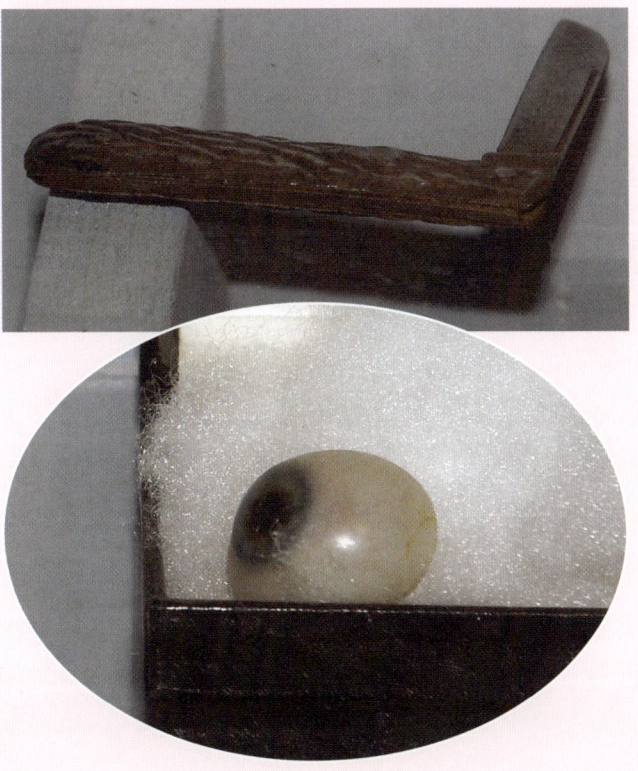

Curse of the Pyramid

A shiny stainless-steel Egyptian pyramid and a fiberglass Rameses II may look a bit out of place in Tennessee. About thirty-two stories tall, it is the sixth tallest pyramid on earth and the only one that is mostly hollow and built as an arena—in Memphis. It's still big enough that the Statue of Liberty could stand up inside it. In 360,000 square feet of space, the pyramid could fit twenty thousand or more people for indoor sporting events and sold-out rock concerts. It could, if it weren't cursed.

In reality, it may be the largest abandoned building in the nation. Beleaguered Memphis city planners have explored the possibility of turning it into an aquarium, an indoor theme park, a gambling casino, a hunting and fishing superstore, or even a mega-church.

In 1992 a mysterious metal box was found welded to the steel support structures of the second-level observation deck. Inside it was an oak box, and inside *that* box was a black velvet box containing a quartz skull, magazines, a fax addressed to a Denver hotel, a photo of wild-haired Indian holy man Sri Sathya Sai Baba, and a cloud of dust.

House of Blues and Hard Rock Café founder Isaac Tigrett, of the wealthy Memphis family that made its fortunes in lumber, cotton, and railroading, had secretly placed the items there in homage to Sri Baba. When he found out that local government had removed the skull from the Pyramid, he said, "You don't have any idea what you have done," and hinted darkly that the entire cosmic balance of the earth could be undone.

This wasn't the first time that dire consequences had befallen the arena, nor the first curse to be aimed at it. A cataclysmic thunderstorm had nearly prevented the construction from getting off the ground in the first place, after a Native American shaman warned the builders that the site was a sacred spot and that nothing good would

180 ROADSIDE ODDITIES

ever come of disturbing it. His predictions seemed to be borne out on opening night when one of the few capacity audiences ever to fill the space rushed to the bathrooms. The city sewer system overwhelmed and the unseemly overflow flooded the arena floor. This infamous disaster made the annals of civil engineering, since all new arenas and stadiums in the country must now pass the "Pyramid Test" before they're opened to the public. Soon other problems became apparent as well: narrow seats, too-steep stairs in the nosebleed sections, poor lighting, and an echo with a fifteen-second reverb.

One of the more bizarre events connected with the Pyramid had to do with two fellows who burglarized a Memphis house and made off with two TVs, a stereo (and CDs), all the clothes (including underwear), an ab roller, and some basketball tickets to see the Los Angeles Lakers challenge the Memphis Grizzlies at the Pyramid the following week.

Grizzlies management issued new tickets, but when the victimized couple attended the game, they spotted the two thieves, who had not only used the stolen tickets to take their seats but had shown up at the game wearing the stolen watch and white leather jacket as well. Tony Rosser and his cousin Stanley Stanback were arrested during the second quarter and charged with the burglary.

At the trial, Rosser's attorney admitted that his client had perhaps exercised "poor judgment."

Music City Parthenon

Talk about a roadside attraction! The giant figure of Athena in Nashville's Centennial Park is the largest indoor statue in the Western world (a number of Buddhist temples in Asia contain much larger statues, but never mind). Still, at nearly forty-two feet she's a pretty big girl. Like the original statue of Athena Parthenos ("Athena the Virgin," Greek goddess of wisdom) she stands inside a Parthenon. Unlike the old one in Athens, Greece, the one in Nashville is intact and made of concrete covered in yellowish brown pebbles dredged out of the Potomac River. But otherwise, it's an exact replica (to within about one-sixteenth of an inch) of the temple of wisdom built some 2,450 years ago.

This is the second Parthenon in Nashville. The first one was a lath-and-plaster affair created as a temporary display during the Tennessee Centennial and International Exposition of 1897. Although originally intended to be torn down at the end of the six-month-long fair, the citizens of the city kept it propped up like last year's Christmas tree

to remind them of their glory days for two more decades. The new one, built of brick, stone, reinforced concrete, and concrete aggregate, took ten years to complete. The original, made of solid marble (making it the largest marble building on earth) and using no machinery and no ready mix, took only nine years to build. Most of the original is still standing after thousands of years; the new one needed a $12 million renovation in 1991. But it is looking good once again.

If you go to see it, you can get some sense for how awesome it is by comparing the little statue of Nike (the Greek goddess of victory) in her hand. Nike is 6'4", just about perfect to make a great center for the University of Tennessee Lady Volunteers basketball team.

Athena in Nashville's Centennial Park is the largest indoor statue in the Western world.

Cannonball Church

Greenville's Cumberland Presbyterian was built just as the Civil War began. Four years later a skirmish broke out in the streets surrounding it as Union cavalry raided the town on September 4, 1864. During the fight, former cannabis farmer and disgraced Confederate general John Hunt Morgan hid in stables on the ground floor of the church (the sanctuary is upstairs) and then tried to make a break for it. He was shot in the back and killed just across the street when he refused to halt after being ordered to do so by Pvt. Andrew J. Campbell of the Thirteenth Tennessee Cavalry, who had been on the Confederate side earlier in the war—an irony, since Morgan had begun the war as a Lincoln supporter. A small stray cannonball, fired during the scuffle, lodged in the bricks in the front of the new church. Rather than remove it, the congregation chose to let it stay there as a reminder of the incident.

Nashville's "Nun Bun"

The Nun Bun, a pastry that had an uncanny resemblance to the famed Mother Teresa of Calcutta, was spotted in a tray of cinnamon rolls by Bongo Java Coffee Shop's store manager Ryan Finney in October 1996. Somehow, some phenomenally inexplicable baker's alchemy had yielded an instantly recognizable replica of the would-be saint. From then on, the bun was displayed next to a photo of Mother Teresa for folks draw their own conclusions.

For the next decade, both those thirsting for coffee and those famished for faith made the pilgrimage to Bongo Java on Belmont Boulevard. On Christmas morning 2005 someone forced their way into the shop while it was closed and made off with the miracle marvel. Puzzled police surmised that the theft must have been carefully orchestrated. Perhaps the burglars had been the shady minions of the Vatican, or maybe a rival coffee brewer's cronies had spirited the priceless pastry away to a locked vault in Seattle. In time, the fickle attention of the world turned back to the Holy Tortilla, the Virgin Mary Grilled Cheese, the Holy Ghost on Toast, the Pope Tart, and other inspirational eidetic edibles.

Meanwhile, so as not to disappoint the public, a gilded plaster replica of the original Nun Bun holds its place beneath the front counter.

Totems of Terror

In certain parts of Memphis you may occasionally find yourself passing by a telephone pole covered with children's toys like dolls, stuffed Teddy bears, and plush rabbits. These almost always occur in front of abandoned houses or derelict stores, if there are any standing buildings at all remaining in the vicinity. Puzzled by the phenomenon, we finally pulled over and asked a passerby why the poles were decorated like that. "Drive-by shootings," he muttered, before turning up his collar and quickly heading the other way.

Oh.

ROADSIDE ODDITIES

Bible Covered Bridge

If anyone tells you to go check out the Bible Covered Bridge, don't expect to find a span papered with pages torn out of the King James Version. Turns out the bridge is named after an early settler whose name was Christian Bible (talk about covering your bases!) who built a log house nearby in 1783. In 1923 the bridge was financed by one of Bible's descendants, who got tired of wading across Little Chucky Creek to get to the main road.

Contrary to popular belief, covered bridges weren't covered to prevent horses and mules from being frightened of running water but to keep the bridge timbers dry so they'd last longer. But whatever the reason they were built, they remain magnets to lovers, who like to get in a few quick smooches while passing through the local tunnel of love. On the other hand, covered bridges are also favored places for suicides.

The Bible Covered Bridge is located at the junction of Highway 349 and Bible Branch Road in western Greene County.

Yee-Haw Time

No true aficionado of the oddball should pass through Knoxville without making at least a stopover to visit Yee-Haw Industries, at 413 S. Gay Street downtown. Even if you don't walk out with some of their peculiar "art-like products" (to use their term), you'll get more than an eyeful of some of the strangest (and funniest) graphics. Yee-Haw is the demon offspring of self-styled West Virginia hillbilly designer and bluegrass musician Julie Belcher and antique letterpress printmaster Kevin Bradley, a native of Greenville.

Since 1996 the two have partnered to run a shop that probably has more ancient wood type and old printing machinery than anyone except, possibly, the Smithsonian. But unlike the Smithsonian, Yee-Haw's gear is all still in daily use. Specialty work is still done by hand-carving blocks of wood or linoleum, inking by hand, and air-drying the printed posters and handbills that are the shop's forte and that bring in business from all over the world. Computer graphics, according to Bradley, is "the Devil's work."

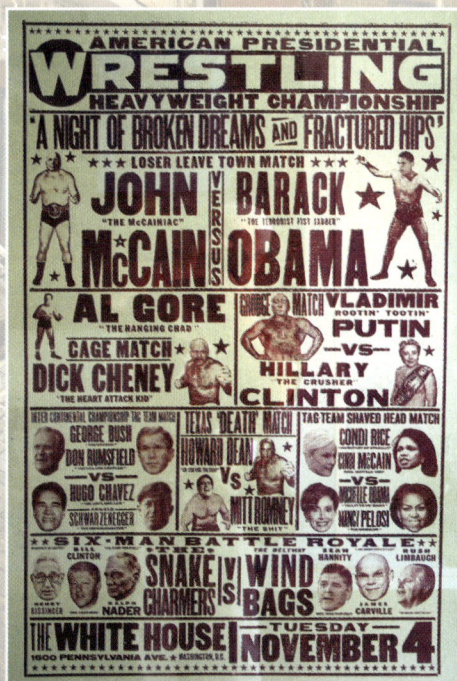

Immaculate Concept, a Shiny Happy Hotel

We found this place to be truly eerie. Not because it was dark; quite to the contrary it was dazzlingly illuminated. Nor was it dirty, for it was shiny and clean. And not because it smelled of rot and mold; in fact, it had that new-car smell that car dealers and rental agencies know their customers associate with vehicular virginity.

Dogwood Manor, a bed-and-breakfast near Pikeville in Van Buren County, has all these qualities because it is built almost entirely of polyvinyl chloride. That means nearly every bit of it is covered in bright, gleaming-white vinyl, including the walls, ceilings, doors, and furniture. A similarly outfitted wedding chapel complete with vinyl altar, artificial flowers, and vinyl pews complements the restaurant (with all nonstick cookware in the kitchen) and the bedroom suites.

The conception of B. J. and Janice Starnes, Dogwood Manor opened to the public in 2006 and caters primarily to the over-fifty ultraneatnik germphobic crowd who values squeaky cleanliness above everything else.

"Locals call it the Plastic Palace," a neighbor told us. "They say the owners must of *[sic]* put the hospital in hospitality."

All that sparkling spotlessness gave us the shivers, too.

Coin-Op Elvis

A few years back there was a fabled Memphis weirdness site called the First Church of the Elvis Impersonator, resoundingly dedicated to all things Elvis. Alas it is no more, but one of the more popular features of the old FCEI—a coin-operated shrine to the dark-haired deity—was saved from destruction and resurrected just a few doors down at Goner Records at 2152 Young Avenue. There, inserting a love offering of a quarter will activate a device outfitted with disco lights, spinning turntable, and animated mementos that, together with the sound of The King's voice, provide enough momentary dazzle to convey a feeling of his presence. And isn't that, after all, a significant part of what real worship—whether fan, hero, or divine—is all about?

Inserting a love offering of a quarter will activate a device outfitted with disco lights . . .

Is That *the* Chattanooga Choo-Choo?

America's first megahit was a song-and-dance act featured in the 1941 movie *Sun Valley Serenade*. Within less than a year "Chattanooga Choo Choo" sold well over a million copies to become the first gold disc awarded by the recording industry. The huge popularity and success of the song owed at least as much to the amazingly acrobatic tap dancing and singing of Dorothy Dandridge and the Nicholas Brothers as to Glenn Miller and his orchestra, but because they were black, little of the fame (or profits) the song earned trickled down to them in their lifetimes. Historical plaques instead commemorate the restored 1880 locomotive that once pulled trains for the Cincinnati Southern Railroad to form a central connection in the primary mass transportation link between New York, Baltimore, Atlanta, and Miami. The old engine now sits behind Chattanooga's Choo Choo Holiday Inn, the city's former Terminal Station. Forty-eight of the unusual hotel's rooms are located in railroad cars parked along the platforms, where guests can experience some of the thrill of sleeping on an overnight train without actually waking up in a different place from where they started.

Towing for Fun and Profit

The International Towing and Recovery Hall of Fame and Museum in Chattanooga celebrates its heroes and shows you why they should be considered heroic in the first place. You'll leave this museum amazed that there are so many different ways of cleaning up the messes the rest of us make.

But why in Chattanooga? Because it was here that in 1916 local mechanic Ernest Holmes first rigged up three poles and a pulley on the back of a 1913 Cadillac to help pull a friend out of a vehicular pickle. According to the museum, this is where the idea of one vehicle pulling another really began. Not too many years before that, that the idea of a vehicle pulling *itself*—and not being towed by horses—was considered a big breakthrough. The original Holmes workshop, which manufactured the first wreckers, is just a few miles away.

In addition to displays that feature all the amazing vehicles and curious contraptions that have been created to facilitate towing, there is a serious side to the museum as well. A Wall of the Fallen honors the men and women of towing who lost their lives in what is—along with firefighting and coal mining—one of the most dangerous civilian occupations.

The International Towing and Recovery Hall of Fame and Museum is located at 3315 S. Broad Street in Chattanooga. Open daily except holidays.

Thin Blue Lines

When we were kids, one of the minor thrills of family road trips was crossing state lines. The GOODBYE FROM and WELCOME TO signs were proof that progress was being made at long last, and that "there" (as in, "Are we there yet?") was getting a little closer. Other signals—the changes in road surfaces, or signs posting new regulations—provided further evidence that we were entering new territory. One thing that might have helped us was another visual clue that we'd crossed the state line: the ubiquitous dotted line on road maps.

As far as we know the dotted line that separates Copperhill, Tennessee, from its cheek-by-jowl neighbor McCaysville, Georgia, is one of the only places where you can actually see a state line. Amazingly—that is, if you are as easily entertained as we are—the only other place we know of is in downtown Bristol, where a short row of brass plates between the double lines down State Street indicates the divide between Bristol and its Siamese twin counterpart, Bristol, Virginia. Somehow, though, that isn't quite as satisfying as the Copperhill line, which cuts through parking lots and sidewalks, goes up poles and over buildings before finally fizzling out at the river.

Occasionally it creates a bit of confusion. Sales taxes in Bristol are more than four percent higher on the Tennessee side of State Street—but conversely, Tennessee has no income taxes, so it more or less evens out. Each Bristol has its own school system, police force, and city council, but shares the same post office, library and chamber of commerce. The newspaper (the *Bristol Herald Courier*) is headquartered in Virginia but is published in Tennessee. Getting permission to exhume a body from Bristol's East Hill Cemetery entails twice the usual amount of paperwork, since a number of graves are occupied by people with their feet in one state and their head in the other.

The community was founded as a railroading and real estate venture, but for many years the railroads were licensed and regulated differently in each state and therefore weren't allowed to connect. A three-foot gap between the rails ending on each side of the boundary meant that all cargo and passengers needed to be taken off in one state and reloaded onto another train across the line before everything could go on to its eventual destinations.

In Copperhill/McCaysville, the line causes similar confusion since it divides buildings as well as streets. It's possible to shop in Georgia and pay the cashier in Tennessee without ever leaving the store, or, we were told, to decide which state to get married in, depending on which side of the church aisle you stand to take your vows. The Ocoee River even changes names here, becoming the Toccoa as soon as the water flows under the bridge that straddles the state line.

Roads Less Traveled

In a frank and open reply to Bob Dylan, we must admit that we really don't know how many roads a man must walk down before you can call him a man, but we can say with a certain degree of confidence that until you've gotten off the beaten track and headed down a fair number of back roads, you can't call yourself a true Tennessean. The real blood and bones of what makes this state Tennessee only begins where all the franchises and four-lane bypasses leave off. You can't fully appreciate local flavor until you go slow enough and let yourself get close enough to see them.

Happily, Tennessee has plenty to offer the wayward traveler, and a remarkably diverse landscape to wander in. The roads that get you there often offer chances for weird—and sometimes darkly frightening—experiences, too. You do need to be careful, of course. The Dead Man's Curve near Monterey has claimed its share of victims, and another bend by the same name awaits the unsuspecting along Gap Creek in Carter County. Ghosts there are said to jump out at cars and try to send them careening off the pavement.

Tennessee's hollows may leave you hollering, too. A ghostly figure in Shipley Hollow, Hamilton County, haunts the stretch between Daughtry Ferry and the Mill Dam. A full seven haints hang out in Golden Hollow near Kelso, Lincoln County, eager to hitch a ride. Meanwhile, Dark Hollow's lonesome female spirit may even try to get in the car with you as you pass through the northern end of Washington County, and Chinquapin's Haunted Hollow ends with a road that will leave your head spinning.

Bridges, too, are places to be wary. Ancient folklore has it that evil spirits can't pursue you over running water, but that doesn't seem to stop them from getting stuck halfway. There are certainly plenty of stories about phantoms lurking on and around the lonesome viaducts and solitary spans across the state. From Ardmore to Springville and from Burntmill Bridge to Silver Cove, have your wits about you on these roads and byways. Try these out for starters.

Dark Hollow Road

There is a lonely stretch of road in northern Washington County that passes by a cemetery where it is said that one occupant is decidedly not resting in peace. The road, which traverses deep forests, is appropriately named Dark Hollow, and the restless spirit is said to be that of a woman named Delinda, who was buried in the Morgan Branch cemetery more than a hundred years ago.

Legend states that Delinda, while never married herself, was quite popular with the menfolk in her day, most of whom were married. This naturally made their wives rather upset and they branded Delinda a witch. One day the women of town banded together and decided to put an end to Delinda's beguiling ways. But when they made their way to her house to confront her, she had disappeared, never to be seen again.

One of Delinda's more scandalous affairs was with a man named Jankins. After getting no satisfaction from her trip to Delinda's house, Mrs. Jankins returned home and promptly shot her husband square in the chest, killing him. At his funeral there was still no sign of Delinda, who was thought to have beat a hasty retreat out of town to avoid the wrath of the angry mob. After the funeral, however, the pallbearers remarked on the unusually heavy weight of the casket, leading some members of the congregation to speculate that Delinda had hidden herself in the coffin in an attempt to follow her one great love to the grave.

It is said that if you drive down Dark Hollow Road at night you will feel a bump as you pass the cemetery, as if somebody had jumped into the backseat of your car. Some claim to have seen Delinda sitting in their backseat in their rearview mirror! Because Delinda was denied a proper Christian burial, her spirit can never be at peace in the consecrated ground of the cemetery. And so it would seem that Delinda's poor restless soul is forever doomed to bumming rides with late-night passersby on the shadowy lane of Dark Hollow Road.

Dark Hollow Road in the Wee Hours

In the mid-1970s, my husband and I and two friends ventured through the area in the wee small hours of a Sunday morning. The tales we had heard told of footsteps following young men who had to walk the area at midnight as a passage to manhood. Our friend, who accompanied us on the drive through the area on that dark and stormy night, had walked the area at midnight, alone. He heard footsteps behind him, drawing ever closer, and stopping when he stopped. He continued the trek and escaped unscathed, never knowing what made the footsteps.

When the four of us ventured to Dark Hollow, we stopped the car in front of the haunted area, to assure ourselves we really wanted to do this. Of course we girls were all for it; my husband thought the legend was just a big story. So, he began to drive slowly down the road. . . . Suddenly the car began bucking and jumping, as when you apply the gas and brakes simultaneously. I thought my husband was just doing it to scare us and accused him of this. However, I saw he was telling the truth.

> **Suddenly the car began bucking and jumping.**

This jumping and lurching of the car continued until we had reached the end of the area at which time the car began to drive smoothly and normally. I was shaken by the experience and asked my husband to drive the long way home and not return the short way through Dark Hollow. He said he was not driving an extra ten miles and turned the car around and proceeded back the way we had come. The car began jumping and lurching as soon as we reached the designated haunted area again. —*Letter via e-mail*

Dark Hollow Road Hitchhiker

Growing up in Roan Mountain, I had always heard about the mysterious hitchhiker, whom if you were on the road at dark, would end up in the backseat of your car.

I had heard that the woman, whose name was Delinda, was very popular with the men of the community. Her popularity seemed to upset the men's wives to the point of murder. I've heard different stories about how Delinda met her untimely demise, but the one that comes to mind is that a few of the wives invited her to a quilting bee, and upon her arrival she was tarred, feathered, and hung. The tree she was supposedly hung from is still standing and the last time I saw it, a noose was hanging from one of the limbs.

I've heard that if you are driving on Dark Hollow Road at night, you'll hear your car door open and shut. If you look in the backseat, you can see the impression of someone sitting there. —*Dorah Caulfield*

Red Hart Road: Hell's Portal?

In Jackson, in Madison County, just off Beech Bluff Road, is an old gravel road named Red Hart Road. The street sign stands on the corner. The road is little wider than a truck, and after you've been down it a minute you can see an old preacher's house just off the road, behind some trees. After another minute, you come to a small church. If you go into the church, you can see where people have spray painted stuff like "666," "Devil's Bed," "Sleep Here and Go To Hell" and "Hell's Portal: Enter and Die." The road wraps around the church so that you can turn around, and behind it is a downward slope with a graveyard on it.

There are a few stories about the church and the preacher's house. One is that it was a black church and the KKK ran the people off and used the buildings for ritualistic things. Another says that a cult was using the buildings. They were supposedly taking homeless people from downtown Jackson and killing them there, after which they would keep the bodies in the house for several days on plastic beds so they could fold them up and clean them easily. Others just claim that it is haunted. When we asked our teachers about "Red Heart" Road they all knew about it. One teacher even said that you could go to the library and read old newspaper articles about the area and the people who had died out there.

One of my friends stopped to ask this old good ole boy gas station attendant where it was, and the attendant said that that was a bad place to go and he didn't recommend it. Upon further prodding, he said that one time he was riding around drinking and happened to drive up the road. Someone pulled in behind him and blocked him in, so he kept driving and pulled around behind the church, where he was completely blocked in by some cars parked ahead of him. He said he was jerked out of the car and threatened with castration and death if he ever entered that road again.

Another friend said he had just pulled away from Red Hart Road onto Beech Bluff when a long line of cars started pulling into the road. His lights caught the inside cab of one of the trucks, where he could see that the people in the truck were dressed in black and had face paint on.

I have gone back only a few other times with several buddies and many flashlights and it is as spooky and scary as ever. The trees are so close and the ole timey feel of the place makes everyone uneasy. The last time I was there, just the back third of the church was still standing. The graffiti is still clearly visible. —*Joe St. Georges*

Rotting Flesh on Red Hart Lane

Red Hart Lane is an old gravel road that passes by an old shed that's caving in, and past it is the old broken-down church. If you look it's got "Welcome to Hell" written in blood (maybe spray paint). It's said to have been run by devil worshippers before the church finally fell apart. My friend actually went up there and seen cats that had been hung. I guess they sacrificed cats. . . . I've been out there numerous times. On the road before you get to the caved-in church there is an old schoolhouse on the right side of the road. I did a little research and found out that the KKK performed some ceremonies out there. Anyway, when I used to go out there, after driving around the left side of the church and returning to the main road there is this one spot where you can stop and it smells like rotting flesh. Every time I have ever been out there I have smelled the same smell and others have also. I don't know what the deal is with it though. —*Anonymous*

If you look it's got "Welcome to Hell" written in blood . . .

Old Dr. Bell of Cayberry Hill

If you hear enough ghost stories, you start to see patterns and repetitions for restless spirits who've gotten a little bored with the Hereafter and want a chance to return and interact with the living, even if only under limited circumstances. There are always plenty of run-of-the-mill roadside hauntings. In fact, we wonder if there might be a Central Casting agency for phantoms.

We picture the scene: a waiting room filled with ghastly wannabes and a bored receptionist who calls out the available job openings. "We got a 'cry-baby bridge' opening at East Valley Bridge outside of Jasper," the receptionist announces. "All you gotta do is make crying sounds whenever someone parks there. And if they honk three times, you just step up, show your face, and they scream. Easy money! No takers? Okay, how about this one? We need a headless conductor to stand on the tracks and wave a light at people. Nothing to it!"

There's a great example of phantasmic hitchhikers between Vanleer and Charlotte in Dickson County. Called Cayberry (or Cabury) Hill, it's on a steep stretch of the old Vanleer Road, just above Fagen Chapel Road. Many years ago "Old Dr. Bell" (to distinguish him from the current Dr. Bell, his great-grandson who still serves the community) was returning from a house call when he reached the bottom of this hill. A stranger stood near Lane Cemetery, apparently getting ready to walk up the incline. The kindly doctor offered him a lift in his buggy, and the man climbed aboard.

They chatted all the way to the top of the hill, but when the doc turned to ask him whether he needed a ride all the way to Charlotte, snap!—he was gone.

By the 1930s people in the area had stopped offering the fellow a ride. They found that if they passed him without slowing down, he'd jump on the running boards of their automobiles and ride up the hill anyway, hanging on until he got to the top and then disappearing without a word of thanks. Locals were more outraged than spooked by the phantom.

Now that Highway 49 cuts across to avoid this part of Old Vanleer Road, the sightings aren't quite as common. But try it for yourself: Make a little dogleg over toward Fagen Chapel and go the old way up the hill and maybe you'll see him.

Lost Flyers of Billy Hollow

Near the county line, not far from Defeated and even closer to downtown Difficult, there is Billy Hollow Road in Pleasant Shade. About thirty or forty years ago, so we hear, a small private plane crashed here on a stormy night, killing all five people aboard, including the pilot and a newborn baby. Ever since then, Billy Hollow Road has been the locale for a number of paranormal encounters, including four very bloody and mangled adults (one of them carrying an infant) walking alongside the road. They are usually glimpsed during rainstorms, walking the curve near the top of the ridge. But if you stop and roll down your window to see who they are or to offer them any help, there's no one there.

Perhaps they are all still lost and confused? Maps for this part of Tennessee often conflict. On the ground, for example, the sign on the pole says BILLY HOLLOW. But on some topographical maps, it is called Green Hollow. On old county roadmaps it is identified as Kaiser Hollow. Who knows what it was called on early flight maps.

Believe it or not, "Billy" is a name that descends from "Kaiser." In much the same way that French fries were given the absurd name of "freedom fries" in 2003 (after the French thought fighting a war in Iraq was a bad idea), back during World War I many German-sounding names were changed to reflect our anti-German sentiments. Sauerkraut was renamed "liberty cabbage" and German measles were called "liberty measles," for example. The German leader, Kaiser Wilhelm II, was often mockingly called "King Billy," so Kaiser Hollow probably became Billy Hollow to Americanize it.

But if that silly name change wasn't made on the flight maps used by the pilot that night, it might account for the crash. There is another Kaiser Road over in Dickson County, but it is two hundred feet lower in elevation. If you're flying below the clouds at night in a storm, having an incorrect map could prove fatal.

Scared Senseless in Sensabaugh

Ask any teenager in Kingsport who's old enough to have a driver's license where the scariest, most haunted place in the area is, and chances are you'll be told to check out Sensabaugh Tunnel. You get there by heading west out of town on the Netherland Inn Road, past the creepy old (1802) tavern for which the road is named, and crossing Rotherwood Bridge—itself believed to be haunted too—and then taking a turn to the north on Big Elm Road along the North Fork of the Holston River for about three miles. At a sharp turn, Sensabaugh Hollow Road heads off to the left through a gloomy, sparsely inhabited valley before making a bend and entering the tunnel. But just because the road enters doesn't mean *you* should. For one thing, the road is wide enough to accommodate only one car at a time.

But before we go further, we should say that we know this is not, technically speaking, the "real" Sensabaugh Tunnel. In fact it is not, technically speaking, a tunnel at all, nor was it originally built for cars to drive through. When the Clinchfield Railroad extended its tracks through this part of the mountains almost a hundred years ago, Sensabaugh Tunnel was bored through Sensabaugh Ridge, while Click Tunnel went through Click Ridge. In between, the tracks had to cross Sensabaugh Creek, so an extended "archway" was built to channel its water. That's what the road goes through now—the archway. In other words, it's essentially a 348-foot-long glorified culvert occasionally used by cars. But since everyone knows this old archway as the Sensabaugh Tunnel, that's what we'll call it, too.

Screams and disembodied cries heard in the tunnel on too many occasions suggest that something truly awful happened here in the past. But exactly what that was, no one seems sure. The most-repeated story is about a bum who jumped off a slow-moving freight train and showed up at the farm at the far end of the tunnel, asking for work. The young farm couple gave him some odd jobs and then invited him to stay for dinner.

But when he entered the house and saw their nice silverware, he was overcome with greed and grabbed it. The farmer ran to get a gun, so the thief snatched the baby out of her crib and made a mad dash out the door, thinking the farmer wouldn't dare shoot as long as he held onto the infant. He ran into the tunnel to make his escape.

Some accounts say that, while stumbling in the darkness halfway through the tunnel, he accidentally dropped the squirming child and its head split open on a sharp rock. Others say that he intentionally stopped and, not wanting to be weighed down by his tiny hostage any longer, drowned the baby in the creek that flows through the passage. Still others claim that the farmer caught up with the hobo and shot him, but accidentally killed the baby as well.

Some stories dispute the whole narrative and insist that a baby was drowned here by a woman who got pregnant out of wedlock. Or they say that her father killed it when he found out, to avoid the shame that she'd brought down on the family. Still other stories say that a family of escaped slaves hid here long before the railroad came through, in what was then a naturally eroded cave. According to this story, when the slave trackers came hunting for them, the mother smothered her own baby (or smashed its head) to save the rest of the family from capture.

Those are only some of the local legends. Anyone can see that this is the kind of place that cries out for some kind of story to explain it. This place is creepy-looking and things actually do happen here. Hundreds of witnesses have heard the sound of a baby crying. Others report cars refusing to start. Strange lights have often been seen darting down the

length of the old tunnel. Dark figures often show up in rearview mirrors. A general feeling of dread permeates the place. Clearly *something* is haunting the old tunnel.

There's one more story worth retelling. It has to do with an Italian immigrant named Francisco Antonio Colisco, who worked on the Clinchfield Railroad when it came through this part of the country. Around 1900, Colisco left his home in Sicily to seek work in France while his wife remained at home to take care of their baby. He was hoping to save up enough money in France for the couple to buy a farm when he returned. He had only been there for a few months, however, when he got word from some of his relatives at home that his wife was cheating on him with a neighbor.

Colisco headed back to Sicily without telling anyone. When he reached his village he looked through the window of his own home and found his unfaithful wife and neighbor together. In his rage he shot them both, but accidentally killed his own infant child as well. Running to the waterfront, he jumped aboard a ship just as it was pulling away from the docks, and sailed to America.

Colisco remarried, and the couple moved to Tennessee to be part of the railroad. All of it was hard work, but the segment approaching Kingsport proved especially treacherous. Seven men—all Italians—were killed in an explosion in the "real" Sensabaugh (railroad) Tunnel, a quarter of a mile south of the tunnel where the road passes through the long culvert. They are all buried at the Ross Camp Ground cemetery, just on the other side of Sensabaugh Ridge. Locals knew Colisco only as "Frank the Italian" or "Frank Tally."

But what accounts for the sound of the crying baby in the Colisco tale? Perhaps it has to do with the ancient belief that crimes, especially murders, have a way of catching up with you. The goddesses of vengeance—the

Furies—follow the guilty disguised as a guilty conscience or the ghost of victim, trying to drive you insane. Only a blood sacrifice could appease them and stop their relentless pursuit. Perhaps, in this case, the blood sacrifice was the group of Italians who died in the railroad explosion.

Thwarted in its desire for atonement, perhaps the spirit of that lost baby can find satisfaction only by frightening the dickens out of us.

Light at the End of the Tunnel

After driving down two of the creepiest roads I've ever seen we arrived at the tunnel at about 10:30. We didn't stay long because the locals did not seem friendly. It is seriously the creepiest place I have ever been to. Unfortunately this time we didn't hear any of the rumored crying. However, there was a light that came from nowhere I could find and illuminated part of the tunnel entrance. We all saw this light and confirmed we had seen the same thing. —*Rev*

Black Dog of the Tunnel

If you drive your car into the tunnel and turn it off, it won't turn back on. Then a horrible ghost flies at you, shrieking an unworldly scream.

Also, a huge black dog haunts a nearby mansion. A cruel man lived there, and while in bed one night flies crawled into mouth and nose, which suffocated him. When they buried him, a black dog jumped out of his casket, and it still haunts the grounds. —*Drew Masters*

Baby Prints on Foggy Windows

It was about 9:30 P.M. when we went through the first time. I turned the headlights off and drove in, and once inside I stopped for a minute and my friend freaked out. He said he heard a train, and then I heard it too, so I drove out of there. We drove down the road, built up the courage to do it again, and went back. Once again I turned the headlights off and started through the tunnel. When we got to the middle, I stopped and waited. Then all of the sudden, the windows fogged up and we could see baby's handprints all over them. Needless to say, we got out very fast. We all laughed at the thought of ghosts before tonight, but I have a change in attitude now. —*Weston Castle*

Tales of Two Tunnels

The original tunnel is less than a mile from my home. There's a river that always runs through it, unlike the newer tunnel, which only has a river going through it when it rains a lot. You cannot drive through the original tunnel because of huge rocks and other stuff in it. I know this from experience: I tried one time and got stuck, then almost died trying to get out of the tunnel because I lost control of my car and it went across the street and almost flipped over. Thank goodness an old, fallen tree stopped us. —*Irot*

Ghost of Sensabaugh Tunnel

There are many stories of murders taking place within the tunnel. One says . . . that a young pregnant girl was kidnapped and murdered within the tunnel. Both her spirit and that of her unborn child remain behind to torment any and all who enter.

There is [also] the story of Mr. Sensabaugh. He lived near the entrance of the tunnel with his family, until he lost his mind. He killed all of his family, including his newborn son, and hid their bodies in the creek inside the tunnel.

All of these legends (which oddly all feature tales of babies dying) have attracted many thrill seekers to the tunnel over the years. People report hearing screams and footsteps, as well as the wailing of a baby. —*Erika Galbraith*

Horrifying Harahan, Bridge-a-Doom

When the old Harahan Bridge in Memphis opened in 1916, it was one of the most remarkable bridges in the country. A cantilevered through-truss steel monster, it is nearly a mile long and built to carry two sets of railroad tracks across the Mississippi. A year after it opened for trains, it began carrying vehicular traffic as well, on two one-way lanes slung off the side of the main truss. Just fourteen feet wide (they were called "wagonways" and originally designed for cotton wagons), ten stories above the water, and with decking made of wooden planks, the vehicle lanes were a source of genuine fear for many an automobile driver who used them, especially when loaded trains made the bridge bounce. They had no alternative, other than to grit their teeth and tough it out, for until 1930 the Harahan was the only vehicular bridge across the Mississippi anywhere south of Cairo, Illinois.

Not only did the bridge boards need constant replacement, but they were dangerously flammable. Small fires were often a problem (soaked in creosote, the boards lit up like torches if sparks from passing trains fell on them) and in September 1928 just such a fire destroyed a good chunk of the bridge and crippled transport routes for months. Repairs required the replacement of nearly a thousand tons of steel supports.

By then, people had long been familiar with the Harahan Curse, some saying that the bridge had been doomed from the outset. (For one thing, the bridge—and therefore the curse, too—was named for James T. Harahan, president of the Illinois Central Railroad, who was killed in 1912 when his car was struck by a passenger train.) Some blamed the curse on the frantic and dangerous conditions under which the bridge was constructed. (Twenty-three workers were killed.) During the years when cars crossed the bridge, people often complained to authorities that men in

muddy work clothes had been seen standing in the roadway above Pier Five, even though no living workers were on the bridge. Others attributed the bridge's ongoing problems to the fact that it had no proper dedication ceremony. (Because of this, the trolls may not have been properly exorcised.) Historians say that the bluffs on the Memphis side of the bridge were once Chickasaw holy sites, and that several mounds were destroyed by bridge construction.

Car traffic ceased crossing the bridge in 1949, when the new Memphis and Arkansas highway bridge opened downriver. The Harahan Bridge has become a magnet for daredevil urban explorers lured by stories of its "secret room" (where leftover dynamite from the construction era was discovered in 1972), but recent reports say that the room has now been sealed.

Lest you be tempted to explore the bridge yourself, be forewarned: Not only is it very dangerous (more than twenty daily trains still cross the bridge), but both ends are under twenty-four-hour video surveillance. Luckily, the Harahan is still plenty scary to look at, making trespassing unnecessary.

Vampire Bridge?

Persistent rumors that the 1882 covered bridge over the Doe River in Elizabethton (Carter County) was once a roosting place for vampires may have a recent origin in a television broadcast in the late 1990s by Tim Cable of WJHL in Johnson City. For a Halloween special on his show *Cable Country* the TV journalist hung from the rafters of the bridge upside down like a bat during the entire segment.

It is possible, though, that the vampire legend is much older. Locally, the old span is known as the "Kissing Bridge" for the tendencies of amorous couples to take advantage of the momentary passage through darkness and privacy to get in a little tonsil hockey. It takes no great leap of the imagination to realize that sometimes the osculation must have been unappreciated, unexpected, or unwanted by one member of the couple, who might then see the other as an opportunistic bloodsucker.

Near one end of the bridge is a chunk of a tree identified as the site of the first court held west of the Alleghanies. Wood you happen to know why? We're stumped.

Long Fall of Hannah Ward

The only good way to get to Hannah Ward Bridge, at Ward's Bluff over the Elk River in Giles County, is by boat. Since we didn't have one, we had to content ourselves with an old photo of the bridge taken about a century ago, and imagine why it's haunted.

According to local lore, Hannah Ward was one of the earliest white settlers in this area. As a teenager, Hannah reportedly escaped an Indian raid and ran to the top of the bluff. Rather than let herself be captured, scalped, or worse, she jumped to her death in the river two hundred feet below. People who have been there insist that if you know exactly where to look along the edge of the cliff on the north bank, you can still see the full impression of a right foot and the toes and the ball of the left foot from where she took her fatal plunge.

Another version of the death of Hannah Ward, told by Grady Ezell, the man who actually owned the cliff in the 1920s and 1930s, starts with Hannah attending a nearby camp meeting revival—her husband refused to go. She invited the revival preacher home for dinner. At mealtime, the minister turned to Mr. Ward for the blessing. Annoyed at being put on the spot, Ward grimaced, bowed his head, and said, "I prayed to the Lord to send me manna; instead the devil sent me Hannah."

Hannah was so embarrassed and ashamed she ran out of the house crying. Her husband ran after her, insisting that he'd only been teasing. He tried to embrace her at the edge of the precipice, but she jerked away in a tearful rage, then slipped and fell over the edge. For the rest of his life her husband attended church, but he went to his own grave many years later never having forgiven himself.

For decades, a wooden bridge near this cliff was named the Hannah Ward Bridge. It was washed away in the Great Good Friday Flood of March 28, 1902 (one of the worst natural disasters in the state's history), along with most of the mills and other bridges in central Tennessee.

If you go, be very careful, because we're told the bridge is a rickety old truss, while the cliff is as high and steep as it ever was and it's far away from anyone who might hear your screams.

Murder and Mystery at the Watauga River Bridge

Elizabethton's Watauga River Bridge, sometimes called the Old Steel Bridge, has stood for over three quarters of a century. Teenagers used to gather under it when they wanted a secluded area where they could make out. That all stopped in the early 1930s, after a brutal and still unexplained event shattered the tranquillity of this community.

Tom Jackson and Wanda Smithson were ready to head home when they noticed movement in the woods and saw a shadowy figure coming toward them. They assumed that it was simply another couple coming to take advantage of the bridge's privacy, and thought nothing of it.

As the shadow drew closer, they realized that it was no couple; it was a large man who seemed intent on making unwanted contact. Before they could react, he lunged at them, stabbing and instantly killing Wanda. Tom took off for the road, but the man managed to slash him on his way. Still, Tom managed to flee. He got up to the roadway and jumped in front of a passing car. When the driver slammed on the brakes, the blood-soaked teen wrenched open the rear door and clambered in. A woman in the car screamed while her husband floored it just as the knife-wielding murderer appeared in the rearview mirror. The couple took Tom to the hospital, where he was barely able to tell his story before he, too, died.

The killer was never found. Neither was Wanda's body, nor any sign of blood or a struggle. Ever since then, the bridge has been a hotbed of strange activity. For decades, people have reported hearing strange thumps pounding against the side of their car as they drive across it, or the sound of someone attempting to open their car doors, even though no one is there.

A new concrete bridge will soon replace the Old Steel Bridge, but we hope they'll leave the old one anyway. We think portals to the unknown are places of genuine worth.

Crazy George's Bridge

Ask any five different people how Crazy George's Bridge got its name and you'll get five different answers. Some say a man was hanged there, or else hung himself from the old span (once wooden, now replaced with concrete) that crosses the railroad cut on Woodcliff Road near Bilbrey. Others will tell you about the guy who slipped from the bridge, broke his legs when he fell to the tracks below, and was neatly severed in three pieces by a train. Still others claim the bridge earned its name from a Charles Manson–like creature who organized his cohorts in a 1970s cult into murderous sprees that involved flinging their victims from the bridge just as trains rounded the bend.

The oldest and therefore most plausible of the many stories tells of a nineteen-year-old who had befriended an elderly railroad night watchman in the early 1930s. Tennessee Central had erected a small shack there for the watchman's convenience in inclement weather. Here the old railroader regaled the young fellow with colorful stories of far-off metropolises like Memphis or Louisville. The teen often passed by the little shack at night after going coon hunting, and in exchange for a story or two, he would often walk along the tracks with the older man and help him clear away any recently fallen debris.

At age twenty, he went to visit the old man in his shack after receiving a positive response his proposal of marriage. The next morning mangled pieces of the boy's body were found flung all along the tracks under the bridge, where a train had obviously run over him.

A special train consisting of just a locomotive and a flat car came from Monterey to retrieve the hastily reassembled corpse. On the way back it stopped off at Woodcliff Church to tell the gathered congregation the awful news. The boy's fiancée was there, and she screamed and fainted the moment the news was announced.

We don't know if Crazy George was the boy—made crazy enough with newfound love to walk down a track at night and not hear an oncoming train—or the old man, crazy with sadness at what had happened.

The bridge is a gathering place for local teens, as the campfire ashes and beer cans and bottles strewn through the woods attest. We feel sure that the tale of Crazy George is still rehashed around those campfires.

If Tunnels Could Talk

Vanderbilt University Medical Center in Nashville used to be called simply Vanderbilt Hospital. The old edifice is at the corner of Medical Center Drive and Twenty-first Avenue South (now called Medical Center North). It was built in the early 1920s, incorporating what was then considered a radical new concept: a double grid layout designed to allow every room to have windows to let in light and fresh air—a critical advantage in the days before central air-conditioning was invented. Even the operating room was outfitted with big windows that let in more light than the weak electric bulbs of the day could provide, while at the same time letting out the stench of the cauterizing irons. During the summer, at least one OR technician always stood beside the surgeons armed with a fly swatter to try to keep their incisions sterile until the unfortunate patient could be sewn up again.

The hospital's floor plan, however, proved a bit awkward, since getting gurneys or wheelchairs from one part of the building to any other involved zigging and zagging along routes that both patients and new interns found confusing and disorienting. Matters were only made worse over the years as remodeling and expansion meant still more corridors, stairways, and tunnels intended to link older parts of the building with more recent additions. Nearly ninety years of such "improvements" have resulted in a labyrinth of forgotten corridors, tunnels that go nowhere, faux doors and windows that open onto brick walls or elevator shafts, and "secret" stairs and passageways that have been walled in behind drop ceilings or side panels.

Some of these areas see so little traffic that homeless people have been known to take up temporary residence in them and escape notice for weeks at a time. Other areas, like the notorious D-0200 corridor—aka "Sugar Hill"—are well known as trysting spots for randy young residents.

But it's not all fun and games at Vanderbilt Hospital. The tunnels are among the areas considered haunted. Tales abound of apparitions of dripping, zombielike patients who died on the operating tables back in the good old days of open-air surgery, and who stumble along with their surgical wounds still open and their glistening guts hanging out.

On August 22, 1995, university police responded to a call from a nurse reporting a suspicious-looking individual. They found a man weirdly disguised with a wig, fake beard, and heavy trench coat (remember, it's Tennessee in August). In his bag they discovered an equine syringe filled with boric acid, a hospital floor plan, and a photo of VUMC neurosurgery chair George Allen. The man, still in disguise, was arrested for trespassing.

After the arrestee was identified as Ray Mettetal Jr., a resident at VUMC in the 1980s, out-of-state searches (Mettetal lived in Virginia) revealed additional vials of poisons and various publications like *Silent Death* and *The Complete How-to-Kill Book*. Evidence suggested that he had come to the campus to harm Dr. Allen, his former boss. He was then arrested for attempted murder.

Mettetal was tried twice and convicted twice, but both times his convictions were overturned on appeal. He was set free, and remains free.

Don't Land on Runway 17!

Students at Cookeville High School in Putnam County can be forgiven if they occasionally complain of nightmares involving plane crashes. The bad dreams probably don't have anything to do with fears of flying, but of fears of going to school. Their school, see, sits squarely across the end of the old Putnam County Airfield, which closed in 1997 after sixty-five years of service.

Let's hope that none of the old-timer pilots forget the airstrip is closed and land there out of habit.

Tennessee Ghosts

The *jury is still out as to whether ghosts* really exist, but not very long ago people actually began scientifically testing for the existence of the supernatural. The fact that scientists haven't unequivocally succeeded may not mean much (though there have certainly been enough anomalous data collected to generate some tantalizing discussion). Perhaps we aren't adapted enough yet to understand how to set up the right experiments. Like color-blind dogs trying to prove the existence of color, we might not be equipped to interpret the results, even if they are staring us in the face.

We've definitely seen (and heard and felt) some things we can't explain any other way. We leave the rest to the reader.

Phantom of the Orpheum

There's something inherently creepy about almost *any* theater, but particularly an old one at night after the audience has gone home, the set has been struck, and the lights have been dimmed. Maybe it's the big, echoing space of an empty auditorium, the fading away of the magic illusions of an alternate reality, or the "us versus them" dichotomy that invariably arises between those performing on the stage and the crowd seated in the dark around it. It could just as easily be the confusion of tangled auras from the former occupants of all those vacant seats, the raw fear embodied by stage fright, or the oversized spirits of the performers who left a lingering sense of their larger-than-life presences behind with their autographs and celebrity pictures. Whatever it is, few of us would voluntarily spend an entire night alone in a darkened old theater, and especially one that's known to be haunted.

Happily for those who work at Memphis's grand Orpheum Theatre, however, the several spirits that linger there (possibly up to six) seem to be benign. Most famous among them is little Mary. No one knows for sure if that's her real name, but that's what she's been called ever since she put in her first appearance in 1928. No one is sure why she's there, but most theories connect her with a tragedy that occurred that year, when a young girl was struck down by a streetcar hurtling along the tracks that run along South Main Street in front of the Orpheum's marquee. The unconscious child was rushed into the theater's lobby, where she died of internal bleeding without ever regaining consciousness. With nobody to identify her and claim her body, she died unknown but not unmourned, as the entire staff attended her final services. She was buried in a grave in a city cemetery, the stone marked only with the date of her death and the epitaph, LITTLE GIRL LOST.

Her spirit settled into the permanent role of Phantom of the Orpheum, and many theater employees have encountered her at least once. She's usually seen wearing a white dress that some say resembles a 1920s school uniform, playfully darting around the mezzanine in stocking feet. During performances she is a well-behaved audience member, sitting in rapt attention in seat C-5, Box 5, unless someone else has occupied it first. According to theater organist Vincent Astor, who has seen her many times, "She's a very good ghost."

Astor discovered that Mary has a favorite tune, which the Orpheum's chief administrative officer Donna Darwin told us is "Never Never Land" from the musical *Peter Pan*. When Astor plays it, the little ghost can become entranced enough to remain in full view for prolonged periods of time. Perhaps it's no wonder, since the lyrics would surely speak to anyone caught in her situation with its mentions of time never being planned and people never growing old.

Not all are convinced that "Mary" is the same little girl who was struck in front of the building in 1928. Some believe she was either a girl who died in the theater fire that destroyed the original building in 1923 (which had been called the Grand Opera House until 1907, when it was renamed the Orpheum) or another girl who was killed in a fall from another downtown building in 1921. However, the trolley accident occurred within weeks of the theater's reopening in 1928, which is just too coincidental to be ignored.

And like Mary, the Orpheum is also caught in a perpetual limbo of youth. Stepping into its gilded, crystal-lit auditorium is like flipping back the calendar to the Roaring Twenties. With any luck, Mary will stick around as long as the old building still stands, which we hope will be for a long time to come.

Music Makes Mary Appear

I've heard two different stories on how Mary came to reside there, the first being that she was killed by a horse and carriage while crossing the street to the Orpheum. The other version is that she fell from the upper balcony to her death. The truth is, nobody really knows who she is or where she came from. They do know that she's been around the theatre for a long time.

Unfortunately, with as many times as I've been to the theatre I can't say I've experienced any ghostly phenomenon. But I did know a very old gentleman by the name of Vince who used to volunteer his time as the organ player whenever they had the classic movie showings during the summer. He swore up and down to me that he could make Mary "come out." He explained that she was very shy and reclusive, and whenever the shows were over and the crowds were gone, he would hang around and play tunes on the organ and she would magically appear in the balcony. He said this happened more than once. He said he even figured out her favorite tunes!
—*castleburk22, via e-mail*

Redrum in the Read Room

There are two kinds of people who believe in ghosts: those who don't want to run into them, and those who will go to any lengths to encounter them. The front-desk staff at the Sheraton Read House Hotel in Chattanooga are used to dealing with both kinds, for the hotel has a room that is haunted: 311. Some people ask for any room *but* 311, while others beg to be booked into the room on the off chance that the guest ghost will put in an appearance.

The Read House was originally called the Crutchfield House when it opened in 1847. It was occupied by Union soldiers during the Civil War, burned in 1867, reopened as the Read House in 1871, and was rebuilt yet again in 1926. During the yellow fever epidemics of 1873 and 1878, and in the Spanish Flu pandemic of 1918, the hotel served as a hospital. But the ghost of room 311 is neither from the famous nor the ill. According to most accounts she was a "lady of the evening."

The story is that a young Union soldier invited her into the room in 1863. After her "performance," a loud scuffle broke out. The soldier may have been suffering from the Civil War version of post-traumatic stress disorder, or it could be that, as a Southerner, she got in a dispute with him over the war. One story suggests that she wasn't a prostitute but a local woman who fell in love with the soldier and was enraged to discover that he was already married. Whatever happened, the fighting abruptly ended and the next day when the staff went into the room, they found the young woman dead. Not wanting to rile the population of the occupied city, the Army quickly suppressed any mention of the event. The soldier was never court-martialed and the episode was soon forgotten . . . except by the young woman who paid with her life.

The room has been known ever since for unpredictable and sometimes unpleasant events ranging from relatively innocent nightmares and sudden scalding and freezing water in the bath, to more serious matters like luggage being suddenly knocked over and dumped by an unseen hand, laptops and cell phones being swept from desktops and smashed, or even full apparitional appearances by the screaming young woman herself. This time, however, her screams are never heard outside of the room, so if you stay in it yourself, don't expect anyone to come to your rescue if she shows up in full revenge mode.

Red Dress Screamer of Grant-Lee Dorm

At the top of a hill overlooking most of Lincoln Memorial University campus near Harrogate, Claiborne County, is a stone building called the Grant-Lee Dorm. It stands where, in the late 1800s, a seven-hundred-room hotel called the Four Seasons was being constructed with backing from a consortium of English investors. The project included not only an inn but also a sanitarium and residential hospital for longer-term visitors. The sanitarium was open and the inn was well under way when a financial panic hit England in 1895 and forced the abandonment of the project. The hotel was put up for sale and soon purchased for the purposes of building an educational institution.

When Lincoln Memorial University was established on the hotel grounds in 1897 the sanitarium was still in use, though they weren't accepting any new patients. Sadly, a fire swept through the building in 1904 and two people died: a woman and her infant child. Since patients were often admitted anonymously in those days (when social stigmas were attached to many illnesses) nobody knew her real name. And since the records were destroyed in the fire along with everything else, her name remains unknown to this day. Her presence, however, is very much known.

After the 1904 fire, the sanitarium was rebuilt inside but converted to a dormitory. When the building caught fire again in 1950, firefighters and university personnel were stunned to see a woman in a red dress leaning out of a fourth floor window and screaming as she held a baby—the window of the same room where the 1904 deaths had occurred. When they later went through the scorched wreckage of that room, no remains were found.

The dorm was rebuilt yet again, but it seems the woman in red is no longer taking any chances. Ever since that second fire, students report seeing a running figure or hearing strange noises or crying sounds whenever a match is struck, an iron or hotplate is left on, or someone walks into the building with a lit cigarette. It's like she's determined to act out forever the old proverb "Burn me once, shame on you; burn me twice, shame on me."

John Sevier Center's Ghosts of Christmas Past

When tragedies occur on Christmas Eve, there's always a special poignancy to the news, and by that reckoning, Christmas Eve 1989 was one of the most horrific holidays ever, especially for the people of Johnson City.

The John Sevier Center had once been Johnson City's finest hotel. Built in 1924 above two medicinal springs, it was advertised as "fireproof." Its grand ballrooms and suites were for the social elites of the day, but by the 1960s, the former grandeur of the ten-story hotel had long faded, and it had become a hangout for prostitutes, drug users, and the homeless. In 1978 the property was remodeled to become a retirement home for the indigent elderly. Social Services sent older clients there when they had no other place to go.

Shortly after 5 P.M. on December 24, 1989, fire broke out on the first floor. Within minutes, the flames spread up to the second and third floors, sending poisonous fumes and smoke throughout the entire building. As firefighters rushed to the scene they were aghast at the sight of gray-haired elders in their nightgowns leaning out of windows surrounded by smoke, feebly begging to be saved.

Before long, the men on the hook and ladder trucks began evacuating aged victims in the below-freezing weather and sending them to area hospitals to be treated for smoke inhalation. Construction cranes and helicopters were brought in since some of the highest floors were out of reach of city fire equipment.

Not everyone was lucky: Fifteen residents died, as well as a twenty-nine-year-old man who had been staying in the center for a few weeks to take care of his grandmother.

Survivors talked of strange events during the course of the evening. One woman said that she and her brother thought they had been leading a group of people to a window out onto the patio portion of the building when she looked back over her shoulder and realized that the others had "disappeared." Firefighters talked of seeing faces momentarily appearing the smoke and then vanishing again. After the fire, when construction crews were cleaning out the debris, they sometimes saw elderly people walking in the wreckage, only to find out later that the people they had seen were among the dead.

After the fire, there was talk of tearing the hotel down and starting over, but once it was determined that the building's structure was still sound, it was remodeled as it was before. A new population of elders and the indigent occupy it now. New, that is, except for those who have never left. Sixteen different ghosts are said to wander the halls now, stuck in a place where they came to live out their days, until even those days were taken away from them.

Mollie Woodruff and the Rose Room

Mary Louise "Mollie" Woodruff was lucky to be born into a life of privilege. Her father, Amos Woodruff, was a wealthy carriage manufacturer who moved his family to Memphis from New Jersey in 1845. He became immensely successful and in 1870 bought a large lot on Memphis's "Millionaires' Row" for $12,600, where he commissioned a $40,000 home in the fashionable French Second Empire style. Every room featured different molding and intricate plasterwork surrounding crystal chandeliers, carved marble fireplaces, and sumptuous paneled doors.

The Woodruff family moved into it in 1871, just in time for Mollie's wedding to Egbert Wooldridge. After the wedding, which was held in the house, Mollie and her new husband set up housekeeping on the second floor. Two years later, the yellow fever epidemic took the life of their first child, who died in the room called the Rose Room after its ornate wallpaper of entwined Victorian cabbage roses.

Not long after that, Egbert fell overboard and nearly drowned during a fishing trip on the Mississippi. Although he was rescued, he had inhaled some river water. That, along with the chill he caught that day, led to his death of pneumonia in the Rose Room some days later.

Mollie remarried in 1883 to James Henning and had another baby, but yellow fever struck again, taking the life of her child in the same, by now apparently cursed, bedroom.

So many Memphians died of fever that year that the city government collapsed. When the federal government took over the private railroads, Amos Woodruff's entire business empire began to crumble. In 1883 he was forced to sell the mansion to Noland Fontaine, a wealthy Memphis cotton factor. Mollie Woodruff-Henning and her second husband lived elsewhere until her death in 1917.

After her death, her spirit apparently returned to the house at 680 Adams Street, for according to different accounts, people living there began to hear a faint female voice saying either "Oh dear, oh dear" or "My dear, my dear," especially around the annual dates of the three known tragedies that occurred in the Rose Room. The bed in that room is said to be alternately smoothed and straightened by unseen hands if someone living sits on it or sleeps in it, or, if a living person has remade it and straightened it, then the same unseen hands muss it up. Once in a while, children have reported seeing a sad-looking woman in a Victorian wedding or birthing dress in the Rose Room, while elsewhere in the house the same woman is sometimes seen in black mourning clothes. The ghost is never threatening, just mournful, and only seems to get upset with the living if someone moves or rearranges the furniture in the Rose Room. Ghosts are habitual and like everything just so, the way *they* had it—when they had it.

Little Ghost Girl in the Pink Dress

The Brinkley Female College on South Fifth Street, between East Georgia and East Carolina Avenues in Memphis, was home to a Christian girls' boarding school started by Col. R. C. Brinkley, the building's second owner. It was also home to an eight-year-old ghost named Lizzie Davie, the daughter of the mansion's original owner.

On numerous occasions Lizzie appeared to thirteen-year-old student Clara Robertson, who walked to school each day instead of boarding there. Lizzie's almost transparent figure wore a rotting pink gown splotched with mold. She had an emaciated, almost skeletal face, and her sunken eyes were expressionless and unblinking.

During one such appearance Clara finally steeled herself to ask what the specter wanted. Lizzie previously said that Colonel Brinkley had acquired ownership of the property illegally, and she wanted Clara to find the original deed and assume ownership of the school or face a far less benevolent haunting. Now the ghost pointed toward the side yard south of the mansion and croaked, "The stump . . . all yours . . ." Later, during a séance held at the behest of Clara's father—led by the medium Madame Nourse and witnessed by twelve others—Lizzie said that five feet below the stump, "you will find our papers and valuables," including several thousand dollars' worth of coins, a diamond necklace, and the deed to the Davie estate, proving that it never belonged to Colonel Brinkley.

Sure enough, at Lizzie's instruction, Clara and her father found a green glass jar clouded by mud, containing cloth bags and an envelope.

Clara's father decided to cash in on the widespread fascination, booking the Greenlaw Opera House for the "grand opening" of the jar and selling tickets to the event at a dollar apiece—roughly $17.50 in today's money. Half the profits, he claimed, would go to charity, and the rest would go to Clara. The event quickly sold out, but sadly it never took place.

Three nights before the jar unveiling, robbers threatened Robertson if he didn't hand over the jar, which had been hidden in the outhouse. The jar was never seen again, and none of the robbers was ever caught.

Disappointed ticket buyers demanded their money back, and Robertson lost his professional credibility. A happier outcome awaited Clara, who married a wealthy seventy-two-year-old spiritualist five years later (she was eighteen) and moved to Arkansas, where she became a full-time medium and psychic.

Little Brinkley Female College didn't last long. It was torn down in 1972 to make way for the Wurzburg paper products warehouse that occupies the block now.

Once the old mansion was gone, local memory of what had been most famous ghost in the history of Memphis faded as well. Even so, a few old-timers claim that a pale, skeletal girl still shows up from time to time in the vicinity of the big warehouse door that marks the exact spot where the six tall columns once stood. She's still wearing that rotted pink dress, and she still seems desperate for someone to take up her cause and right the wrongs of her lost legacy. If you're interested, it's easy to ride by sometime and see if she's still there. Just go around behind the warehouse and look for Door 13.

Skull's Bones

Cutting through a block of downtown Nashville between Third and Fourth avenues and Union and Church streets is a little world-within-a-world called Printers Alley. In the 1880s and 1890s, printers and presses ran all night long to get out the morning editions of the papers and keep up with their backlog of orders. Saloons and gambling halls were natural entertainments for a nocturnal workforce.

By the early 1900s, Printers Alley was already a semisecret "Men's District" where anything went—except women who wanted to maintain their respectability. During Prohibition, it was the one part of Memphis where you could buy alcohol without worrying about the law: The city police protected the district from the feds and G-men, while the local politicians patronized it.

The golden age of "the Alley" lasted through the late 1960s, when the county finally voted to permit liquor sales by the drink—a move that led to the opening of bars elsewhere in the city and suburbs. By then, nearly all of the printing companies had moved out of Printers Alley, and, to maintain their clientele, the remaining bars became strip clubs. Skull's Rainbow Room was among those.

Skull's Rainbow Room was named for David "Skull" Schulman, a gaunt, six-foot-four impresario of burlesque who was nationally known for his wild clothing, flashy jewelry, friendly manner, and pack of poodles, one of which was always named Sweetie. Skull opened his first Alley club in the early 1940s as an adult alternative to family-friendly Grand Ole Opry at the Ryman Auditorium downtown. Patrons considered him a "fixture" they could count on seeing every time they returned to Nashville, while locals began calling him the Mayor of Printers Alley. Ever since his club opened in 1942 he could be found sitting in front of the Rainbow Room from 1 P.M. to 3 A.M. every day but Sunday, never missing a single day's work—not even when he was brutally attacked and robbed one afternoon in 1981. Skull was back at work that evening. In 1986 he said, "I'll be right here until I die."

Those words turned out to be sadly prescient. On the evening of January 21, 1998, the seventy-eight-year-old Skull was found on the floor of the Rainbow Room with his throat slit. He died several hours later at Vanderbilt Medical Center with singer Tanya Tucker by his bedside. The entire country music establishment went into a state of shock, and friends like Chet Atkins and Willie Nelson commented to the press about how senseless his death seemed. Meanwhile, the killers remained at large for two years, as TV shows such as *America's Most Wanted* tried to help drum up clues to catch whoever had perpetrated the murder. In 2000 police arrested two men, one a former employee of the Rainbow Room, for Skull's murder.

Several months after Skull's death, thousands of personal mementos were auctioned. It was the end of an era, but not, as it turns out, Skull's exit from Printers Alley. Even though the Rainbow Room was closed, patrons and employees of the other clubs on the block began seeing a tall, elderly man walking a small dog up and down the Alley. Snapshots taken in an alcove near Skull's old club often revealed the face of a sad-looking man with a prominent nose and ears looming behind whomever was posing for a photo. And even though the Rainbow Room is locked and abandoned now, lights often appear inside it.

Once in a while Skull shows up wearing a long-sleeved white shirt beneath the bib of his *Hee Haw* overalls. Those in the know take this as a good sign. Skull decided to remain a lifelong bachelor after his fiancée, the love of his life, died while wrapping Christmas presents in the 1940s. As his sister Ethel told the Nashville *Tennessean*, "Her gift to him was a long-sleeved white shirt that he kept all his life" and never wore.

Headless Gownsman of Sewanee

The campus of the University of the South (aka Sewanee) atop Monteagle Mountain in Franklin County is rife with Gothic and medieval-style pointy arches, and it's practically crawling with creepy spirits. There's Sidney the Suicide in the Dubose Conference Center (as well as ghostly Dr. Dubose himself, namesake of same), the Hunter of Tuckaway Dorm (who's been known to choke students pulling all-nighters) as well as the three student suicides who haunt a third-floor room of Tuckaway, the Phantom Soldier of Walsh-Ellet Hall, the Woman in White in the old cemetery abutting the campus, the Ghost of Rebel's Rest, not to mention the "demonic entity" in the baby grand piano practice room of Van Ness, the Ghost Nurses of Cleveland, and a number of still-ambulatory Civil War veterans who wander about the campus.

The most famous, though, is the Headless Gownsman, who tends to show up on campus for homecoming and convocation, but especially during exam periods. He is thought to be a former member of the Order of the Gownsmen, a student honor society whose membership wears robes after they've been inducted ("gowned") into the semisecret organization.

The headless guy's origins are a little garbled. According to legend, he was decapitated in a car wreck on the winding roads leading to the campus, and now his head and body are engaged in a perpetual effort to reunite, with the body clumping around in gown, khakis, and wingtips and the head thumping up and down stairs on its own. Talk about a headache!

Alas, these tales conflict with others who insist he was a Wyndcliff Hall seminary student in the 1880s—even though there were there no cars in Tennessee in the 1880s (the first successful vehicle with an internal-combustion engine was made in 1885 in Germany).

But the lack of adequate or accurate explanations for why something exists is not the same thing as saying it doesn't exist, and whatever his origins, the many sightings and remarkable rendezvous with this particular acephalic phantom suggest that there are indeed brainless scholars on Sewanee's campus.

Signal Mountain School Spirit

People had been living on Signal Mountain since the 1870s, but it was the yellow fever epidemics of the early 1900s that sent people into the mountains from the Tennessee River Valley during the summer months. In 1913, the Signal Mountain Inn opened, and it became a popular resort. The Signal Mountain Grammar School, built of local stone, served the local children from 1926 until 1998, when a newer school replaced it.

Now used as a community center, the former school might be haunted by a little girl who suffered some sort of traumatic experience in the past. She's sometimes heard running down the hall, shrieking, "My dolly is burning, my little dolly is burning!" but no one recalls even a small fire in the school that could account for it.

There might be some kind of paranormal overlap going, though, since fires had been a very common event on the ridge. Signal Mountain was named, in fact, for the promontory's former use as a place where Indians, and later Union soldiers, lit fires to signal the approach of visitors from the river valley far below.

Ketron Flute Girl

The spirit of a girl who played flute in the Ketron Middle School band is said to hang out around the stage in the gymnasium. She's often seen walking around well after school, when all the living kids have bolted. Two stories of her demise circulate around the Kingsport school. One has it that she fell down a flight of stairs and accidentally jammed the flute down her throat in the process, while in the other (more likely) version is that she died of a heart attack in the gym room. An assistant principal performed CPR but couldn't revive her.

McCullough Chapel Ghost

There's a haunted chapel in Dyer County at the intersection of McCullough Chapel Road and North Walker Lane. Several friends and I decided to go check it out, and before we went, my friend's mom told us the story behind it.

A woman tried getting pregnant for years and couldn't until one year she finally had a little boy He was diagnosed with a rare disease and died only a few months later. She was devastated but kept trying and about two years later had another son. Sadly, he also had the same disease and died in a few months. This pushed her completely over the edge, and within a year she killed herself.

The mother was buried across the road from her two children, who were interred side-by-side inside a small fence. Her ghost was sometimes seen late at night crossing the road to feed her babies, and many fatal car crashes that have happened in front of the church are blamed on sightings of her. After many years, they exhumed her body and moved it near her children, but you're supposed to still be able to see her feeding her babies.

The night we were there was very creepy, but there was no encounter with this ghost. I was sitting in the middle of the car with both windows down on each side when a cold gust of air came through one window and stayed there (this was a clear night with no wind). The person beside me noticed it, too. I turned to my other side and it felt a couple degrees warmer. I could see my breath on the side of the car this presence came into but on the other side, no matter how hard I tried, I couldn't get the same effect. So I spoke and asked the spirit to go away and quickly rolled the window up. —*Jessi, via e-mail*

Seven Islands

On a hill overlooking the French Broad River Valley about a half mile north of the Kimberlin Road and Seven Islands Road intersection is Seven Islands Church. The church was constructed in the 1850s, but the cemetery that slopes down toward the river to the east of it dates back to at least 1802. The church has no ghost stories, but one of the graves bears the epitaph KILLED BY INDIANS IN VIRGINIA and several Revolutionary War soldiers and early pioneers are buried here.

Paranormal researchers frequently record electromagnetic disturbances, cold spots, and the appearance of strange lights.

Old Green (or Yellow) Eyes

Since the days when Yanks and Rebs fought and killed one another in the woods of Chickamauga and the steep slopes of Chattanooga, there have been reports of a strange humanoid figure with wild, bloody hair, who's often found lurking around the old battlefields. Local stories say it is the ghost of a Yankee killed by his Confederate brother, and he's usually referred to as Old Green Eyes or Old Yellow Eyes, though neither nickname is quite accurate. "Old Greenish-Yellow Eyes" seems closer to the color of this specter's glow-in-the-dark optical organs.

He tends to haunt the observation towers that overlook the Civil War battlefields. One of the towers where he has been spotted most frequently is the Wilder Tower just across the state line in Georgia, where they say there are bloodstains on the top four steps that no amount of cleanser can remove.

All we can do, then, is recommend that if you climb up for the view, don't forget to watch your step.

Fraternity of Fraterville Spirits

In the Leach Cemetery behind Clear Branch Baptist Church in Lake City, Anderson County, is a sad monument to one of the greatest tragedies in the state's history. Carved into the sides of a central obelisk at the back of the graveyard are 184 names, and surrounding it are several concentric rings of 89 individual graves, all marked with the same date: May 19, 1902.

The Fraterville Mine was considered among the best-run, safest mines in the country. It enjoyed reasonably good relations between its workers and owners, and the jobs it offered were critical to the survival of local families. The towns of Fraterville and Briceville grew up around the mine. Schools, churches, and even an opera house were built in the valley. People looked forward to the future.

On the morning of May 19, 1902, shortly before the graveyard shift ended, workers in the Fraterville Mine broke through the wall of an abandoned adjacent mine. Three miles from the mine entrance, gassy stagnant air from the older mine seeped into the Fraterville tunnels. The rear shafts were ventilated but at 7:20 A.M., black smoke and thick dust belched out of the ventilation shafts and mine entrance. The abandoned mine had ignited and exploded.

Rescuers found their first victim within two hundred feet of the entrance, but the gas and dust were so thick and poisonous that they were forced to retreat. More than eight hours passed before the air cleared enough to go back in, and the rescuers found dismembered corpses and body parts mingled with the shattered wreckage of mine carts and the bodies of the pony mules that were used to pull them. Meanwhile horrified throngs of wives and children gathered outside as the remains of their loved ones were brought out, often only one piece at a time.

An exact count of how many had died was never determined, but estimates range from about 212 to 226. A few dozen miners were itinerant bachelors or had left families someplace else. Without anyone to recognize and claim their body parts, it was impossible to count the dead. Every man who'd entered the mine that morning was killed, leaving more than a thousand children fatherless. There were only three adult men left in the town of Fraterville. More than 180 bodies were claimed and were given church burials, while the itinerants were buried in hastily dug pits near the mine marked with fieldstones.

On dark nights, the rings of graves behind the Clear Branch Church are said to light up with the faint glow of the old oil and carbide headlamps of the lost miners. After they appear and glow for while, they slowly wink out until, finally, none are left. GONE BUT NOT FORGOTTEN is the way most of their graves are marked.

Maybe this is why the itinerants are more restless still. It's said that if you listen carefully you can hear the forgotten men desperately whispering their names as if to say, "Do not forget us. We were there, too."

Ghosts of Militia Hill

Heading into the Coal Creek Valley on Road 116 from Lake City in Anderson County you soon come to a curve where Beech Grove Road turns off to the right. Take that road, cross the bridge over Coal Creek, and take Sharp's Lane, which heads left. A few hundred feet later you'll see the Vowell Mountain Road. A mile or so up this lane, past the second hairpin switchback, you'll come to the shoulder of a ridge called Militia Hill. This is where the Tennessee State Militia (precursor of the National Guard) set up their cannons and Gatling guns in a crude fortification they called Fort Anderson, and where they took on the avenging coal miners of the Coal Creek War of 1891–1892.

There is no monument at the site, although there should be, for the battles fought here spelled the end of the infamous convict leasing system in the South, making it one of the key events in the labor reform movements of the late nineteenth and early twentieth centuries. The convict lease system had, in effect, replaced slavery with something that was, in many cases, worse. Slaves, at least, were considered valuable property, while convicts could be worked to death and replaced for free. Perhaps the failure to recognize the importance of this site is one of the reasons an angry ghost plagues the area.

Dick Drummond was a young "free miner" who joined the group protesting the use of convict labor. He became a martyr to the cause when a group of militiamen captured and dragged him to the old railroad bridge in Briceville and lynched him. Ever since then, the trestle has been called Drummond Bridge. Locals say that his ghost walks up and down the valley, still howling in righteous anger at the unfairness of the cruel system that ended his short life.

Bellwood Horror

At the end of Bellwood Landing Road in Stewart County, east of Dover, is a lone house near the ruins of an old iron furnace, where a terrible atrocity has left an indelible stain. Bellwood Furnace was built in 1829 and was operated by slaves. The house is where John Bell, owner and overseer of the furnace and its employees, once lived. (Bell was no direct relation to the Bells of Adams or their famous witch [see Local Legends], although he might as well have been.)

In 1856 there was widespread panic in middle Tennessee spawned by the idea that slaves throughout the region were planning an insurrection. After a barrel of gunpowder was found beneath a church near the Louisa Furnace in Montgomery County, slaves in the vicinity were captured and tortured until a story began to emerge. They said that there had been plans to destroy furnaces throughout the central part of the state, kill the whites in the region, then attack and rob all the banks in Clarksville before doing the same in Hopkinsville, Kentucky, before escaping to the North.

Whether such plans were real or the result of coercion and torture isn't known, but whites went on a state of high alert and carried weapons with them at all times. In nearby Kentucky, locals believe the escaped slaves were already on their way. The terror surging through the region led to the murders of a number of innocent people who merely happened to be in the wrong place at the wrong time.

Allegedly the masterminds of the rebellion that never was were at Bellwood Furnace. Four hapless men were accused there and were horribly maimed, then hanged. At last check, the basement of the Bellwood house still had the rings on the walls and the wooden whipping stocks where the men were bound, chained, and tortured. The house is closed and fenced, and the current owners won't say whether or not the gruesome gear is still there.

Ironically, most of the murdered slaves were skilled ironworkers, and replacing them with equally knowledgeable laborers proved almost impossible. More than twenty-five ironworks were shut down in the panic, and many never reopened.

The Bellwood House and furnace are now considered among the most haunted places in middle Tennessee. Paranormal investigators recorded strange lights and the sounds of piteous screams coming from the basement.

The glassy blue slag found in the ditches and creeks around the ruined furnace is considered to be a powerful talisman for repelling ghosts. Is it coincidental that blue is associated with protective strategies all over the world? It's the color of (anti-) evil eye amulets used in the Mediterranean, holy water used in Catholic churches, and voodoo temple thresholds. Pick up a piece (on public property) and keep it with you next time you go ghost hunting.

Still Standing Watch at Fort Donelson

Fort Donelson on the Cumberland River near Dover was the site of a Civil War battle that began on February 11, 1862. Although battlefield wags later referred to it as an "exchange of iron Valentines" because much of the fighting took place on February 14, it gave the Union its first major victory in the Civil War. It also left at least 850 men dead.

In 1867, 670 Union soldiers were buried at nearby Fort Donelson National Cemetery. Fourteen of them were black soldiers from the U.S. Colored Troops, including Reuben Hammond, whose ghost is said to watch over the cemetery now. Both visitors and staff have seen him and he seems friendly, if a little lonely.

> An "exchange of Valentines" ... left at least 850 men dead.

Scream Scrum

Rugby, in the northern tip of Morgan County, was an experiment that turned into a ghost town. It still is a ghost town—for ghosts.

After British novelist and social reformer Thomas Hughes's Tom Brown's School Days became the Victorian equivalent of a best seller, he had enough money to try out an idea that had been haunting him for years. As the second son of a reasonably well-off family, he was painfully aware of the old English tradition of "primogeniture," which dictated that the family wealth be passed down to the first-born son. By 1880 Hughes decided to found a "colony" in North America where second- and third-born offspring of English gentry could live without the social stigma of having lost the birth race.

He bought a parcel of more than seventy-five thousand acres of remote wilderness on the Cumberland Plateau in East Tennessee and put the word out back in England that here he would build a society where everyone could be treated as equals. He named it Rugby, after the school he had attended as a boy, where the game was invented and where he had set his famous semi-autobiographical novel. Founded under the tenets of Christian Socialism, Rugby would be a place where young British aristocrats could learn to live as tradesmen and farmers.

To the bemused amazement of their backwoods Tennessee neighbors, 450 English gents and ladies built a tidy English-style town, including little Gothic Revival cottages, a church, a library, lawn-tennis courts, bowling greens, ornamental gardens, and bridle paths. The Rugbyites dressed up for afternoon tea and read British newspapers, held formal balls and musical evenings, staged costume plays, went on lavish picnics, and generally carried on like the upper-class Brits they were.

It wasn't easy going. The colony suffered from occasional outbreaks of typhoid, fires, and drought. The typhoid epidemic prevented the town from cashing in on the spa and resort boom that supported many other mountain communities. The town's tomato cannery and pottery businesses failed and administrators of the colony were accused of embezzling funds. Mostly, however, these folks weren't well equipped to handle adversity; and rather than fight to win the war against nature, most gave up and moved back to England to live out their lives as idle dilettantes.

Within a decade of its founding, Rugby began a slow slide into abandonment and ruin. By the time Thomas Hughes died in 1896, the colony was only a shell, to remain largely forgotten for the next seventy years. Depending on how you measure it, the "last British colony in the Americas" came to its bitter end either in 1909, when its last cooperative enterprises were sold to American businessmen, or in 1948, when its last original British inhabitant died.

Amazingly, a teenager rescued Rugby. In 1964, sixteen-year-old Brian Stagg began lobbying the state historical commission to save the twenty original buildings that remained from the colony, which were as they had always been, if a little run down. The town library of seven thousand nineteenth-century books still had every volume in its place, the founder's house still stood, and the guest house still had its original beds and furnishings.

As Stagg's efforts to restore the town generated enthusiasm and enticed new homeowners to recolonize the community, many of the new inhabitants discovered that they shared the buildings with the ghosts of people who had lived there long ago. Roslyn House was where Sophie Tyson was often seen weeping and pacing the halls in her

Victorian dress. Kingstone Lisle House, which founder Thomas Hughes had built for himself, has a snoring ghost who can always be heard in "another adjacent room," but never in the room where visitors happen to be. The old Hughes Free Library shelters the ghost of former librarian Eduard Bertz, a German described as the fussiest man around. Under his hawk-eyed gaze, only twelve books went missing. His faithful dog is also said to remain at the property, growling at any who approach the library after hours.

The most haunted structure of all is said to be the Newbury Guest House. On several occasions, guests staying in the bed in Room 2 upstairs have been awakened after midnight by the specter of a tall man leaning over them. Others have reported that the lights or fan were switched on or off, the heat readjusted, or the bedsheets tucked in, even though the door was locked from the inside. Cold spots and orbs have often been detected in that room. Most people think that it is probably the spirit of Charles Oldfield, who died in the bed in Room 2 in 1882, and may never have left. But others say that it's the bed in which Mr. Davis, who ran the guest house, slashed his wife's throat, then killed himself.

Today Rugby is booming once again, with about eighty inhabitants of the kind that still need to be fed several times a day, and at least an equal number who are getting by just fine on nothing at all.

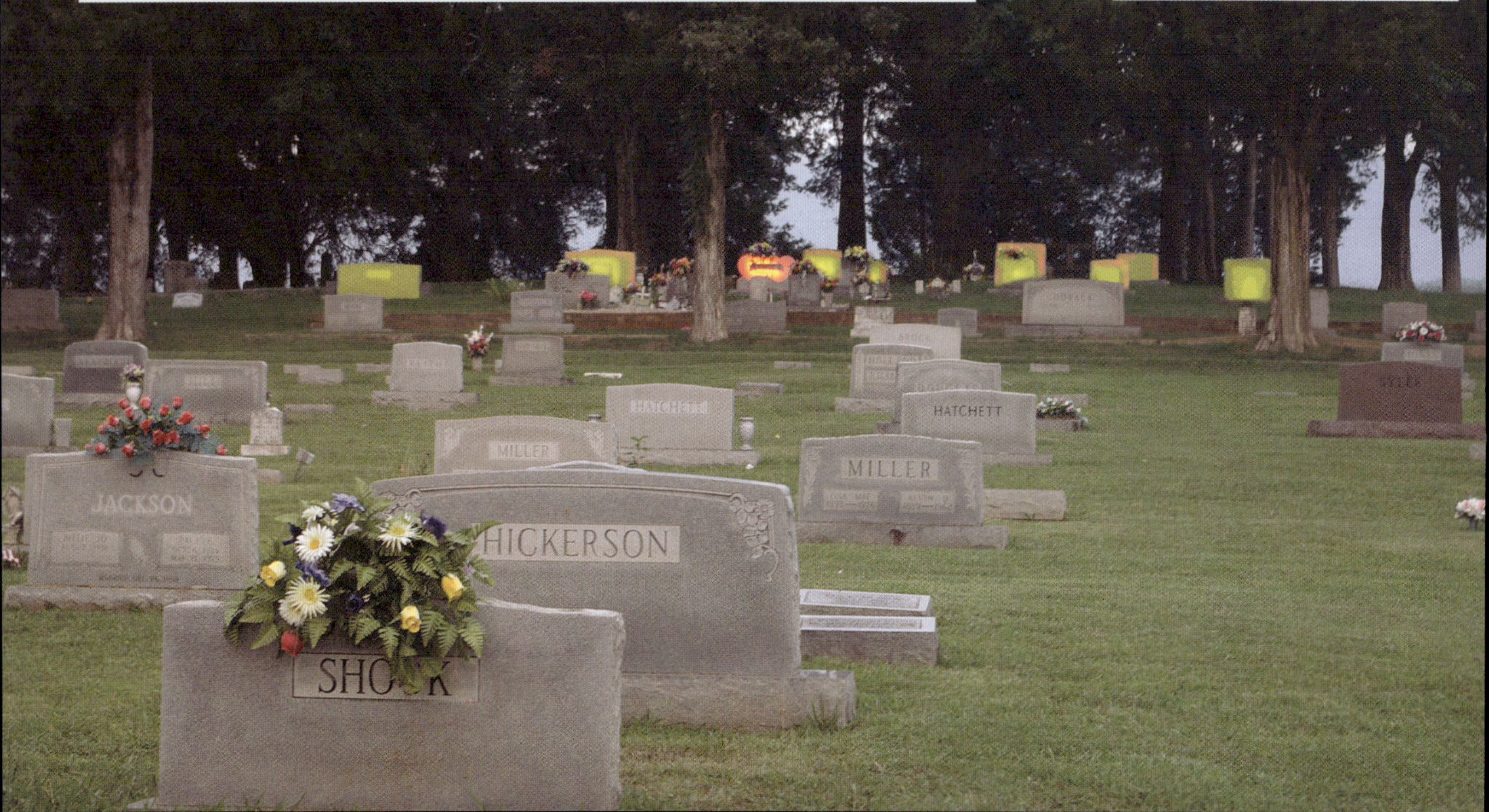
JACKSON
HICKERSON
MILLER
MILLER
HATCHETT
HATCHETT

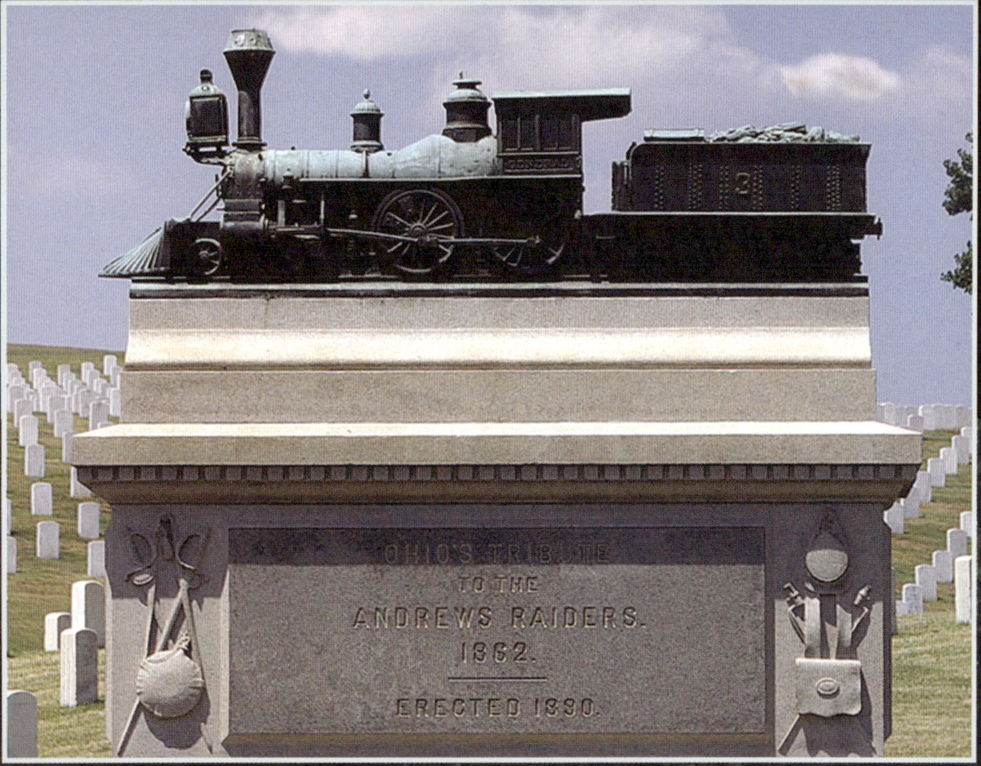
OHIO'S TRIBUTE
TO THE
ANDREWS RAIDERS.
1862.
ERECTED 1890.

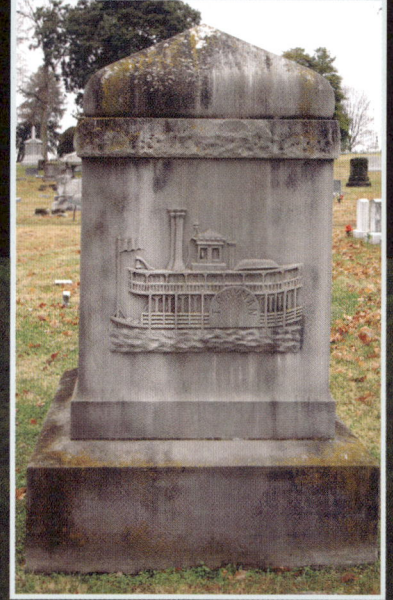

Cemetery Safari

The biggest, most emotion-stirring things in life are characterized by the number of ways people avoid talking about them. Love, politics, religion, death—every language on earth has loads of euphemisms for sidling up to each of these topics. Same goes for the subcategories under them that make us a little nervous, too.

Death must be one of the hardest things of all to talk about straight-on, judging from the hundreds of substitutes we've come up with to avoid saying the awful word itself, from pushing up daisies and six feet under, to passing away, flatlining, pulling the plug, answering the call, kicking the bucket, and heading to the great beyond.

There are even more catchy terms for cemeteries. They run the gamut from the dignified to the playful to the downright disgusting. Try hallowed ground, necropolis, eternal care facility, and city of the silent. Or granite garden, endsville, terminal terminal, adiós park, dirtnap dormitory, bone zone, spook nook, cadaverburg, stiff city. Then there's Frankenstein's workshop, field of screams, carcass motel, worm food farm, decay buffet. Even the word *cemetery* is actually a euphemism: It comes from the Greek word *koimeterion*, meaning "dormitory," a place to sleep.

Death and cemeteries are endlessly fun and fascinating to talk about. To see what we mean, take a look at some of the ways Tennesseans cope with "reaching the end of the line" by the things they've erected in their local marble orchards.

The Bleeding Mausoleum

On October 18, 1871, seven-year-old Nina Craigmiles went for a pleasure ride with her maternal grandfather, Dr. Gideon Thompson. They rode in the horse-drawn buggy he normally used for making housecalls, but their joyride ended in tragedy. No one knows exactly how it happened, but for some reason or other the buggy suddenly swerved and headed directly into the path of an oncoming train. Bystanders later said the accident was terrible to behold, with one of the horses killed, the elderly doctor thrown from the wreck, and young Nina crushed beneath the buggy and the flanges of the cowcatcher that projected from the front of the hissing steam locomotive.

The screams and moans of John Craigmiles and his wife, Adelia, were almost unbearable to anyone in earshot. For months afterward their pain was inconsolable, and only began to abate after her father resolved to commemorate his little girl with a church dedicated to St. Luke, the patron saint of doctors, on whose day she had died. Craigmiles was one of the wealthiest men in Cleveland (Tennessee, of course, not Ohio), and built one of the elegant churches in the state to contain his grief. Directly behind the church he commissioned a mausoleum to be built of the finest Italian marble and placed his beloved daughter's coffin within it.

Nina was not to remain alone in the mausoleum for long, though. The couple's second child, a boy, died so soon after his birth that there wasn't even time to name him. In 1899 John Craigmiles slipped on a frozen puddle and scraped open a wound that refused to heal. Infection set in, soon taking him, too. In 1928 Adelia Craigmiles was suddenly run over by a car and killed.

At some point during this string of tragedies, church caretakers noticed that something inexplicable was happening. Although the bright Carrara marble had been snowy white when the sepulcher was first erected, bloody-looking splotches of red and pink had begun to appear in several places—on the top steps, on the side of the mausoleum, and above the door. Even stranger was the fact that the reddish hue intensified each year on the anniversaries of the Craigmiles family members' deaths, particularly Nina's. Attempts to remove the recurrent stains by scrubbing, bleaching, or even replacing parts of the marble facade all failed. No matter what, the stains quickly returned.

Psychic disturbances were also reported in the area immediately next to the tomb. Small children—a young girl clutching a giggling baby boy—could sometimes be seen dashing around the side of the monument, but when chased, they would disappear.

We might never know why events happen the way they do, but whatever the reasons, the results (or effects) are there for anyone to see.

Come Back, Little Nannie!

Easily the most beloved tombstone in Clarksville's Greenwood Cemetery is the one marking the grave of Little Nannie Tyler, daughter of Judge Charles Tyler (and his wife, Mollie), who died of pneumonia in 1885 at age four. Her grief-stricken parents sent a photograph of their young girl to a sculpting studio in France, which carved a highly detailed marble portrait of the pensive-looking little girl in a dress of Victorian lace. She stood on the site for more than a century. In front of the statue was a glass box containing Nannie's favorite toys, which for many years visitors could see embedded in the ground. Eventually it was covered with a stone (now cracked, possibly by desperate antique-toy collectors). For a hundred years, anonymous individuals would place a new flower in the statue's hand every week. Then, in 1996, it was stolen. Descendants of the Tylers and fellow citizens of Clarksville helped the police put out an all points bulletin. Here we had the first "Amber Alert" issued for a missing child made of stone.

Nannie's statue turned up in an antiques shop in Boston. The embarrassed dealer had acquired it for more than $2,000 by what he had thought was a legal purchase; but as soon as he learned it was stolen, he personally returned it to Clarksville. It was reinstalled at Greenwood in a public ceremony.

Since then, Nannie's statue has been treated as a kind of shrine. Folks lightly touch the hem of Nannie's skirt to make a wish.

Little Lil

James Gaines, a Knoxvillian, betrothed Belle Porter of Ohio shortly before the Civil War broke out. The war, of course, separated them when their families wound up on opposite sides. James rose to the rank of colonel in the Confederate Army and lost an arm just before the conflict ended. Realizing that things might have changed since their engagement was announced, he offered to release Belle from their commitment if she were now turned off by his "mutilation and poverty." Belle married him anyway.

Lillien, the youngest of their three children, died of an illness at age seven, not long after they returned to Knoxville. Nowadays, both mourners of young children and star-crossed lovers often leave tokens of loss and affection in the little girl's lap.

Cave of the Patriarchs

There's a place in Memphis Memorial Park Cemetery that's well worth a visit. It's free, weird, and easy to find. Jutting above the carefully landscaped grounds of the modern-style ground-level necropolis at the intersection of Interstate 240 and Poplar Avenue is a tall spire of oddly shaped reddish concrete atop a small hill. The uphill side of the spire looks vaguely threatening and almost skull-like, while an entryway at its base leads down into a cool, damp cave lined with huge quartz crystals and real stalactites, and surrounded with strange niches filled with unusual statuary.

The spire and the grotto hidden beneath it are only a few of the features of a curious "attraction" located in the middle of the cemetery. A large pool of water, artificially dyed a Stygian blue-blackish hue, ripples around a handmade concrete fountain, accessed either by strolling through a giant concrete tree stump, or else by crossing a concrete bridge cleverly formed to look like the intertwined branches of a fallen tree. A fake rock outcropping across the way surrounds an artificial tomb—artificial because it's intended as a replica of the tomb of Abraham, the ancestral patriarch of both the Arabs and the Jews, who lived about four thousand years ago.

The site was the brainchild of cemetery developer Clovis Hinds, who founded and ran Memorial Park from 1924 until 1949. In the early 1930s he hired gifted Mexican concrete artist Dionicio Rodriguez and commissioned him to create the site. Rodriguez worked on it almost

singlehandedly. The statues were carved by local sculptors David Day and Marie Craig, but the rest of the scenery and handiwork is by Rodriguez.

Scattered throughout the rest of Memphis Memorial Park Cemetery are other isolated examples of Rodriguez's concrete artistry, all of it unusual and cleverly naturalistic. One rustic footbridge looks like the hollowed-out log of a giant California redwood fallen across a creek. A concrete bench, resembling a fallen tree, was described by Hinds as having been created ". . . centuries ago [when] a cloudburst caused a great wall of water to surge down this valley, followed by a violent wind storm that blew down this hickory tree, and when the tree struck another tree, the upper part was broken and thrown back with such force that the limbs were driven into the ground."

Some of the decor seems to belong more in a theme park than a cemetery. A stone and concrete chair called "Annie Laurie's Wishing Chair" purports to be a copy of a stone seat in front of a church in Glencairn, Scotland, that was "blessed by fairies" so that whoever sits in it will fall in love successfully. There are even more peculiar items here, and you'll simply have to visit to see them all.

Hinds kept Rodriguez in his hire until 1943, when the Mexican Michaelangelo of molded concrete suddenly vanished. Almost forty years later, other examples of his amazing work began to turn up in other cities, such as North Little Rock, Arkansas, and San Antonio, Texas.

But why did Rodriguez leave Memphis? A handful of surviving letters between Hinds and Rodriguez may offer some clues—like a Renaissance pope, it appears that Hinds tried to maintain control over "his" artist by keeping a tight rein on the purse strings, never quite completing the payments for one project before requesting another. Then, too, the men didn't always share the same vision for the work. —*Thanks to Barbara Bradley*

Has Elvis Left the Building?

Next time you're in Memphis and want to pay your respects to Elvis Presley but don't have time for the long lines or enough money for the admission ticket to Graceland, you can still visit his grave. His original grave, anyway.

On the afternoon of August 18, 1977, two days after his death, a hearse and seventeen white limousines made their way to Forest Hill Cemetery (1661 Elvis Presley Boulevard), where eight pallbearers hefted the nine-hundred-pound copper casket that held Elvis's body and slid it into place in a niche in the cemetery's main mausoleum. Elvis was wearing a white shirt and blue suit, his TCB (Taking Care of Business) ring, and a bracelet. A sealed cylinder with his vital information was included along with his corpse in case archaeologists thousands of years from now want to know which idols our civilization worshipped.

The King didn't rest here for long, however. Only ten days later, several men were arrested shortly after midnight near the gates of Forest Hill on a charge of attempted grave robbery. According to newspapers, the men were planning to blow a hole in the mausoleum, take Elvis's body, and hold it for ransom. Later the charge was reduced to criminal trespass for lack of evidence, when the "explosives" were revealed to be fireworks.

Nevertheless, the Presley family petitioned the Shelby County Board of Adjustment for a zoning variance to move Elvis's remains to Graceland, since the residential area wasn't zoned for human burial. On October 3, 1977, Elvis's final resting spot was moved to its current location near the Graceland swimming pool. His parents and grandmother are buried here as well.

Years later, one of the would-be grave robbers claimed that the whole thing had been a hoax, that he and his colleagues had been hired to pose a threat to the mausoleum to create a public outcry that would encourage the Board to grant the variance. An FBI agent backed up the claim.

A visit to the original tomb at Forest Hill remains free of charge. In 1999 Lisa Marie Presley said that she was sometimes bothered by the carnival-like atmosphere that continued to surround her father's gravesite more than twenty years after his death, and that she would prefer his remains be removed to a secret private location. One theory has it that Elvis was never moved at all, and that the attempted break-in at the mausoleum, the transfer, and the re-entombment were simply an elaborate sleight-of-hand act to make people *think* the body had been moved. They point to how ancient Egyptian pharaohs attempted to trick tomb robbers with false passages and fake sarcophagi in their pyramids.

Finally, there are those who think the death itself was a ruse. Sightings still occur from time to time, and Elvis *would* only be in his mid-seventies. They say the comeback concert will really be worth waiting for.

The Patsy Cline Memorial

It's been more than forty-five years since searchers came upon the awful scene of destruction off Mount Carmel Road, a few miles west of Camden, Benton County, that ended Patsy Cline's life.

By early 1963, Patsy Cline was at the peak of her career. She had topped the country music charts numerous times with a string of successful hits, made the crossover to pop music and challenged the top scores there as well. By her thirtieth birthday she was already ranked with Elvis, Johnny Cash, and other megastars. She had built her dream house in Nashville, found a man she loved (her second husband), begun a family, headlined in Las Vegas (the first female country singer to achieve this), and was *Billboard* magazine's "Favorite Female Country & Western Artist."

But she'd already begun to have premonitions about death. A near-fatal head-on collision had left her so scarred and weakened she could barely breathe deeply enough to record "Crazy," the song that's still recognized as her signature number. Even so, it soared to the top of the charts as Cline became the first country singer to perform in Carnegie Hall. By late 1962, however, she began telling her acquaintances that she didn't think she was going to live much longer, and began giving away cherished personal items to many of her close friends. She spontaneously wrote out a will on Delta Airlines stationery and made arrangements with her friend June Carter to have her children cared for, should anything dire happen to her.

Sadly, it didn't turn out to be paranoia. On March 3, 1963, she gave a benefit concert in Kansas City to raise money for the family of disc jockey "Cactus" Jack Call, who had been killed in a car wreck. Stormy weather delayed her return home to Nashville following the performance until the afternoon of March 5, when she boarded a four-seater Piper Comanche.

About seventy miles west of Nashville, the plane was caught in a turbulent squall with zero visibility. As near as could be reconstructed later, the pilot tried to land the small plane on a stretch of country road, accidentally clipped some trees, and nosedived into a small ravine called Fatty Bottom, three miles west of Camden. Everyone on board was killed instantly.

After an all-night search, Civil Defense member Bill Hollingsworth and his twenty-one-year-old son Jeners made the awful discovery. "We went down the steep hill and saw pieces of the plane scattered around a 300-foot area," Jeners later recalled in the *Camden Chronicle*. "There were parts of bodies on tree limbs and on the ground." A six-foot deep crater made by the plane's impact had begun filling with water.

A state patrolman soon arrived at the crash site, but was unable to keep away the swarm of gawkers and souvenir hunters that quickly invaded the scene. Eventually some three thousand people trampled the site, making off with pieces of the plane, bottles of Cline's hairspray, her cigarette lighter, shoes and lingerie, and the other passengers' belongings. Years later, many of these items were donated to the Country Music Hall of Fame collection (including Patsy Cline's watch, stopped at 6:27 P.M., the exact time of the crash). Parts of the plane and other items from the crash site still occasionally turn up on online auction pages.

A huge boulder at the bottom of the ravine now fills the crater where the plane crashed. Behind it and to the left is a makeshift shrine marking the spot where most of Cline's remains were discovered.

Elmwood—City of the Dead

You'll have to go through a slightly dicey part of Memphis and turn off Boss Crump Boulevard and head south on Dudley Street to get to Elmwood cemetery. Yes, it looks as if the neutron bomb has been tested there, but then suddenly it's like that scene in *The Wizard of Oz* when the movie goes from black and white to color. There are acres of rolling manicured grounds at Elmwood, founded in 1852 as part of a new trend in cemetery design: the necropolis. Not only was parking the dead well away from the living considered a whole lot healthier in a time periodically plagued by yellow fever, cholera, and other epidemics, but it also played into the Victorians' fascination with melancholy. It's a peculiar fact that Victorian Americans felt most alive whenever they were contemplating death. People back then liked nothing better than to take a long carriage ride out to the cemetery for an afternoon of picnicking, wandering around, and basking in the delightfully depressive aspect of it all. Cemeteries also functioned as outdoor sculpture gardens. The competitive streak that today fuels lavish landscaping wars meant that, back then, families often vied with one another to have the grandest, most interesting, or most stylish tombstones for their relatives.

As a result, Elmwood is crammed with both beautiful and peculiar stuff to look at, yet it's well off the beaten track between Graceland and Beale. If you like weird, though, we can recommend it.

No Man's Land

One big section of Elmwood Cemetery was set aside as no-man's-land for all the deaths caused by three yellow fever epidemics that decimated Memphis in the 1870s. According to the marker, "Elmwood was required to handle over fifty burials a day. Due to the sickness and labor shortages, many bodies were piled above ground, awaiting burial. Persons from all levels of society were interred in trenches in an area formerly reserved for paupers and unknowns." In 1878 alone, about 88 percent of the people in the city were struck by the fever, and nearly a quarter of those stricken with the disease died.

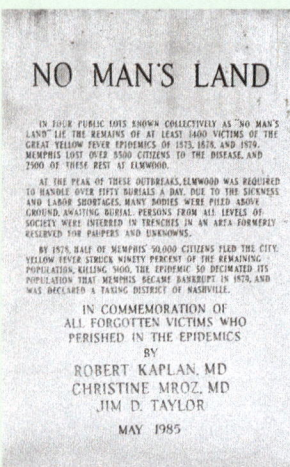

Who Knows, Who Cares

One strange grave marker in Elmwood reads almost like a novel in haiku form. All we know about it is that (according to the county census for that year) Dorothy Ann Whitaker was twenty-one in 1930, so she must have been born in 1907. The daughter of James F. and Lottie M. Whitaker, she had a brother named Gus. But what Dorothy Ann did to deserve her tombstone is a mystery.

The Last Lap

In a little out-of-the-way cemetery near Asbury, in Knox County, there is a tombstone marking the resting place of Pete Kreis. It replicates in miniature the old Indianapolis Motor Speedway as it was in the early 1930s. On May 25, 1934, both Kreis and his riding mechanic Robert Hahn were killed during a practice race when Kreis's car spun out of control on turn one, leapt the embankment at 90 miles per hour, slid along the top of the retaining wall, then fell off and crashed into a tree fifteen feet below the other side. (The car was torn in half.) It's been called one of the strangest wrecks in Indy history. Coincidentally the same tree had been hit two years before, in a crash that killed Harry Cox.

Like most racers in his day, the thirty-four-year-old Kreis wasn't a full-time professional driver. He'd take time off from his regular job as a railroad construction contractor to race in the Indy 500 as often as he could. Had he survived the practice run, 1934 would have been his sixth Indy race.

Kreis's racing career was marked by bad luck. After finishing eighth in his first race in 1925, he returned the following year only to fall sick shortly before the start. His friend Frank Lockhart took his place and, lo and behold, won the race. Kreis never made it to the top ten again. Most of his races ended in various mechanical failures. He was knocked out of the race in 1932 when he crashed in the same turn that would take his life two years later.

Seth Klein, who had also started in the fatal 1934 race, attributed Kreis's string of losses to his overeager driving style. "He had had a lot of hard luck, because he would rather break a car in fast company than lag behind."

The 11,000-pound marble tombstone in Asbury Cemetery replicates the Indy track as it was in its early years, when it was paved with 3.2 million bricks. As cars improved and got faster each year, the brick surface became increasingly dangerous and was replaced by tarmac. Today only a three-foot-wide strip of brick paving remains to mark the start/finish line, but the track is still fondly called the Brickyard.

Giant Among Men

Soldiers' graves are often marked with cannonballs or a helmet on an upended rifle, librarians are buried beneath carved granite books, and firemen memorialized with marble fire hydrants. On occasion, a grave marker is not just a symbol but a functional item as well.

Mills Darden was born in North Carolina in 1799. He probably had a pituitary gland malfunction; the man never stopped growing. He weighed an estimated three hundred pounds by his tenth birthday, and by the time he died, he stood just short of eight feet tall and weighed more than a thousand pounds.

Darden wasn't a porch potato. His strength was legendary and entirely real. Contemporaries loved to tell about the time he lifted a loaded wagon out of a mud hole, or when he hefted a half-ton hogshead of tobacco and set it upright in an oxcart. To impress his in-laws at a family reunion, he lifted an entire table with ten people sitting on it by crawling under the table and standing up.

According to historian Daniel Barefoot, Darden was a mighty eater at those reunions, too. He is said to have eaten eleven watermelons in one afternoon. His typical breakfast consisted of "several dozen buttered biscuits, eighteen eggs, two pounds of bacon, and at least two quarts of coffee." Since no horse or carriage could carry him, Darden walked everywhere or sat in the back of an oxcart while someone else drove.

Darden ran a tavern, managed a hotel, and also farmed in Henderson County. He raised eleven children (by two wives), all of them of normal size. Sadly, his out-of-control growth finally proved his undoing on January 23, 1857, when his throat caved in under the weight of his own neck flesh and he suffocated to death. It took more than five hundred board feet of lumber to construct his coffin, and seventeen men to carry it to the gravesite, memorialized by a picnic table.

To visit the Mills Darden memorial picnic table, follow Highway 200 (Life Road) several miles southwest of Lexington and then turn northwest at Chapel Hill on Darden Cemetery Road. The overgrown graveyard is about 1.5 miles on the right (east) side, just before the creek.

No Hope Hill

At the very back of the old graveyard in Hope Hill Cemetery, Gibson County, is a tiny dollhouse-like structure. If you get down on your hands and knees and peer inside it, you'll discover a few abandoned toys; a musty Bible; perhaps some crayons, photos, or flowers; and a tombstone for Dorothy Marie Harvey, who died in 1931 at the tender age of five. According to a gruesome story that grew up about the place over the years, the little girl was brutally raped and then murdered by a deranged member of her own family (many claimed it was her uncle). In his grief, her father erected the little playhouse as a symbol of protection.

Other explanations insist that the girl was killed by a falling piano mishandled by an inept house mover, or by falling off a pony while being photographed, or, according to the West Tennessee Ghost Hunters and local historians, a severe case of measles. Her own original playhouse (which may actually have been built by her maligned uncle) occupied the gravesite for many years until it rotted away. They say members of the community replaced the dollhouse out of a desire to maintain a cemetery tradition. Whatever the original cause of young Dorothy Marie's demise, nearly everyone says that something strange is going on there now.

Visitors report seeing lights glowing from inside the little structure, hearing the sounds of children's laughter when they turn their back on it, or seeing a small girl's face either behind the glass or in the reflections (a faint childlike image often shows up on photos, too). A shadowy figure of a man is said to appear in the graveyard with some frequency. Since it doesn't appear to be threatening, perhaps it is a protective figure.

Be forewarned also that there are two Hope Hill Cemeteries, about half a mile apart. Both are found on Hope Hill Cemetery Road a few miles northeast of Medina in Gibson County, but one (an old slave cemetery) is located on a rough road through the woods, while the other (with the "Dollhouse Grave") is relatively easy to get to.

Neither is open after dark, and since there have been reports of locals threatening visitors with deadly force, be sure to go only during daylight hours with a trusted friend and behave appropriately.

Singing Slaves at the "Other" Hope Hill

Just down the road from the dollhouse cemetery is an old slave cemetery. Back in the 1800s some slaves were hanged there. My friends and I went down there one night and we could hear the slaves singing very faintly.
—*thefreak9010, West Tennessee Ghost Hunters*

The Great Locomotive Chase

Almost all the tombstones in the Chattanooga National Cemetery are nearly identical and perfectly aligned, but eight of them curve around a monument topped by a scaled-down bronze locomotive.

The real-life train had been hijacked by the men buried here. The death dates are the same because they were hanged on the same afternoon. And yet they were also the very first recipients of the United States' highest military award, the Medal of Honor. Their story is exciting enough that several movies (including one by Walt Disney) have been based on it.

During the Civil War "the General" was a prized piece of Confederate railroad equipment. But even more important to the South's war-making abilities was the network of rails that shipped soldiers quickly from one battlefront to another. Because of this, a civilian spy for the Union, Kentuckian James J. Andrews, concocted a daring plan to interrupt Confederate rail traffic by destroying the tracks between Atlanta and Chattanooga. While the General paused in what is now Kennesaw, Georgia, to refuel and allow passengers to breakfast, Andrews and his cohorts separated all the passenger cars, hijacked the locomotive, and clipped telegraph lines as the Confederates chased after them with all haste.

A few miles north of Ringgold, Georgia, the General, low on fuel and water, blew a valve and lost steam power. The Union raiders jumped off and ran into the nearby woods but a massive manhunt resulted in their quick capture, trials, and death sentences.

Andrews was hanged on June 7, 1862, in a hasty affair, conducted on a scaffold that was too low to the ground. He died slowly by strangulation. The other members of "Andrews Raiders" were tried in a military court-martial in Knoxville, and seven of them were hanged in Atlanta.

Six members of the group were later the first American soldiers to win the Medal of Honor. But because Andrews and one other man were civilians, they didn't qualify for the award no matter how instrumental they'd been in the attempt to cripple the Confederates. Of the others who participated in the raid, eight escaped and made their way back to the North, and another six became prisoners of war who were eventually traded for Confederate POWs.

The remains of the hanged men were exhumed from their unmarked mass grave and moved to the Chattanooga National Cemetery a number of years after the end of the Civil War.

Bright Shining Souls

The old Cowan Cemetery at the end of South Willow Street in Cowan, Franklin County, dates back to 1774, when Hugh and William Montgomery buried the first members of their extended family on a small hill at the northeast corner of the community. The city added more land in 1940. There's a legend that those original graves on the rise shine and glow as twilight falls.

We pulled into the graveyard at dusk and found that it really does happen, except there's a pretty straightforward reason for it. The tombstones face west, so they reflect the setting sun if you enter the graveyard at the right time.

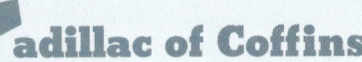

Cadillac of Coffins

One of the treasures of the Museum of Appalachia in Norris is a patented Fisk Metallic Burial Case that came from the Berry Funeral Home in Knoxville. The Fisk coffin, made in the mid-nineteenth century, was form-fitting like the age-old mummy cases of Egypt. According to Fred Berry Jr., such cases preserve corpses better than modern caskets. However, the moment the cases are opened and the body is exposed to the air, it decomposes completely. Best to leave them be.

A Fisk was the "Cadillac of coffins" and many well-known people of the day vouched for them. The Fisk company secured product endorsements from folks like Henry Clay, Daniel Webster, Jefferson Davis, and John C. Calhoun—who ended up buried in one himself.

By the way, there is no technical difference between a casket and a coffin. In the 1960s the funeral industry began using the word *casket* to overcome customers' squeamishness with the word *coffin*.

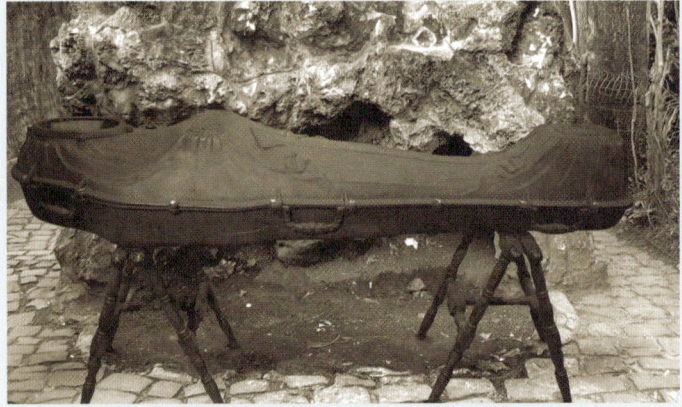

Beautiful Jim Key

A lone gravesite west of the junction of Himesville Road and Singleton Road (Highway 130) a few miles south of Shelbyville, Bedford County, holds the remains of four individuals: two humans, a dog, and a horse. The horse, equine prodigy Beautiful Jim Key, was a popular entertainer.

No wonder crowds were drawn to him. He could compete in spelling bees, read, sort mail, use a specially adapted cash register to make change, make phone calls, discuss politics, and recite biblical passages entirely from memory. Using numbered and lettered blocks he could add, subtract, and tell time, and by holding a special extended pencil in this mouth he could write intelligible sentences and sign his own name.

Jim was trained by "Dr." William Key, a former slave born in 1833. Bill Key grew up on a farm close to the gravesite, where as a very young boy his phenomenal ability to communicate with animals was recognized. By 1889, when Doc Key found the scraggly, part-crippled colt that he named Jim (after a local drunken stumblebum), he'd been earning a living as a horse whisperer and self-taught veterinarian for more than fifty years. William Key's life story is amazing in its own right—among other things, he had been a double agent during the Civil War, won his freedom in a poker game, took over the farm where he'd previously been a slave and supported his former masters for the rest of their lives, married four times; and invented Keystone Liniment and used its profits to fund his ventures in hotels, racetracks, and restaurants. But it was as the trainer of the little wobbly colt that he gained lasting fame.

Taking the horse with him on travels with his Keystone Medicine Show, Doc Key applied his well-honed skills in training animals "only with kindness, never force or punishment." In 1897 at the Tennessee Centennial Exposition in Nashville, President William McKinley saw Jim and Key perform. McKinley later said that this was not only the most amazing thing he'd seen at the exposition, but among the most astounding phenomena he'd ever seen, period. The notoriety this generated quickly vaulted Jim into stardom and his trainer and their newfound partner, Albert Rogers, into riches. They moved Jim to an estate in New Jersey.

Jim's talents and abilities may have put him in the limelight, but it was his good works that kept him there. He performed repeatedly on behalf of the Humane Society and the Society for the Prevention of Cruelty to Animals. He also broke down color barriers decades before Jesse Owens and Jackie Robinson, since wherever Jim went, his African American trainer went as well, including to command performances for President Teddy Roosevelt. Doc and Jim Key were among the most celebrated acts in the world at the turn of the last century, performing for millions. In the days before TV, this was an amazing accomplishment.

Plagued through his life with joint pains, Beautiful Jim was seventeen when he retired in 1906 to Shelbyville. Dr. William Key died in 1909 at age seventy-six, and Beautiful Jim and his dog-friend Monk both died in 1912. The three of them, together with promoter Albert Rogers, share the grave south of town. —*Thanks to Mim Eichler Rivas*

Mount Olivet Cemetery

Founded in 1856, Mount Olivet Cemetery was named for the Mount of Olives to the east of Jerusalem, where Jesus Christ is traditionally believed to have ascended into heaven. A number of Nashville's prominent politicians and civic leaders are buried here.

Many of them seem to have taken to pacing and wandering around the cemetery grounds, for Mount Olivet is regarded as one of the more paranormally active sites in the city. Shadowy figures that some call "black abbeys" are often spotted flitting from one mausoleum to the next, as if the social dalliances and adventures of passion that occupied most of them in life were too exciting to forgo in death. Others seem to be plain old ghosts, like the one of Tom Ryman, so often seen swaggering between his grave and the crest of the hill.

Ryman's Reason

The relatively modest stone that marks the grave of Capt. Thomas G. Ryman in Mount Olivet Cemetery does what many larger memorials often fail to do, which is to capture some of the true essence of the person buried beneath it. As a young boy in Chattanooga, Ryman was a fisherman on the Tennessee River. Later he owned and ran steam-powered packets that plied a route on the Cumberland River from Evansville, Indiana, to Burnside, Kentucky. Nashville was roughly at the halfway point on the seven-hundred-mile circuit, so it was the natural place to settle down when he had to.

In 1885 Ryman experienced a religious conversion during a tent revival led by Rev. Sam Jones. Following his "anointment with the Holy Spirit," Ryman immediately shut down the saloon he owned, decreed that no liquor would be allowed on any of his riverboats, and began construction on the Union Gospel Tabernacle, a huge church in downtown Nashville that opened in 1892. When he died two years later, the building was renamed the Ryman Auditorium at Reverend Jones's suggestion. The building is famous now for being the home of the Grand Ole Opry from 1943 to 1974, and still operates as a major music and entertainment venue. Ryman was so proud of the building, they say, that his ghost still appears in its balconies from time to time.

The Last Laugh

Any Frenchman would immediately recognize Vernon K. Stevenson's crypt, for it is an exact replica of the most famous grave in France, that of Napoleon Bonaparte. As president of the Nashville and Chattanooga Railroad, Stevenson became the first really major railroad magnate in the state.

Stevenson fell out of favor with his fellow Nashvillians during the Civil War, when he put a greater priority on getting his own personal possessions out of the city instead of using his railroads to send much-needed supplies to Confederate forces. His war profiteering in international trade during the war sullied his reputation further, so when the war was over he moved his home and businesses to New York City.

According to Stevenson's obituary in the *New York Times* on October 18, 1884, Napoleon III had been one of the major investors in the Southern Pacific Railroad and had paid Stevenson the princely sum of $100,000 in gold to accept the job of running it, with an annual salary of $35,000 (roughly $600,000 in today's money). What better way to perpetuate the memory of such a sweetheart deal and thank his grand benefactor at the same time, than to model his tomb after the original Bonaparte?

Pyramid Scheme

Iron and explosives gave Maj. E. C. Lewis his toehold on industry, which he later expanded to include interests in textile mills, coal, newspapers, and the Nashville, Chattanooga and St. Louis Railway. When it came time to tap someone to head up the Tennessee Centennial and International Exposition of 1897, Lewis was the obvious choice. Although the fair was a year late opening (it was supposed to mark the hundredth anniversary of Tennessee statehood in 1796), it was worth waiting for. Visitors got their first good look at a working x-ray display, telephones, automatic brick-making machines, electric lights, steam-powered cotton presses, dynamos, gasoline-powered internal-combustion engines, and other wonders of the burgeoning modern age.

The past was celebrated as well. Attendees could explore a real Dutch windmill from Holland, see displays of Civil War artifacts, and enter an exact replica of the Parthenon or a scaled-down replica of an Egyptian pyramid or an exact replica of the Parthenon (see both in Roadside Oddities).

When Lewis died in 1917, his remains were placed inside a scale replica of the Great Pyramid of Cheops at Giza. A bronze arrow embedded in the walkway between the two sphinxes flanking the entry points toward true north, to show that its incline angles and celestial orientation are an exact duplicate of the original built for King Khufu some 4570 years ago. The Lewis pyramid is near the entrance of Nashville's Mount Olivet Cemetery.

The *problem with places that have* long been empty is that they are so *not* empty. A place with people still living or working in it is empty in all the rooms where they momentarily happen not to be—nothing is emptier, after all, than a noisy classroom right after the last bell has rung and the kids have run to catch their bus, or a stage after the applause has died down and the theater has emptied, or a disheveled room after the last wild party guest has finally gone home. It's as if the living presence of all those people had displaced everything else, and the moment they're gone there's only the void left where they had been. Towns where the last inhabitants moved away the day before, factories that have just closed for the last time, houses just after the moving vans have pulled away—those places are truly empty.

But such emptiness doesn't last. Nature, as the old saying goes, abhors a vacuum, and when it comes to abandoned places, once their former occupants have left for good, all kinds of things slowly begin to creep back in to fill up the emptiness. Some of them are visible, like the spiders that begin making cobwebs in the corners, the vines that start sending tendrils under the window sashes or prying up through the weather-boards, or the pigeons making nests under the eaves—and some are invisible, like the gathering memories and spirits that slowly reestablish themselves in any place that stays abandoned for long. In time, all abandoned places that aren't torn down are reoccupied, with new occupants (who are shadows of the old occupants), but that are here for the long haul.

Their stories are told in bits and pieces—literally. A chipped plate, a three-legged chair, an old postcard or photo that had fallen behind a shelf, a scribbled crayon drawing on a wall—each item is a message from the past, if only we take time to read them. Before, that is, the time comes for each of us to leave our own messages for those who will follow.

Accursed Carousel

Its artificial ponds are now thick with green scum, and the cracks in the meandering paths and sidewalks are sprouting weeds faster than any maintenance workers with herbicides could stop them. Holes in the roof are letting rain drip down on the grimy and defunct games in the old video arcade, and it's been so long since any of the rusting rides have stirred that vines have begun growing up through their lifts and bearings. The Round Up is seized up and peeling, and the Spider looks mummified in its lair. As Rod Serling of *Twilight Zone* fame understood, almost nothing feels quite as derelict as an empty amusement park.

It's the silence, as if a pall has fallen over a place that was once filled with calliope music, the ratcheting of roller coasters being pulled to the top of the first big drop, the delightfully terrified screams that followed, mixed with the surprised cries of children whipped about on the Scrambler or feeling a goat's tongue lick their hands in the petting zoo. Missing all that, the silent emptiness of such a place becomes all the more obvious.

Not so long ago, Libertyland was one of Memphis's favorite diversions. The city's only amusement park, it lasted for exactly thirty years—long enough, some say, for a few legends to have taken root there, and possibly even a curse or two. Two of these stories, as it turns out, are true.

The park first opened in 1976, and rode the bicentennial year wave of nostalgia for history-is-fun repackaging of the American past. Independence Hall was there, but only in one-fourth scale, like an overgrown dollhouse. The Revolution had been transformed into a loop-the-loop roller coaster. The Casey Jones train plied a circular route around the park. Twain's Twister was a spinning ride, apparently named that only because the Mississippi flows on the other side of downtown and they needed something alliterative to go with *twister*. Gazebos, antique cars, porcelain doll displays, and red, white, and blue painted features throughout—it was as if all that was worth remembering about American history ended sometime around the beginning of the World War I.

Two of the most famous attractions were also the oldest, actual relics of that same lost past. Indeed, Libertyland had been built around them. Dating back to 1912, the Zippin Pippin is the second-oldest roller coaster in the country, and one of the few wooden coasters still standing in the Western Hemisphere. For a minute and a half, its riders were treated to a seventy-foot plunge and more than five Gs of force as the rickety old trestles wobbled and squealed under the stress.

The Pippin was Elvis's favorite ride—so much so that he would sometimes rent the entire amusement park so that he and his friends could ride it non-stop without being constantly hassled by fans. The King's last public appearance, in fact, was on the day he rented Libertyland for the last time. On August 8, 1977, Elvis and about ten acquaintances remained in the park after hours from 1:15 A.M. until 7 A.M. Wearing a blue jumpsuit with a black leather belt outfitted with a huge buckle encrusted with turquoise jewels and gold chains, Elvis remained on the roller coaster for nearly two hours that night. At one point his heavy buckle flew off into the darkness. It was found the following day and returned, but many of his fans later saw it as an omen. Almost exactly a week later, he was found unconscious in his suite at Graceland and pronounced dead early the following morning. Like the buckle, his soul had apparently spun off into the darkness under the centrifugal force of his chaotic life.

The Grand Carousel was even more well known than the Zippin Pippin. Built in 1909 by William H. Dentzel of the famous Gustav Dentzel Carousel Company of Germantown, Pennsylvania, it had been a major Memphis attraction since its arrival in 1923. One of the largest and most ornate—yes, grandest—carousels in the country, the Memphis Dentzel had thirty-two jumping horses, sixteen standing horses, and two chariots. (By the way, the traditional technical difference between a carousel and a merry-go-round is that carousels have *only* horses or horse-drawn vehicles, whereas merry-go-rounds may feature other species or kinds of transportation.)

For years after Libertyland was built up around it, the Grand Carousel was believed to be haunted. Many visitors thought this only had to do with how its aura of authenticity set it eerily apart from all the other rides except the Pippin, and how the leering jesters and angels on its rounding boards had just enough hand-carved individuality to seem almost spookily real, but people who worked at the park knew better.

On August 2, 1976, not long after Libertyland first opened, a seventeen-year-old named Mike Crockett was put in charge of running the huge old ride as his first summer job. A child mounted on one of the horses let go of a balloon just as the carousel began to move. It drifted into the gears and belts at the center of the machine. When the boy began to cry, Crockett stopped the ride and clambered into the inner workings to retrieve his prize. Suddenly the machine started up on its own, dragging Crockett into the big gears and crushing him to death.

Although the park did everything it could to suppress news of the tragedy (Crockett's name wasn't revealed until 2007) rumors that the machine was possessed persisted for the life of the park. Workers who stayed after closing time to clean and service the rides often spoke of hearing cries and groans from the center of the massive carousel and felt as if the eyes of the jesters were staring at them. Dark shapes were seen flitting in the mirrors that adorned the fancy ornamentation. Old hands were always careful to warn new hires of the dangers of getting within range of the machine's deadly grasp, while even longer-term employees had a foreboding sense that the park would ultimately be doomed to failure as long as the resentful spirits of the old rides were surrounded by the newer, less demanding attractions.

For now, neither the carousel nor the roller coaster are likely to have a chance to strike again. Libertyland closed at the end of the 2005 season, the Zippin Pippin was sold, and in October 2009, the Grand Carousel was dismantled and put into storage. The future of both old rides—both of them now listed on the National Register of Historic Places—remains uncertain. But anyone familiar with legends like the Mummy's Curse knows that haunting spirits can be very patient. Time is always on their side.

Dropping Acid in the Tennessee Badlands

Until recently, Tennessee could boast the largest desert east of the Mississippi. As far as the eye could see, not a sprig of greenery grew, and not a bird or mammal interrupted the landscape with signs of life. Clouds of reddish dust whipped up every time the wind blew, and a hellish acrid smell like fire and brimstone permeated the air. The fact that it was all manmade only added to the strangeness of the scene. The thirty-two thousand acres that made up the Copper Basin were one of America's first major demonstrations of the polluting power of acid smoke and rain.

Copper was discovered near Ducktown, Tennessee, in 1843, by a prospector who presumably was looking for gold. Copper was almost as good as gold, though, because it was so much more generally useful, for making everything from kitchen wares and roofing shingles to firearms and moonshine stills. Before long, mule trains began hauling the rich ore from mines around Ducktown down to Dalton, Georgia, where it could be loaded onto freight trains bound for smelters in Boston that would turn it into pure copper.

Although the railroads eventually reached the mines around Ducktown, by the 1880s it became obvious that smelting the raw ore locally would be cost-efficient. Since there was plenty of timber and no population centers nearby, a process called "open roast" smelting was used. Starting in 1891, the ore would be layered with heaps of wood and the whole giant pile set on fire to melt the copper directly out of the rock. But Polk County copper ore had a high sulfur content, so the burning piles of ore instantly created clouds of sulfuric acid fumes, which soon

killed every plant and animal for many miles around. The miners burning the ore could run around and stand upwind of the fires to avoid inhaling so much of the acid, but the trees and wildlife and their nonmining neighbors couldn't avoid it.

As a result, the locals mounted one of the first major environmental lawsuits. By 1906, the Supreme Court had sided with the agriculturalists, but by then the environmental damage was already done. Ducktown, Copperhill, and the surrounding area looked as desolate as the surface of Mars, accented by gaping sinkholes such as that created from the Burra Burra Mine. At three thousand feet deep, Burra Burra was once one of the deepest vertical shafts in the country.

Today, more than a century later, and after some 16 million trees have been replanted, the "Tennessee Badlands" have dwindled to only a fraction of their former size, most of it in large tailings ponds that have solidified into hard-packed clay.

The Isabella Mine nearby, now hidden behind gates marked with big NO TRESPASSING signs, was almost as big, and is said to be haunted. Before the gates and fences were put up, paranormal researchers often reported hearing what were described as the anguished cries of miners wafting up from bottom of the huge pit. These pitiful spirits were said to have died in the 1890s when an air pump broke down.

Nowadays both the Burra Burra and Isabella mines are filled with liquid, so any paranormal studies from here on out will likely require the use of scuba gear. Just one word of advice, though: Check to make sure the liquid is water. You won't want to dissolve from the acid, even in the name of research.

Got Milk?

Got about seven thousand gallons, in fact?

If there's still anything in that rusty old "bottle" sitting atop the abandoned building at Beechwood and Bellvue in Memphis, any remaining milk would have soured by now, since the building's been defunct since 1983. That's when Midwest Dairies, the last in a long series of dairy companies to occupy the site, moved out.

Since then it has been left vacant, turning slowly into an overgrown ruin known only for the curdling I-screams emanating from urban explorers udderly horrified to come face-to-face with white-mustachioed phantoms drifting among its old pipes and vats. In this case it's probably butter to stay at home, we think.

Tenn State Pen

Of all the abandoned buildings in Tennessee, the scariest of all is almost certainly the state prison, whose residents did everything imaginable to get out of it for ninety-four years. The old Tennessee State Prison may be abandoned, but it is still considered verboten to trespassers. Anyone caught wandering around it without permission may be invited to spend some quality time in one of the several other facilities run by the Department of Corrections.

The fortresslike prison at the end of Bomar Boulevard in northwest Nashville opened on February 12, 1898. Even though it may bring to mind Count Dracula's castle or the entrance to Auschwitz, in its day it was touted as the latest thing in modern prison architecture. It was built with no wood, which was heralded as making escapes considerably more difficult, but it also cut down on vermin and reduced the chances of fire. The cellblocks still had fire hoses, but they were used mainly for flushing out cells, subduing berserk inmates, or quelling riots. Newspaper articles proudly ticked off the new prison's other new amenities, including "a kitchen equipped with 1st-class steam equipment, equivalent to luxury hotels," a large basement that housed the "shower baths and a large heated swimming pool," its newfangled air-conditioning system (cooled by evaporating water as it trickled through burlap), and the institution's "adjustable windows, making it the most modern, up-to-date prison in the country."

The reporters who wrote such glowing articles would undoubtedly have given them a somewhat different spin if they'd ever had to spend a few days trapped in the prison they seemed so awed and delighted by. The "heated pool"—actually a large bath—was closed within days of the prison's opening after inmates found they could drown their rivals in it. Meanwhile the evaporation system cooled air only when outdoor humidity was very low, which is almost never the case during a Nashville summer. Instead, most of the time it only made the cells even hotter and steamier. The marvelous new adjustable windows soon rusted in the open position, which meant that the top cells in the crowded cellblocks averaged 10°F in winter and 120°F in summer. Those windows were refitted with glass bricks, which not only blocked both air circulation and any view of the world beyond the walls, but were just as unforgiving for maintaining normal temperatures.

Overcrowding was by far the biggest problem. Seven hundred feet wide and fifty feet high, the prison was built to house a maximum of eight hundred inmates in single-occupancy cells, but on the day it opened, more than fourteen hundred prisoners were hauled to the site. The prison often held up to twice that number in six-by-eight-foot cells.

Old Sparky, the state's electric chair (built in 1913), was housed in a special chamber retrofitted with a fume hood after official witnesses to the first several executions ran out of the room gasping and gagging at the horrible smell of burning flesh. "It boils the blood," former warden Vince Thompson once explained, "and just cooks 'em from the inside out." The last person to die in the arms of Old Sparky was William Tines in 1960. (He was death number 134.) The current electric chair, just a few miles away at the Riverbend Maximum Security Institution, was built from wood salvaged from both the old chair and the original state gallows. It was most recently used to execute Daryl Keith Holden on September 12, 2007.

The old state prison was finally closed in 1992, after federal courts decided that keeping even hardened criminals in such a hellhole ran afoul of the U.S. Constitution's restrictions against "cruel and unusual punishment." Nowadays the rusting and peeling cellblocks provide only temporary quarters to folks like Tom Hanks and Robert Redford. The tiers of iron cages rattle and echo to the sounds of directors yelling "Action!" and "Cut!" as they try to tap into the authentically spooky horror of the place to make films like *The Green Mile*, *Against the Wall*, *Furnace*, *The Walls*, and *The Last Castle*.

Although the Department of Corrections receives occasional revenue from renting the grim facility as a realistically gruesome set, the main reason they haven't torn it down yet is the sheer cost of doing so. With reinforced stone and concrete walls three feet thick and built to withstand any efforts to knock them down, the prison promises to remain a magnificently monstrous ruin for many years to come.

Western State Hospital

You almost never see real-life burglars dressed the way they are inevitably shown in cartoons, faces covered in little black bandannas with eyeholes. Bankers and politicians never lug around sacks of coins, spies rarely wear trench coats anymore, and most real-life heroes don't look like handsome Hollywood movie stars. So it's almost a relief whenever something really looks the way it does in movies. Western State Hospital in Bolivar is a creepy mental institution that looks exactly the way you'd imagine a creepy lunatic asylum should look. There are tall, pointed turrets and towers, bars on the windows and fences around abandoned outlying buildings, certain entire floors shuttered and boarded over, and guards in white trucks patrolling the grounds.

Western State was the last big insane asylum of its type built in Tennessee. Constructed in 1885 to provide humane treatment for, at most, 300 patients, by the 1950s it had become a crowded warehouse of the insane with thousands of people who gradually declined into madness by the "therapies" offered here. Today, the patient population is back down to 260, tended by a staff of 650, a much better ratio, though the place still looks as grim as ever.

Western State, along with mental institutions built through the country in the late nineteenth century, was constructed according to a scheme called the Kirkbride Plan, which intended to provide safe, humane quarters for the insane. Quaker reformer Thomas Kirkbride, superintendent of the Pennsylvania Hospital for the Insane in 1840, called it "Moral Treatment" and promoted the concept as a big improvement for its time.

Dozens of gigantic Kirkbride buildings—all of them featuring massive central structures with long wings of dormitory wards extending out from them—were built all around the country. They were hard to maintain, but by then it was too expensive to replace them, so most declined and were abandoned.

Western State isn't abandoned—yet—but it still looks pretty foreboding. Many stories circulate about the nightmarish events that happened there in the past. Legend has it that one of the steeples lights up from the inside on dark nights, in a room where a deranged man hung himself from a light fixture. The fourth floor is rumored to be where the lobotomies and insulin and electric shock therapies were once carried out. Other outdated treatments once performed at Western included hydrotherapy (plunging patients in freezing cold baths or spraying them with high-pressure water), and laxative "therapies." We were told that that floor is now boarded up and the elevator no longer stops there, although sometimes screams are heard emanating from

behind its sealed doors. The elevator itself is said to be haunted by a nurse who fell down the shaft when the doors malfunctioned and opened accidentally. Tunnels connecting the various units are thought to be haunted as well, especially by patients who were raped by their doctors.

In Luton Hall, an all-male facility, patients have been known to murder one another (usually by strangulation) over something as minor as snoring, although since it already has prisonlike security, usually no charges are filed since nothing would be achieved by moving the perpetrators to a regular prison if they were convicted. In the bad old days, the most violent patients were often left chained to their beds, and staff would punish them by withholding food, often to the point of death by starvation. One of the rooms where this is said to have happened was on the third floor of Luton Hall, where a human face now peers out of the grain of the wooden door. If it had been there before, no one had ever noticed it until the death occurred. Another building, called Timber Springs, is reputed to have a room on the top floor with cuffs and collars chained to the wall for restraining violent patients.

Do not trespass or attempt to visit the old asylum without permission, since it is heavily guarded. There are cameras everywhere, looking for not only trespassers trying to sneak in, but patients trying to sneak out. You won't want them to mistake you for someone who belongs there.

Sinking of the *Sultana*

In terms of loss of life, neither the *Titanic* or the *Lusitania* sinkings nor the attack on the battleship *Arizona* in Pearl Harbor can top the awful incident on April 27, 1865, just a few miles north of Memphis. The steam packet *Sultana* was overloaded with thousands of passengers when its boilers exploded. In the mayhem that followed, 1,547 people died and nearly 500 were severely injured.

The *Sultana* was among the most modern Mississippi riverboats of its day. Only two years old, it was 260 feet long and 42 feet wide, but had a draft so shallow that it could still operate on only three feet of water. Two steam engines, powered by four high-pressure boilers, could deliver twice as much steam using half as much coal as conventional boilers. Its thirty-one wood-paneled staterooms were among the largest of any boat on the river. Outfitted with carpeting and crystal chandeliers, on a typical run *Sultana* could accommodate seventy-six passengers in private rooms and up to three hundred deck passengers, plus a crew of eighty and up to 660 tons of freight.

On that particular day, however, the *Sultana* was carrying far more than an ordinary load. Under the command of Capt. Cass Mason, *Sultana* was traveling from New Orleans with a normal-capacity load. But in Vicksburg, Mississippi, thousands of haggard, malnourished Union soldiers—most of them just released from hellish POW camps such as Andersonville—lined the banks of the river, desperate to get back home to the North. Dozens of steamboats like the *Sultana* jammed the riverfront, each hoping to cash in on the sudden demand for transport by charging higher than their standard rates for deck space. Greed led many of the boat captains to succumb to a kind of feeding frenzy, agreeing to take on far more than their usual number of passengers. By the time the *Sultana* pulled away from the Vicksburg docks, more than 2,300 people were jammed on board a vessel with only seventy-six life preservers and one lifeboat, all of them intending to go at least as far as Cairo, Illinois.

When the *Sultana* reached Memphis, some cargo was unloaded and the vessel was refueled. Just before midnight that evening it departed the docks in the midst of a major thunderstorm. Due to the rain, the river was higher than usual, but the *Sultana*'s engines were powerful, and despite its load it made headway against the strong currents. But then around 2 A.M. the next morning, after passing Paddy's Hen and Chickens (a string of little islands now consolidated as Chicken Island, or Island No. 42–45), first one and then two more of the four boilers exploded.

The blast destroyed the bulkhead supporting the main deck as it ruptured the furnaces beneath the boilers, simultaneously heaving tons of embers, red-hot firebricks, and body parts high into the air while dumping hundreds of other bodies directly into the flames. Scalding steam shot through the passageways and filled the main cabins. Amid screams, the boiler deck sagged and caved in, and the twin smokestacks towering over the superstructure began to totter and fall.

Survivors of the initial explosions jumped into the frigid river. Over the next hour or so, the *Sultana* burned and sank as other survivors managed to cling to bits of wreckage and float down the river or were rescued by other riverboats. One Union soldier later told of how, after he finally washed ashore in Arkansas, he passed out, only to wake up many hours later covered in a dry Rebel uniform. He never found out who the compassionate Samaritan was. Others said that when they jumped into the river to escape the flames, their biggest fear was that the pet alligator on board had gotten out of his pen and was now somewhere in the water among them.

Most of those who were aboard the *Sultana* that day didn't survive to tell such stories. "For weeks afterwards," one witness recalled, "the Mississippi below Memphis was strewn along its shore with stark, mangled bodies, lodged in the crotches of trees, [or] caught horribly in the undergrowth of willows and cottonwoods."

What caused the disaster? No one knows for sure. Some blamed hasty repairs done in Vicksburg, some attributed it to the incredible overloading, and some pointed to the ship's tubular boiler design, which was still new and prone to building up internal deposits of dried silt residue when the muddy river water was converted to steam. One final possibility was sabotage. Former Confederate agent Robert Louden bragged on his deathbed that he had used a bomb disguised as a lump of coal to blow up the boat, though few historians credit his claim.

Despite the magnitude of the disaster, the sinking of the *Sultana* soon slipped from the public consciousness. In fact, no one knew where the wreck of the *Sultana* itself was until 1982, when Memphis attorney Jerry Potter finally located what remained of the ship buried fifteen feet below a soybean field a mile and a half from the river. A monument was erected in Memphis's Elmwood Cemetery in 1989, near the three unmarked graves of some of the victims.

Boom Town in Happy Valley

When the Manhattan Project came to Tennessee in the early 1940s and began construction on several major secret facilities to build the first atomic bombs, thousands of workers were hired to build and then operate the immense plants. K-25 was the encoded designation of the secret gaseous diffusion plant, slated at the time to be the largest building under one roof on earth.

The covert town, officially named the J. A. Jones Construction camp but referred to by residents as Happy Valley, was begun in 1943. The first 2,500 Happy Vallians slept in bunk beds in crude shacks called "hutments" that were heated with woodstoves, but within a few months there were 900 trailers, 4 big dormitories, 8 large barracks, and more than 100 "victory homes" for the rest of the inhabitants. (Local historian Bill Wilcox points out that patriotic-sounding terms like *victory* were almost always euphemisms meaning "temporary.")

At its peak, Happy Valley boasted a cafeteria-style mess hall, three recreation centers, a movie theater, a bowling alley, and numerous other facilities. Since workers could neither leave Happy Valley nor communicate directly with the "outside world," the recreational and entertainment activities were key to enduring the hardships of life in this instant town. Unbeknownst to any residents, a similar boomtown existed in the next valley over, built for workers at the equally secret Y-12 plant, which used a different technique for generating radioactive material.

Even more quickly than it boomed, it went bust. With the war over and the gates open once again, by 1946 most inhabitants had left. The last remaining hutments and residential structures were dismantled in the 1950s, and today only a few fire hydrants, scattered bits of paved road, and fragments of concrete foundations remain.

INDEX

A
Acid rain, 256–257
Acuff, Roy, 42
Adams, Tennessee, 15–18
Adamsville, Tennessee, 128, 129
Adgent, Skip, 84–85
Airplane Filling Station, 176
Alcatraz Island, 139
Alexander Inn, 80
American Phalanx, 146
Amis, Thomas, 74
Anderson, Charles, 145
Andrews, James J., 246
Angel Crowns, 107
"Angel hair," 89
Arcadia, Tennessee, 14
Armstrong, Zella, 48–50
Asbury Cemetery, 243
Astor, Vincent, 215
Athena, 182, 183
Atomic bomb, 78, 79, 81, 91, 263

B
Bacon, Willard, 50
Ball lightning, 99
Banks, Floyd, 156–157
Barefoot, Daniel, 244
Barnes, George ("Machine Gun Kelly"), 138–139
Barnum, P. T., 102
Bat Creek, 38–40, 97
Bates, Finis L., 64–65
Batts, Kate, 16–17
Bear Creek house, 168
Beautiful Jim Key, 249
Belcher, Julie, 186
Bell Witch, 15–18
Belle of Riverview, 149
Bellwood Furnace/House, 230
Berry, Fred, Jr., 248
Bertz, Eduard, 233
Bible Covered Bridge, 186
Big Bone Cave, 42
Bigfoot, 112, 118
Bilbrey, Tennessee, 209
Billig, Otto, 95
Billy Hollow Road ghosts, 199
Blackman, Luther, 40
Bleeding Mausoleum, 236
Bloodfalls, 89
Blue Spring Cave, 42
Bolivar, Tennessee, 260
Bonaparte, Napoleon, 251
Bongo Java Coffee Shop, 186
Booger Swamp, 63
Boone, William, 26–27
Booth, John Wilkes, 64–65
Bradley, Kevin, 184
Brassell, George Andrew "Teek," 148
Brassell, Joseph Lewis, 148
Breast-feeding, 120
Breazeale, Felix "Bush," 136
Brentwood, Tennessee, 51, 93
Briceville, Tennessee, 113
Brick collection, 59
Bridges, haunted, 186, 192, 200, 204–205, 206, 207, 229
Brinkley Female College, 220–221
Bristol, Tennessee, 110, 178, 191
Bryan, John Neely, 48
Budhai statue, 165
Buffalo Bill, 142
Bullard, Joe, 100
Burger, J. M., 103
Burgess, Horace, 158
Burial mounds, 38, 41, 50, 51, 52–53
Burials, premature, 131
Burke, Thomas, 119
Buster, Frank "Cuz," 116, 117
Byrne, Thomas S., 98

C
Call, "Cactus" Jack, 241
Camden, Tennessee, 241
Campbell, Andrew J., 184
Campbell Beast, 113
Campbell, Edmund, 135
Cannonball Church, 184
Cannonball Express, 133
Cardinal, Tom "Bird," 163
Castell Coch, 153
Castle Gwynn, 152–153
Catfish, large, 118
Cato Cave, 44
Cayberry Hill ghost, 198
Centaurs, 66
Centennial Park, Nashville, 183
Chapel Hill Light, 84–85
Chattanooga Choo-Choo train, 189
Chattanooga National Cemetery, 246–247
Chattanooga, Tennessee, 28, 110, 169, 190, 216
Cheatham County, 87
Cherokees, 24, 30, 58, 62, 67, 111
Chickasaws, 52, 54
Chisca Mound, 54
Chopper Heaven, 163–164
Chota Mound, 97
Civil Rights Act of 1871, 73
Clark, William, 76
Clarksville, Tennessee, 42, 149, 237
Clinchfield Railroad, 200, 202
Cline, Patsy, 241
Clinton Engineering Works, 78
Coal Creek War, 229
Coffee County, 47
Colisco, Francisco Antonio, 202
Collinwood, Tennessee, 22–23
"Comb" graves, 12–13
Compton, Greg, 46

Convict leasing system, 229
Cookeville High School, 211
Cookeville, Tennessee, 63
Cooper, Gol, 179
Copper mines, 256–257
Copper Ridge Baptist Church, 100–101
Cox, Harry, 243
Cox, P. E., 48
Craig, Marie, 239
Craigmiles, Nina, 236
Crazy George's Bridge, 209
Creeping Bear, 142
Critter from Sugar Flat, 116–117
Crockett, Davy, 11
Crockett, Mike, 255
Crop circles, 96–97
Crosses, 100–101

D
Dandridge, Dorothy, 189
Darden, George, 96
Darden, Mills, 244
Dark Hollow Road, 194–195
Davie, Lizzie, 220
Day, David, 239
Death Crowns, 107
Dellinger, Melvin, 137
De Soto, Hernando, 48, 54
Devil worship, 19, 197
Devil's Looking Glass, 62
Dickens, Darrell, 88
Dickson County, 198
Disappearances, 104–105
Dixie Mafia, 128
Doe Mountain Fireball, 99
Dogs, military, 143
Dogwood Manor, 187
Donahue, Harve, 32
Dorris, William, 130

Drownings, 28–29, 32, 200
Drummond, Dick, 229
Dubose, Dr., 224
Ducks, 125
Dunbar Cave, 42

E
Earthquakes, 32–34
Ebbing and Flowing Spring, 74
Eclipses, 84
Eephing, 81
Eldridge, Otis/Kathy, 137
Elephants, 122–124, 177
Elizabethton, Tennessee, 170, 206, 208
Elmwood Cemetery, 242
Emmert, John W., 38, 40
Erin, Tennessee, 26
Estes, Evelyn, 142–143
Etheridge, Pete, 21
Evans, Daniel, 135
Ezell, Grady, 207
Ezell, Robert, 95

F
Fain Witch, 14
Faulkner, Charles, 50
Fault lines, 34, 83
Fawcett, George D., 91, 92
Feather balls, 107
Fell, Howard Barraclough, 55
Fermi, Enrico, 80
Fewkes Mounds, 51
Finney, Ryan, 184
Fire balls, 86
Fire, Pillar of, 87
Fires of Dyer Road, 86
First Church of the Elvis Impersonator, 188
Fisk Metallic Burial Case, 248
Flatt, Lester, 136

Fontaine, Dean, 155
Fooy, Sam, 135
Forest Hill Cemetery, 240
Forrest, Nathan Bedford, 73, 127, 130
Fort, Charles Hoy, 84
Fort Donelson, 231
Foster, Stephen, 131
Franklin, Ben, 131
Fraterville Mine, 228
Freeman, Michael, 152–153

G
Gaines, James/Lillien, 237
Gallatin, Tennessee, 104
Galvanism, 131
Gardner, Joshua, 15, 17, 18
Garland, Sallie, 120
General Shale Museum of Ancient Brick, 59
Ghost Nurses of Cleveland, 224
Ghosts
    of Bell Witch, 15–17
    at Bellwood House/Furnace, 230
    at Billy Hollow Road, 199
    at Booger Swamp, 63
    at Brinkley Female College, 220–221
    at Chapel Hill, 84–85
    at copper mines, 257
    of Craigmiles, 236
    at Dark Hollow Road, 194–195
    at Devil's Looking Glass, 62
    of drowned woman, 28–29
    of Dubose, 224
    at Fort Donelson, 231
    at Fraterville Mine, 228
    at Grant-Lee Dorm, 217
    at Hanging Rope, 20
    at Harahan Bridge, 204–205
    of hitchhikers, 198

Ghosts (cont.)
　　at Hope Hill Cemetery, 245
　　at Hughes Free Library, 233
　　of Hunter of Tuckaway Dorm, 224
　　at John Sevier Center, 218
　　at Ketron Middle School, 225
　　at Kingston Lisle House, 232–233
　　of Lady of the Lake, 25
　　of Lewis, 77
　　at Libertyland, 255
　　at McCullough Chapel, 226
　　at Midwest Dairies, 257
　　at Mount Olivet Cemetery, 250–251
　　at Newbury Guest House, 233
　　of Nurses of Cleveland, 224
　　of Oldfield, 233
　　at Orpheum Theatre, 214–215
　　of Petrified Soldier, 70
　　of Phantom Soldier, 224
　　at Printers Alley, 222
　　in Read House Hotel, 216
　　of Rebel's Rest, 224
　　of Schulman, 222
　　at Sensabaugh Tunnel, 200–203
　　at Seven Islands Church, 227
　　of Sidney the Suicide, 224
　　at Signal Mountain School, 225
　　testing for, 213
　　of Tyson, 232
　　at University of the South
　　　(Sewanee), 224
　　of Walker, 147
　　of Ward, 207
　　at Western State Hospital, 260–261
　　White Screamer and, 114
　　at Wilder Tower, 227
　　of Woman in White, 224
　　of Woodruff, 219
Giants, 124
Gibson, Brian, 46

Glass eyes, 179
Godsey, Susan Caroline, 102
Goodman, Sam, 163, 164
Gordon, Cyrus, 39
Graceland, 240, 254
Grand Carousel, 254–255
Grand Guitar shop, 178
Grant-Lee Dorm haunting, 217
Grassy Cove, Tennessee, 70
Greenberg, Neil, 66
Greenhill, Catherine Sophie, 131
Greenwood Cemetery, 237
Grinder, Priscilla, 76–77
Gustav Dentzel Carousel Company, 254
Guy, Larry, 120

H
Hackberry trees, 24
Hahn, Robert, 243
Halliburton, Richard, 140
Hamilton, James, 93
Hammond, Reuben, 231
Hanging Rope, 20
Hangings/lynchings
　　of "Andrews Raiders," 246
　　at Bellwood House/Furnace, 230
　　in Collinwood, Tennessee, 22–23
　　at Crazy George's Bridge, 209
　　at Drummond Bridge, 229
　　of Joseph and George Brassell, 148
　　by KKK, 73
　　in Lebanon, Tennessee, 21
　　by Maledon, 134–135
　　at Western State Hospital, 260
Happy Valley, 263. *See also* Oak Ridge, Tennessee
Harahan Bridge, 204–205
Harris, Washington "Wash," 162
Harrogate, Tennessee, 88, 217

Harvey, Dorothy Marie, 245
Headless Gownsman ghost, 224
"Hell Hole," 42
Helms, Johnnie, 97
Hendrix, John, 78, 79
Henning, James, 219
Hidden Hollow Park, 166
Hieroglyphs, 38, 56, 157
Hill, Churchill Winston, 170
Hinds, Clovis, 238, 239
Hinson, John W. "Captain Jack,"
　　144–145
Holmes, Ernest, 190
Hooper, Isaac Hooston, 56, 57
Hootenauger, Herbie, 178
Hoover, J. Edgar, 139
Hope Hill Cemetery, 245
Hoskinson, Danny, 172–173
House of the Almighty, 156–157
Hubbard's Cave, 42
Hughes Free Library, 233
Hughes, Thomas, 232
Hunter of Tuckaway Dorm ghost, 224

I
Indiana Jones, 68–69
Indianapolis Motor Speedway, 243
Indian statue, 177
Inscribed Wall of Chatata, 56–57
International Towing and Recovery
　　Hall of Fame and Museum, 190
Irwin, John Rice, 106

J
Jacksboro, Tennessee, 112
Jackson, Asa, 106
Jackson, Tennessee, 33, 132
Jackson, Tom, 208
Jacobs, Earl, 163
J. A. Jones Construction, 263

Jefferson, Thomas, 76, 77
Jewish culture, 39–40, 41, 57
John Sevier Center, 218
Johnson City, Tennessee, 111, 134, 135, 218
Johnson, Kittie, 142
Jones, Casey (John Luther Jones), 132–133
Jones, John Luther. *See* Jones, Casey (John Luther Jones)
Jones, Joseph, 48
Jones, Thomas, 72
Jones, William "Reelfoot," 32
Jonesboro, Tennessee, 89

K
Katy's Kitchen, 81
Kelly, George R.. *See* Barnes, George ("Machine Gun Kelly")
Kenton, Tennessee, 120, 121
Kentucky Fried Chicken, 177
Ketron Middle School, 225
Key, William "Doc," 249
Keystone Medicine Show, 249
Kingsport, Tennessee, 200, 202
Kingston Lisle House, 232–233
Kirk, Lowell, 40
Kirkbride, Thomas, 260
KKK (Ku Klux Klan), 72–73, 130, 196, 197
Knoxville, Tennessee, 110, 111, 131, 143
Kreis, Pete, 243
Kwas, Mary L., 40

L
Lady of the Lake, 25
Lake City, Tennessee, 228, 229
Lang, David, 104–105
Laughing Eyes, Princess, 32
Leavenworth Prison, 139
Lebanon, Tennessee, 21, 89, 94, 116–117
Lee, Arda E., 166
Lennon, Vince, 112
Lewis and Clark Expedition, 76
Lewis, E. C., 251
Lewis, Meriwether, 76–77
Libertyland, 254–255
Lincoln, Abraham, 64
Lincoln Memorial University, 217
"Lindbergh Baby Law," 139
Littleton, Aaron, 156
Lockhart, Frank, 243
Lost Sea, 42
Louden, Robert, 263
Lowe, W. W., 144
Lyons, Beauvais, 66

M
Machine Gun Kelly, 138–139
Mad Monkeys, 113
Mahan, Joseph, Jr., 39
Mainfort, Robert C., Jr., 40
Maledon, George, 134–135
Manhattan Project, 80, 81, 91, 263
Marquette, Leon, 30, 31
McConnell, Warren, 118
McCullough Chapel, 226
McKinley, William, 249
McNeil, Nicky, 114
Medal of Honor, 246
Memory Lane, 167
Memphis Memorial Park Cemetery, 238–239
Memphis, Tennessee
  Bigfoot, 118
  Booth's mummy, 64–65
  Creeping Bear, 142
  Davie haunting, 220
  eclipse, 84
  Halliburton, 140
  Lady of the Lake, 25
  Libertyland, 254–255
  Machine Gun Kelly and, 138, 139
  marching ducks, 125
  snake shower, 90
  Sultana riverboat and, 262
Mettetal, Ray, Jr., 210
Midwest Dairies, 257
Militia Hill, 229
Millard, George, 142
Millennium Manor, 154–155
Miller, Glenn, 189
Minié ball ammunition, 75
Mining, 30–31
Misty Mountain Ranch, 137
Monroe County, 96, 97
Monterey, Tennessee, 124
Montgomery County, 160
Montgomery, Hugh/William, 248
Moonshine, 32, 42, 137, 256
Moore, James, 135
Morgan County, 232
Morgan, John Hunt, 184
Morrell, Joe, 178
Morristown Tablet, 41
Morroni, Chloe, 112
Mother Teresa, 184
Motorcycles, 163–164
Mount Olivet Cemetery, 250–251
Munday, John, 30, 31
Murfreesboro, Tennessee, 19
Museum of Appalachia, 179, 248
Myer, William, 53

N
Narragansett Tribe of the Improved Order of Red Men, 58
Nashville, Tennessee, 93, 98, 182, 258

National Register of Historic Places, 255
Newbury Guest House, 233
Nicholas Brothers, 189
Nicholson, William, 154–155
Nickle, Elmer/Henry, 176, 177
Norris Lake, Tennessee, 112, 113

O

Oak Ridge, Tennessee, 78–81, 91–92. *See also* Happy Valley
Oak trees, 24
Officer, William/Cynthia, 35
Old Cowan Cemetery, 248
Old Green/Yellow Eyes, 227
Old Stone Fort, 47–50
Oldfield, Charles, 233
"Open roast" smelting, 256
Oppenheimer, J. Robert, 80
Orpheum Theatre, 214–215
Overton County, 12–13, 19
Overton, John, 93
Ozier Mound, 53

P

Parker, Isaac, 134, 135
Parrottsville, Tennessee, 137
Parthenon, 182–183
Peabody Hotel, 125
Peach pit carvings, 141
Perpetual motion, 106
Petrified Soldier, 70–71
Phantom Soldier, 224
Pictograms, 38, 56
Pinson, Joel, 52
Pinson Mounds, 52–53
Pitts, Joe Bradlow, 118
Polk Art Park, 172
Polk County, Tennessee, 120, 256
Porter, Belle, 237

Pot Cave, 44–46
Potter, Jerry, 263
Powell, Richard, 15, 17, 18
Powell, Tennessee, 32
Presley, Elvis, 170, 188, 240, 254
Price, Charles Edwin, 111
Primates, killer, 112–113
Primm Park, 51
Prince of Hangmen, 134–135
Printers Alley, 222
Prohibition, 138, 222
Prostitution, 149
Pulaski, Tennessee, 72, 73
Pusser, Buford, 128–129
Putnam County, 13, 211
Pyramids, 179–181, 251

Q

Queen La Tara, 102

R

Rainbow Lake, 25
Ralston, A. L., 57
Ramsey, Edward, 112
Ravis, Seymour, 139
Read House Hotel, 216
Rebel's Rest ghost, 224
Red Hart Road, 196–197
Reelfoot, Chief, 34
Reelfoot Lake, 32, 33, 34
Rhodes College, 140
Ripley, Robert, 136
Rives, Richard, 69
Robertson, Clara, 220
Rock Springs, Tennessee, 35
Rodriguez, Dionicio, 239, 240
Rogan, John P., 38
Rogersville, Tennessee, 74, 110, 167
Rooster, barking, 120
Rose Room haunting, 219

Rosser, Tony, 181
Rugby, town of, 232–233
Rumbling Falls Cave, 42
Ruskin Cave, 42–44
Ruskin Cooperative Association, 42–43
Ryman, Thomas G., 250

S

S&G Custom Cycles, 163, 164
St. Elmo's Fire, 99
St. Thomas Sanitarium, 98
Sanders, Harland, 177
Sasquatch, 112
Sathya Sai Baba, 179
Sauls Mound, 52, 53
Sayle, W. P., 89
Scales, J. L., 119
Schulman, David "Skull," 222
Schutt, Frank, 125
Scott, Winfield, 67
Scruggs, Earl, 136
Séances, 105, 220
Sells, George, 59
Sensabaugh Tunnel, 200–203
Seven Islands Church, 227
Shaffer, Basil, 59
Shelby County, 94, 162
Shootings, 21, 35, 185
Sidney the Suicide ghost, 224
Signal Mountain School, 225
Skull's Rainbow Room, 222
Skunk Apes, 113
Slaves, 14, 35, 146, 229, 230, 245
Smith, Roger, 141
Smithsonian Institution, 38, 39, 48, 52, 57
Smithson, Wanda, 208
Smoker Mankiller, 135
Snakes, 90, 103, 119
Sodom and Gomorrah, 68, 69

Solar halos, 88
Solstices, 50, 53
Sons of Confederate Veterans, 130
Spanish culture, 48
Sparks Circus, 122
Sparta, Tennessee, 12
Spontaneous combustion, 93
Spring of Blue Tears, 67
Squirrels, white, 120–121
Stagg, Brian, 232
Stamps cemetery, 13
Stanback, Stanley, 181
Standing Stone monolith, 58
Starnes, B. J./Janice, 187
State Line Mob, 128
State lines, 191
Stevenson, Vernon K., 251
Stone, Fred, 168
St. Paul Spiritual Temple, 162–163
Strunk, Fred, 46
Sugar Flat Road, Tennessee, 116
Sultana riverboat, 262–263
Sun dogs, 88
Sutton, Marvin "Popcorn," 137
Swift, George, 30–31

T
Tate, Edmund, 75
Taylor, Thankfull, 103
Tennessee Centennial and International Exposition, 182, 251
Tennessee State Militia, 229
Tennessee State Prison, 258–259
Tennessee Wesleyan College, 24
Thacker, Larry, 112
Thomas, Cyrus, 38, 39, 40
Thompson, Gideon, 236
Thompson, Vince, 259
Thorne, Kathryn, 139
Thunder Hole, 46

Tichenor, John, 139
Tigrett, Isaac, 179
Tow trucks, 190
Trace Creek, Tennessee, 114
Tree house, 158–159
Trenton, Tennessee, 102
Triune Terror, 119
Troost, Gerard, 89
Turpin, Gordon Willis "G.W.," 163, 164
Tyler, Nannie, 237
Tyson, Sophie, 232

U
UFOs (unidentified flying objects), 89, 91–92, 94–95, 96, 99, 169
Union Gospel Tabernacle, 250
University of the South (Sewanee), 224
Urschel, Charles, 139
U.S. Colored Troops, 231

V
Vampires, 206
Vanderbilt, Cornelius, 146, 147
Vanderbilt Hospital, 210
Venable, Francis Preston, 89
Virgin Mary, 98
Voodoo Hill, 19
Voodoo Village, 162–163

W
Walker, William, 146–147
Wampas Cats, 110
War Dog Memorial, 143
Ward, Hannah, 207
Ward's Bluff, Tennessee, 207
Watauga River Bridge, 208
Webb, George "Creeping Bear," 142
Webb, Sim, 133
Wells, Karen, 155

Western District, Arkansas, 134
Western State Hospital, 260–261
West Tennessee Ghost Hunters, 245
Whitaker, Dorothy Ann, 242
White Bluff, Tennessee, 114
White Screamer, 114–115
Whitehead Cemetery, 120
Whitley, Will, 21
Whittier, John Greenleaf, 84
Wickham, Enoch "Tanner," 160–161
Wickham Stone Park, 160–161
Wilder Tower, 227
Wilkinson, James, 77
Willers, Bill, 66
Witches, 12–13, 14, 15–18, 19, 86, 111
Wittington, John, 135
WJHL radio station, 206
Woman in White ghost, 224
Wood, George, 55
Woodruff, Mary Louise "Mollie," 219
Woolard's Corner, 21
Wooldridge, Egbert, 219
WOPI radio station, 178
Wyatt, Ron, 68–69

Y
Yee-Haw Industries, 186
Yellow fever, 146, 216, 219, 225, 242

Z
Zippin Pippin roller coaster, 254, 255

WEIRD TENNESSEE

ACKNOWLEDGMENTS

With three Grand Divisions of Tennessee to take on, nothing was more useful than having somewhere to roost at night in each of them. Carol Crown and Richard Ranta made it possible to roam the backstreets of M-Town and the wilds of the western plains from the serenity of their backyard in Memphis; Chris and Bettie Card provided a snug hideout in College Grove for investigating central Tennessee; and Julie Belcher and Kevin Bradley let me venture into the eastern hills and mountains from their kimchi-perfumed cabinet of curiosity in Knoxville. Without the hospitality of such friends, this book would have been a lot less fun to do.

I'm also grateful to convention and visitors bureaus and chambers of commerce throughout the state for lodging and guidance, but especially to Amy McColl, Jud Teague, and Heather Jones of Kingsport; Andrew Clark of Johnson City Holiday Inn; Brenda Pierce, Corinne Wells, and Jane Springer of Columbia-Maury; Cathy Hannaway and Barbara Stagg of Historic Rugby; Connie Landrum of Meigs-Decatur; Howard Hatcher of Sequatchie; Joelle Cavitt and Melissa Woody of Cleveland; Kaye Ireland of Sumner; and Melody Norris, Ivy Gardner, and Christine Higgins of Crossville.

Edward Meyer of Ripley's Believe It or Not! helped get my research launched, while I was greatly helped along the way by John Rice Irwin of the amazing Museum of Appalachia; Bill Wilcox of the Oak Ridge Heritage & Preservation Association; Rich Newman of Elsinore Productions; Donna Darwin of the Orpheum; Beauvais Lyons of the Hokes Archives; Egyptologists Colleen Manassa and Terry Wilfong; and historian Jack Neely of Metro Pulse.

Libraries, museums, and local scholars were inevitably supportive, but I especially want to thank Patricia Austin, Jeffrey Ayres, Tom Evans, Brenda Fiddler, Kay French, Caroline Gilmore, Rhonda Jones, Lisa Lutts, Carol Morgan, George Newman, Judy Peiser, Jean Powers, Bob Raines, Bill Reece, Jerry Russell, Cathy Smith, Crystal Smith, Brenda Summers, Paula Swallows Stover, Alice Swanson, Stephanie Tayloe, Frank Thomas, and Daphne Windham for their active involvement.

This is not the first book to sample Tennessee's weirdness. Margaret Butler, John Norris Brown, James Ewing, Randall Floyd, Jensen Lacey, Tim O'Brien, Allan S. Mott, Jack Neely, Charles Edwin Price, Darren Shell, Larry Thacker, and William Uchtman trod many of these paths well before me, and I am indebted to them.

Although he died long before I was born, Richard Halliburton of Memphis probably had as much to do with why I wound up writing this book as anyone. His Complete Book of Marvels was my childhood guide to life. The fact that I am able to continue living much that way has everything to do with my co-adventurer, Theadora Brack. Without her, it's hard to imagine how anything would ever get done.

PICTURE CREDITS

All photos and illustrations by the author or public domain except as indicated below:
Page 7 Dan Walworth; 9 Theadora Brack; 30 © iStockphoto.com/wolv; 44–45 Trousdale County Sheriff's Office; 61 Richard Rives; 66 Courtesy of Hokes Archives; 68 Richard Rives; 108 Ryan Doan; 109 bottom left © Bill Asmussen; 110 Ryan Doan; 113 Ryan Doan; 114 © Bill Asmussen; 119 © Barton Nunnelly; 120 © Stephen Kniatt; 195 © iStockphoto.com/Casarsa; 201 © Mike D'Angelo; 202 © Three Miracles Shy.

SHOW US YOUR WEIRD!

Do you know of a weird site found somewhere in the United States, or can you tell us about a strange experience you've had? If so, we'd like to hear about it! We believe that every town has at least one great tale to tell, and we're listening. It could be a cursed road, haunted abandoned site, odd local character, or bizarre historic event. In most cases these tales are told only in the towns in which they originated. But why keep them to yourself when you could share them with all of America? So come on and fill us in on all the weirdness that's lurking in your backyard!

You can e-mail us at: Editor@WeirdUS.com,
or write to us at:
Weird U.S., P.O. Box 1346, Bloomfield, NJ 07003.

www.weirdus.com